ADVANCE PRAISE FOR *COMING BACK TO LIFE*

Renowned activist and teacher Joanna Macy is a woman of uncanny courage and ferocious compassion — a boddhisattva ablaze! For twenty years she has been inviting individuals and groups to acknowledge and honor the shadowed darkness of this era, and to walk through the gates of grief into a new joy at their utter interdependence and solidarity with the rest of the earthly cosmos. Here, with her colleague Molly Brown, she offers a medicine bundle of alchemical group techniques for waking our slumbering souls to the astonishing beauty and travail of the Earth.
— David Abram, author of *The Spell of the Sensuous*

The material in this book works!
Joanna Macy has trained a generation of experiential educators and spiritual activists. This book is her generous gift to us of her teaching methods. Read it. Use it. Experiment with it.
Join in the healing of our world!
— Elizabeth Roberts and Elias Amidon,
editors of *Earth Prayers and Prayers for a Thousand Years*

Based on the insights from contemporary systems science and the world's spiritual traditions, *Coming Back to Life* presents a series of transformative processes that move one from apathy to compassion, from fear to creative energy, and from alienation to a felt realization of our radical interconnectivity. The significance of this book is truly immense. *Coming Back to Life* offers our human species a powerful initiation into a new era of planetary well-being.
— Brian Swimme, Professor of Cosmology,
California Institute of Integral Studies

Joanna Macy is one of the most inspiring voices calling us to our power and healing. She sees the pain we're in, she understands the anguish of today, and is one of the truly wise and compassionate leaders of our time. She leads the way to a life lived with passion, joy and purpose. In *Coming Back to Life*, Joanna Macy and her coauthor Molly Brown take us by the hand and guide us, step by step, into the discovery of what we can do to restore wholeness, harmony and peace in our lives and in our precious and endangered world. A marvelous book!
— John Robbins, author of *Diet for a New America*
and *Reclaiming Our Health*

Joanna Macy's new book represents a major lifework contribution in the effort to catalyze a revolutionary shift in perception and action towards the environment. This newly expanded overview of her theory and exercises presents a pioneering model for liberative environmental education. Macy invites people to contact their own authentic experience-based responses to the deteriorating environment and then to choose effective actions based in personal motivation. The exercises draw out feelings of concern for the state of the world, fostering compassionate action as antidote to numbness and paralysis.

Macy believes firmly in the power of the group to generate courage and creativity rather than any single individual. This is critical, she says, in resisting the enormous juggernaut of environmentally-destructive globalizing forces. Macy's pedagogy is strong and effective; this source-book offers academics and other teachers powerful tools for building community among concerned peers and engaging students in meaning-ful, transformative dialogue. By combining cognitive and ethical elements with empathic, imaginative reflection, this teaching promotes radical breakthroughs, releasing tremendous energy for the healing of our world. Macy's glimpse into the grandeur of the human heart is an inspiration for all those trying their hardest to keep hope alive for a more ecologically sustainable world.
— Stephanie Kaza, author of *The Attentive Heart*

COMING BACK TO LIFE

Practices to Reconnect
Our Lives, Our World

COMING BACK TO LIFE

Practices to Reconnect
Our Lives, Our World

Joanna Macy

Molly Young Brown

Foreword by Matthew Fox

NEW SOCIETY PUBLISHERS

Cataloguing in Publication Data:
A catalog record for this publication is available from the National
Library of Canada and the Library of Congress.

Cover design by *The Salamander,* Berkeley, CA, using *"The Web"* design
by Mara Loft.

Printed in Canada on acid-free, partially recycled (20 percent post-
consumer) paper using soy-based inks by Transcontinental, Best Books
division.

Paperback ISBN: 0-86571-391-X

To order directly from the publishers, please add $4.00 postage to the
price of the first copy, and $1.00 for each additional copy (plus GST in
Canada). Send check or money order to:

New Society Publishers,
P.O. Box 189, Gabriola Island, BC V0R 1X0, Canada.

New Society Publishers aims to publish books for fundamental social
change through nonviolent action. We focus especially on sustainable
living, progressive leadership, and educational and parenting resources.
Our full list of books can be browsed on the world wide web at:
http://www.newsociety.com

NEW SOCIETY PUBLISHERS
Gabriola Island BC, Canada and Stony Creek CT, U.S.A.

TABLE OF CONTENTS

Permissions

The authors thank the following publishers and authors for permission to reprint material copyrighted or controlled by them.

Anita Barrows for "Psalm" from *We Are The Hunger,* unpublished manuscript, 1998. Reprinted by permission of the author.

Jane Hirshfield, for the excerpt from her translation of *Ghalib.* Reprinted by permission of the translator.

Reprinted from *The Collected Poetry of Robinson Jeffers* Volume I, 1920-1928, edited by Tim Hunt, with the permission of the publishers, Stanford University Press. ©1995 by the Board of Trustees of the Leland Stanford Junior University.

Denise Levertov from *Poems 1968-1972.* Copyright © 1972, by Denise Levertov. Reprinted by permission of New Directions Publishing Corp.

MESSAGE FROM THE DALAI LAMA

Although it is increasingly evident how interdependent we are in virtually every aspect of our lives, this seems to make little difference to the way we think about ourselves in relation to our fellow beings and our environment. We live at a time when human actions have developed a creative and destructive power that has become global in scope. And yet we fail to cultivate a corresponding sense of responsibility. Most of us are concerned only about people and property that are directly related to us. We naturally try to protect our family and friends from danger. Similarly, most people will struggle to defend their homes and land against destruction, whether the threat comes from enemies or natural disasters such as fire or flooding..

We take the existence of clean air and water, the continued growth of crops and availability of raw materials, for granted. We know that these resources are finite, but because we only think of our own demands, we behave as if they are not. Our limited and self centered attitudes fulfill neither the needs of the time, nor the potential of which we are capable.

Today, while many individuals grapple with misery and alienation, we are faced with global problems such as poverty, overpopulation, and the destruction of the environment. These are problems that we have to address together. No single community or nation can expect to solve them on its own. This indicates how small and interdependent our world has become. In ancient times, each village was more or less self-sufficient and independent. There was neither the need nor the expectation of cooperation with others outside the village. You survived by doing everything yourself. The situation now has completely changed. It is no longer appropriate to think only in terms of even my nation or my country, let alone my village. If we are to overcome the problems we face, we need what I have called a sense of universal responsibility rooted in love and kindness for our human brothers and sisters.

In our present state of affairs, the very survival of humankind depends on people developing concern for the whole of humanity, not just their own community or nation. The reality of our situation impels us to act and think more clearly. Narrow-mindedness and self-centered thinking may have served us well in the past, but today will only lead to disaster. We can overcome such attitudes through a combination of education and training. This book by Joanna Macy and Molly Young Brown contains a wealth of advice drawn from their own experience for putting such training into effect, both on a personal and on a public level. It gives me great pleasure to express my admiration for such work and to encourage readers not only to give their approval, but to act upon it for the benefit of all sentient beings and this earth that is our only home.

HIS HOLINESS TENZIN GYATSO
THE FOURTEENTH DALAI LAMA OF TIBET

September 7, 1998

FOREWORD

by Matthew Fox

A TURN OF A MILLENNIUM, a time of planetary destruction but also planetary communication, the loss of legitimacy among our religious institutions, youth alienation, species' disappearance—all these realities of our time require a book like this one and deep thinkers and activists like Joanna Macy and her colleague, Molly Young Brown. This is a source book in the true sense of the word. It returns us to our source, our spiritual roots, so that our action will come from nonaction, our action will be from our freedom and not from our acting out.

Joanna Macy represents the best of her generation's (and mine) efforts to replace the dualistic, secularist and anti-mystical biases of the modern era with compassion and loving action. Though descending from an impressive line of Calvinist preachers, Macy's deepest spiritual gift is her application of Buddhism's principles that acknowledge the deep suffering of the world and resolve to assist a great turning beyond that suffering. Like the mystics of old, she invites us into the despair and darkness and fear that grips all of us, and dispels the notion that denial, numbing, or escape are valid options. She challenges us to analysis as well as action and she gifts us with exercises that will strengthen our minds and hearts for the struggle ahead.

In many ways this book can be called a manual for mystics and prophets as we enter the twenty-first century. It is deep in its ecumenism, drawing not only from rich Buddhist spiritual practices but also from exercises from other traditions and the authors' imaginative experience in leading workshops in healing of despair all over the world.

It has been my privilege to be present at several of those workshops, often co-leading with Joanna, and I have always gone away deepened and strengthened by her gifts of spiritual leadership. I recall our work

together on an ecojustice workshop in Munich, on bringing the virtues of
darkness and awareness of suffering to the Findhorn people in northern
Scotland, and our doing "Cosmic Christ and Buddha Nature" workshops
in Santa Barbara, California, and at the University of Creation Spirituality
in Oakland, California. All these experiences rise to the surface on reading this book, and blessings of strength and spirit fill my consciousness
on recalling them. That is what is so special about Joanna Macy's work—
not just her passionate commitment (this may be a hint of the healthy zeal
she inherited from her Calvinist predecessors) and not just her strong
analytical mind—but especially her awareness that learning takes place
not only in the head but in the heart and indeed with the benefit of all the
chakras. With Macy, her process experiences are just as valuable as her
theory. Praxis and theory come together in this book as it does for other
liberation theologians the world over.

This book, deriving from over twenty years of inner work and of
work in the field, emanating from the wisdom of our ancestors East and
West, and coming from the heart, mind and experience of a spiritual
visionary and a committed activist for eco- and social justice, is a blessing
for our times.

To write a book entitled "Coming Back to Life" implies that death is
around us and has overtaken us. How can there be a return to life without an acknowledgment of death? This seems to be the case, namely that
ours has become a culture overwhelmed with death—some of it real and
much of it brought on ourselves by ourselves. When one hears that the
Pope grants Rupert Murdoch a papal award as a citizen of conscience,
one senses that healthy religion has a long way to go to be born anew and
that death has permeated much of religion's existence. When one sees the
young lost, cigarette corporations targeting thirteen-year-olds to render
them addicts, the Nike Corporation growing rich on exploiting women
and child labor in Asian factories with substandard working conditions
while the Nike logo is displayed on numerous American university ath-
letic jerseys and at the Olympic Games, one becomes more and more
aware of the presence of death. Moral death. Spiritual death. Even physical death.

And so, in times like ours, one rejoices to see this book by two persons who have committed their hearts, work, and considerable passion to
the theme of resurrection, of ways out of death. How do we go about
coming back to life, i.e. spirit, in these troubled days? Macy and Brown
offer us both theory and practice on how to do this. This is a spirit book.
This is spirit work. It heals and it gives us hope, thereby empowering us

on the way to a healing life. Meister Eckhart, the great Dominican mystic and prophet of the Middle Ages who was condemned by the papacy because he supported the peasants, women, and other outcasts, once wrote that "a healing life is a good life." A healing book is a good book.

This book is a wisdom book because it operates from the perspective of cosmology and spirituality, which are integral to wisdom traditions the world over. It does not settle for knowledge alone. In addition, because so many of its stories and teachings have come from or been tested by thousands of persons around the world in workshops of healing, that, too, assures the wisdom of the collective. Indeed, the wisdom of the community is strongly felt on these pages. Furthermore, the attention given to future generations not yet born adds to the role of wisdom in leading us to spiritual awareness and action—as does the passion for the more-than-human beings with whom we are called to share community.

This work is a healing work; it comes from a healing person, a priest in her own right, a midwife of grace. It holds the promise to awaken healing in society and its institutions, in religion, and in the hearts and minds of all workers for justice and ecojustice. Joanna Macy is one of those rare voices in our time who is a prophet speaking out on behalf of the poor and those without a voice, the young, the dispossessed, the ecologically threatened. But she does not stop there. She also passes on this prophetic voice to others, she draws it out, she coaxes us not to be afraid and not to be in denial. She encourages us; that is, she builds our courage up to find our prophetic voice and to contribute as teams and as communities to the healing work our times and pain require. We are grateful for her voice and for our own. And we all welcome this book that is sure to unite many voices, hands, and hearts. May it fulfill its promise! May we all fulfill our promise.

Matthew Fox is president of the University of Creation Spirituality in downtown Oakland, California, and author of 23 books including *Original Blessing*, *The Coming of the Cosmic Christ*, *A Spirituality Named Compassion*, and *The Reinvention of Work*.

PREFACE

by Joanna Macy

THIS IS A GUIDEBOOK. It maps ways into the vitality and determination we each possess to take part in the healing of our world. It describes a body of work that has grown up over the last twenty years and helped hundreds of thousands of men and women around the globe to find solidarity and courage to act, despite rapidly worsening social and ecological conditions.

This work can be done alone, and has reached into countless private lives. It is most effectively done in groups. Its methods, developed in and for workshops, yield remarkable openings to the truth of our common condition when brought into classrooms, churches, conferences, and organizational settings. Because it reconnects us with each other and all beings, arousing our passion for life and our power to protect it, we call it simply the Work that Reconnects.

It has been known under other names. At the outset, my colleagues and I called it "despair and empowerment work," thanks to its central dynamic—the profound existential changes that occur when we own and use, rather than repress, our pain for the world. As such, it was described in my book *Despair and Personal Power in the Nuclear Age* (1983). Later it became known as "deep ecology work," because it taps the power of our interconnectedness with all beings in the web of life. In *Thinking Like a Mountain: Towards a Council of All Beings* (1988), my coauthors and I described some of the fresh insights and practices that developed with our understanding of deep ecology.

These names are still valid. Both are used by many groups and guides around the world to refer to this continually expanding body of work. In writing the present book, however, my coauthor Molly Young Brown and I were reluctant to use these labels lest they confuse people

("Despair? Who's feeling despair?") or give the impression that the work belongs to a particular school of thought ("What's deep ecology?"). The work is too practical and too universal in nature for it not to be shared as widely as possible. Along with the numberless men, women, and young people who have benefited from it and contributed to it over the last two decades, we feel that it belongs to all who have a stake in the future.

That future seems ever more fragile. With wars igniting around the globe, the forests falling, the hungry and homeless on our streets, the poisons in our food, water, air, and breast milk, and the extinction of whole species and cultures, it grows harder to take hope in our common journey. We are tempted to shut down, narrowing our sites to our own and our family's short-term survival. In the face of all the bad news, the challenge of creating a sustainable civilization can seem absurdly unrealistic.

Yet it is germinating now, that sustainable society on which the future depends. Its seeds are sprouting in countless actions in defense of life, and in fresh perceptions of our mutual belonging in the living body of Earth—bold, new perceptions deriving from both science and spirituality. Although it doesn't feature in the day's headlines or evening news, a silent revolution is occurring, bringing unparalleled changes in the ways we see and think and relate. I imagine that future generations will look back on this period and call it the time of the "Great Turning." It is the epochal shift from a self-destructive industrial growth society to a life-sustaining society.

The work presented here aims to help each of us play our role in this Great Turning. Its value lies not in dispensing any ideological diagnoses or prescriptions so much as in awakening our will. Its interactive practices uncover our deepest motivations to take part in the healing of our world. They take these yearnings and help us find in them the courage, commitment, and community we need to change our lives and move into action for the healing of our world. These methods not only draw from understandings offered by new science and those reclaimed from ancient spiritual teachings, they make these concepts experiential, vivid, practicable.

In the Great Turning, on which our future depends, many traditions and fields of inquiry have riches to offer. Strong currents in my own life nourished and shaped the Work that Reconnects. Thanks to my Protestant preacher grandfather, Judeo-Christian teachings—especially those of Isaiah and Jesus—infused my early years with the notion that we're here for something bigger than our private pursuits. My doctoral studies in general living systems theory have provided valuable insights and conceptual tools. And so has Buddhism, which has deeply informed and illumined the last thirty-five years of my life. The Buddha Dharma prompts me to think of the work this book describes as bodhisattva training. The bodhisattva is the Buddhist embodiment of compassion, who acts simply and boldly for the sake of all beings, and who lets herself be vitalized—indeed liberated—by her interconnections with them.

Each person, as he or she undertakes the Work that Reconnects, has comparable resources to offer. My coauthor Molly Brown draws from her childhood in Los Alamos as well as her training and practice in psychosynthesis. Other colleagues bring in their backgrounds and skills as artists, naturalists, clergy. And I hope that you who read these pages will find that they enlist your own particular experiences and strengths.

You hold in your hands a guide to the Work that Reconnects. Please use it as such.

The first three chapters summarize the premises on which this work is based. Do not let your interest in the exercises we offer distract you from reading these portions, for they provide the conceptual bases of the work. To skip over them weakens your grasp of the work and your authority in leading it.

Chapters 4 and 5 spell out the aims and principles of the work itself, as well as our advice to you in facilitating groups.

All subsequent chapters and their relevant appendices offer specific group exercises, along with introductions detailing their assumptions and aims. The design of these methods did not precede the doing of the work; they grew out of it through experimentation and interaction with countless colleagues. While Molly and I can attribute certain ones to particular individuals, the authorship of many others is too interwoven to honor any source other than life itself, as it lives through us in this time.

These practices are essentially a "give away." They are given in profound trust that you who read and use this book are aligned with Molly, me, and our publisher in our commitment to a livable world for all beings of Earth. We welcome your responses and counsel. And we appreciate your acknowledging the source of these exercises when you use them.

Since the Work that Reconnects has brought me great learning and immeasurable joy, I offer these pages in gratitude. I am thankful for my coauthor Molly Brown and our editor and publisher, Chris Plant. I am grateful to my children Peggy, Jack, and Chris, who have buoyed me with their love and wry respect for this work over the past twenty years. For my husband Fran, who sharpens this work with his keen political perceptions, who brings it to his coworkers in the countries of the former

Soviet Union, and who coleads it with me in many lands, my gladness is too great for words. Most of all, I am grateful for the thousands of incandescent hours with people in North America, Europe, Asia, and Australasia, as they opened their hearts and minds to the suffering and challenges of this planet-time.

Even after all these years in doing the work, I am continually surprised by the grandeur of the human heart. Ever again, walking into a room of people to share this work—ordinary people I could pass on the street—I am awestruck to discover their caring for the world. It is an anguished caring that extends far beyond the personal ego with its individual wants and needs. I am moved, ever again, by their readiness to face the bad news, and indeed articulate the effects of the global crisis on their lives and communities. As they seize this opportunity to give voice, without agendas and debates, I am humbled by their grief and rage, and by the courage and creativity that is unleashed. The changes they go on to make in their lives, and the actions they go on to take in their communities, teach me. These changes are so real and bold, they challenge me to take seriously the very premises of the work itself. That is our profound, innate allegiance to the web of life, our true nature as compassionate beings—as bodhisattvas.

This work has been an ongoing revelation to me. I offer it with the hope that you too will find blessing in it, and a homecoming to our true nature.

PREFACE

by Molly Young Brown

I FIRST MET JOANNA MACY IN 1987 when I attended a gathering of Interhelp, an organization founded by Joanna's friends and colleagues who wanted to explore the psychological and spiritual dimensions of world problems, and help people respond to threats to their common survival. I was intrigued by the "despair and empowerment" process practiced by this group because it seemed so compatible with psychosynthesis, a holistic transpersonal psychology which I had studied, practiced, and taught since 1971.

My appreciation of Joanna deepened when I took a workshop with her in the winter of 1991, and learned of her vision of "nuclear guardianship." I was especially drawn to this work because of my childhood in "the Atomic City" of Los Alamos, New Mexico; I felt a kind of karmic connection to the problem of radioactive materials and began to work with the Nuclear Guardianship Project which Joanna had inaugurated. I became convinced that Joanna was the woman teacher and mentor I had longed for, and so when I began my studies at Starr King School for the Ministry at the Graduate Theological Union in Berkeley the following fall, I enrolled in Joanna's class in deep ecology. I was not disappointed. Joanna's teaching brought me more fully into the worlds of systems thinking, deep ecology, and engaged Buddhism (all of which had intrigued me for some time), and helped me understand their common threads. It also enriched my thinking in the book I was completing that year, *Growing Whole: Self-Realization on an Endangered Planet* (Hazelden/Harper San Francisco, 1993).

Soon we were working together: editing (along with Wendy Oser, Fran Macy, and others) three pithy issues of the "Nuclear Guardianship Forum," and teaching a year long class in applied living systems thinking

at the California Institute of Integral Studies. I began offering workshops
in this work through my connections in the psychosynthesis world, and
created a class in systems thinking at John F. Kennedy University in
Orinda, California, modeled on the CIIS course.

When Joanna asked me to coauthor this book with her, I jumped at
the chance to bring together my love of writing, my love of this work, and
my love for this woman. In his Foreword, Matthew Fox writes of Joanna's
prophetic voice, and her ability to pass it on to others. Writing this book
with Joanna has helped me develop my prophetic voice and build my
courage to write and speak and act on behalf of Earth, something I have
sought to do all my life, through various disciplines and situations.

I would like to share a little of my life story, to make clearer what has
called me to this work. Being raised in Los Alamos, New Mexico, gave me
an intensive experience in what historian Hannah Arendt called "the
banality of evil."[1] It has taken me a good part of my adult life to fully
grasp how deeply flawed were the assumptions of the scientific/military
culture which predominated there, and how good and loving people
could perpetrate such harm.

Los Alamos is nestled in the forested mountains of northern New
Mexico, so my childhood playground was nature. From an early age, I
camped, picnicked, and played outside, establishing a strong relationship
with trees, mountains, creeks, and critters. I was also subtly shaped by
the Native American and Hispanic cultures in the region. But my family
was part of a scientific community (although neither of my parents were
scientists themselves) so I learned to worship the god of Science along
with the Christian God. I remember going to Family Days Open House at
the Lab, the rare opportunity to go behind the security fences and see a
little of what they did there. I was enchanted by the apparatus, the cloud
chambers, the accelerators, the glove boxes, and the tissues studied under
microscope. I wanted to be a scientist when I grew up. I wanted that
access to the mysterious inner workings of the world.

I also learned that there was a correct way of thinking: "logical,"
"rational," backed by scientific data and framed within measurable para-
meters. If it couldn't be measured and replicated in the lab, it probably
didn't exist. Even then, one would have to defend one's understandings
and hypotheses against the rigorous (and often hostile) critique of other
scientists. I learned that feelings and fantasy had little place in scientific
thinking, and that I had best keep those kinds of things out of the discussion. Feelings and dreams were fine for girls' slumber party chatter,
but had no place in the Real World.

Nearly fifty years later, on a solo "vision quest" at the beginning of 1996, I saw more clearly than ever before how this "mere purposive rationality" (to use Gregory Bateson's term)* distorted people's innate morality at Los Alamos, and led them to do grievous harm to the world. I was finally able to break through my own denial about my community of origin and see how profoundly this distortion affected me as I grew up there. During the vision quest, I felt sick to my stomach, perhaps due to fasting, and remembered how often I had stomach aches as a child, how I spent much time in the school nurse's office, especially during kindergarten and first grade. I focused on the sensations of discomfort and pain I was experiencing because they seemed very similar to what I had felt as a child. I found myself asking, "What is the secret? What is this deeply hidden trauma which I have defended myself from all my life?" And suddenly I knew.

My family moved to Los Alamos a few months after the bombing of Hiroshima and Nagasaki in 1945. I believe now that I knew, as a small child can, that something wrong was going on. I doubtless heard radio news and conversations about bombs and Hiroshima and Nagasaki. I must have known—perhaps psychically—that people in Los Alamos had something to do with what happened there. I knew that the town existed solely for the Lab to carry on atomic research, primarily focused on nuclear weapons, and instinctively I must have known that this work was wrong. Even "Atoms for Peace," highly touted in Los Alamos in the fifties, was an elaborate self-justification for the main work of the Laboratory: building weapons of mass destruction. The good that came from the Lab's work could have come anyway. It didn't make the bad okay. As a child I "knew" all this at a deep unconscious level.

Yet from everyone around me, all the important people in my life, from the entire community, I heard only rationalizations, justifications, and deceptions. We were special people doing important and special work, protected from the rest of the world by fences and pass gates. Even while I felt proud of the title "Atomic City," I felt pain and confusion in my heart about its implications. Although I may never have consciously thought about this deep contradiction, I carried it in my body, primarily in my digestive system. I couldn't stomach it. But neither could I, as a dependent child, speak of it. How could I let myself know that nice, good people that I loved and admired were engaged in destructive work, when they themselves could not possibly acknowledge it? How could I challenge the myth of my whole community?

I can play the tapes of "rational" justification in my head, and they

---

* See Bateson's brilliant article, "Style, Grace, and Information in Primitive Art," in *Steps to an Ecology of Mind* (Ballantine, 1972).

still have the power to confuse me. "We had to invent the bomb before the Nazis did" and then, after Germany was defeated, "we had to stop the Japanese." We have all heard the justifications for the bombing of Hiroshima and Nagasaki, and yet we know the deep anguish most of us feel for the massive suffering engendered by that "justified" act. I recall a conversation I had several years ago during the arms race with a friend who is a nuclear physicist at Los Alamos. He was complaining about people in the Nuclear Freeze movement being "so emotional." I said rather vehemently that I couldn't imagine not being emotional about something which threatened the lives of my children and everything I loved. Somehow in Los Alamos, however, such emotions became taboo. Emotions might call into question the behavior so elaborately rationalized by thought.

Los Alamos is not alone in this practice of covering up and denying its wrong-doing, and inventing elaborate "rational" justifications for it. Our whole economic structure today participates in this kind of self-deception, as we ignore and cover up the enormous harm we do to the environment, to our fellow creatures, and to oppressed peoples around the world and within our own country. As Ed Ayers, editor of *World Watch*, writes in a recent editorial,[2]

> The greatest destruction in our world is not being inflicted by psychopathic tyrants or terrorists. It's being done by ordinary people—law-abiding, churchgoing, family-loving "moral" people—who are enjoying their sport-utility vehicles, their vacation cruises, and their burgers, and are oblivious to where those pleasures come from and what they really cost. Oblivious not to what those things cost at the store, but to what they cost when all the uncounted effects of their production and use are added up.

Living within a society which does this engenders deep conflict within us, but the taboos against speaking of it, or even seeing it, are subtle, strong, and complex. Being nice—even being "intelligent"—means going along with the communal deception, like the mutually shared trance of an alcoholic family. Yet we do ourselves and the larger world real damage when we go along with the taboos, and deny the truth of our inner knowing, as I did for so long.

The work presented in this book is a precise antidote to the collective self-deception of our industrial growth society. Helping Joanna to write this book has been a precise antidote to the communal deception of my childhood, and the confusion I have carried from it for most of my life. I am profoundly grateful for the experience.

I am also grateful for a supportive circle of family and friends, especially my husband Jim and our sons Gregory and Cassidy. I am grateful for the patience and vision of Chris Plant, our editor and publisher. And I am grateful for the inspiration and goodwill of the colleagues I have met through the years of doing this work.

Chapter 1

TO CHOOSE LIFE

I call heaven and earth to record this day to your account, that I have
set before you life and death, blessing and cursing: therefore choose life,
that both you and your seed shall live. —Deut. 30.19

WE LIVE IN AN EXTRAORDINARY MOMENT ON EARTH. We possess more technical prowess and knowledge than our ancestors could have dreamt of. Our telescopes let us see through time to the beginnings of the universe; our microscopes pry open the codes at the core of organic life; our satellites reveal global weather patterns and hidden behaviors of remote nations. Who, even a century ago, could have imagined such abundance of information and power?

At the same time we witness destruction of life in dimensions that confronted no previous generation in recorded history. Certainly our ancestors knew wars, plagues, and famine; entire civilizations, such as Phoenicia and Imperial Rome, foundered when they cut down their trees for warships and turned their lands to desert. But today it is not just a forest here and some farmlands and fisheries there; today entire species are dying—and whole cultures, and ecosystems on a global scale, even to the oxygen-producing plankton of our seas.

Scientists may try to tell us what is at stake when we burn rainforests and fossil fuels, dump toxic wastes in air, soil, sea, and use chemicals that devour our planet's protective ozone shield. But their warnings are hard to heed. For ours is an Industrial Growth Society.* Its economy depends on ever-increasing consumption of resources. To maintain its engines of

* We are indebted to Norwegian ecophilosopher Sigmund Kwaloy for his formulation of this term.

15

progress, Earth is both supply-house and sewer. The planet's body is not only dug up and turned into goods to sell, it is also a "sink" for the poisonous by-products of our industries.* If we sense that the tempo is accelerating, we are right—for the logic of the Industrial Growth Society is exponential, demanding not only "growth," but rising rates of growth. Like Alice on the chessboard of the mad queen, we must run ever faster to stay in the same place. What is in store for our children's children? What will be left for those who come after? Too busy running to think about that, we try to close our minds to nightmare scenarios of want and wars in a wasted, contaminated world.

We've come so far. We have survived so many trials and evolved through so many adventures in our planetary journey, and there is so much promise still to unfold—yet we can lose it all. As the intricate web of living systems unravels, we can bring it all down with us. Jahweh's words through Moses now bear a literal truth: "I have set before you life and death, therefore choose life."

THE CHOICE FOR A SUSTAINABLE WORLD

We can choose life. Dire predictions notwithstanding, we can still act to ensure a livable world. It is crucial that we know this: *we can meet our needs without destroying our life-support system.* We have the technical knowledge and the means of communication to do that. We have the savvy and the resources to grow sufficient food, ensure clean air and water, and generate the energy we require through solar power, wind, and biomass. If we have the will, we have the means to control human population, to dismantle weapons and deflect wars, and give everyone a voice in democratic self-governance.**

To choose life means to build a life-sustaining society. "A sustainable society is one that satisfies its needs without jeopardizing the prospects of future generations," according to Lester Brown of Worldwatch Institute. In contrast to the Industrial Growth Society, a Life-sustaining Society operates within the "carrying capacity" of its life-support system, regional and planetary, both in the resources it consumes and the wastes it produces.

To choose life in this planet-time is a mighty adventure. As people in all countries and walks of life are discovering, this adventure elicits more courage and enlivening solidarity than any military campaign. From high school students restoring streams for salmon spawning, to inner city neighbors creating community gardens on vacant lots, from forest activists

* Just as a continually growing cancer eventually destroys its life support systems by destroying its host, a continuously expanding global economy is slowly destroying its host — the Earth's ecosystem." Lester Brown. *State of the World, 1998.*
** World Game Institute, 1997: As of 1997, $19 billion was spent worldwide on weapons every week. United Nations Human Development Report, 1997: $80 million would grant access to clean water, social services, and basic education for the world's poor for ten years; this equals financial assets of the world's seven richest men.

sitting in trees to delay logging until environmental impact studies are done, to windmill engineers bringing their technology to energy-hungry regions—countless groups are organizing, learning, taking action.

This multifaceted human activity on behalf of life may not make today's headlines or newscasts, but to our progeny it will matter more than anything else we do. For if there is to be a livable world for those who come after us, it will be because we have managed to make the transition from the Industrial Growth Society to a Life-sustaining Society. When people of the future look back at this historical moment, they will see, perhaps more clearly than we can now, how revolutionary it is. They may well call it the time of the Great Turning.

They will see it as epochal. While the agricultural revolution took centuries, and the industrial revolution took generations, this ecological revolution has to happen within a matter of a few years. It also has to be more comprehensive—involving not only the political economy, but the habits and values that foster it.

The Great Turning

Let us borrow the perspective of future generations and, in that larger context of time, look at how this Great Turning is gaining momentum today, through the choices of countless individuals and groups. We can see that it is happening simultaneously in three areas or dimensions that are mutually reinforcing. These are: 1) actions to slow the damage to Earth and its beings; 2) analysis of structural causes and creation of structural alternatives; and 3) a fundamental shift in worldview and values. Many of us are engaged in all three, each of which is necessary to the creation of a sustainable civilization.

I. "Holding actions" in defense of life on Earth

These activities may be the most visible dimension of the Great Turning. They include all the political, legislative, and legal work required to slow down the destruction, as well as direct actions—blockades, boycotts, civil disobedience, and other forms of refusal. Covering a wide variety of endeavors, such holding actions include:

- Documenting the ecological and health effects of the Industrial Growth Society, including those of fossil fuels, nuclear power and weapons production, heavy metal mining, clearcutting, incinerators and toxic landfills, pesticides, food additives, and factory farms.

- Campaigning for laws to mitigate the effects of pollution, poverty, and loss of habitat—such as the Endangered Species Act, the Clean Water (and Air and Food) Acts and the raising of the minimum wage in the U.S., and internationally, the Comprehensive Test Ban Treaty, the abolition of nuclear weapons, and the protocol on limiting greenhouse gases.

- Promoting appropriate regulations to implement environmental and social legislation, and their just enforcement through citizen monitoring of government and business, participation in public hearings, and litigation.

- Lobbying against international trade agreements which endanger ecosystems and undermine social and economic justice, such as GATT (the General Agreement on Tariffs and Trade), NAFTA (the North American Free Trade Agreement), and MAI (the Multilateral Agreement on Investment).

- Blowing the whistle on illegal and unethical corporate practices.

- Boycotting corporations that endanger living systems through pollution and weapons production, or exploit their workers with low pay and harmful working conditions.

- Blockading and conducting vigils at places of ecological destruction, such as old-growth forests under threat of clearcutting, construction sites of malls and motorways, nuclear dumping grounds, weapons labs and testing sites.

- Protesting against the global arms trade at ports, military depots, and arms bazaars, especially in the U.S. (which exports more weapons than all other countries combined).

- Providing shelter and food to the poor and homeless.

This first dimension of the Great Turning is wearing. It is heroic work, and when we're in the spotlight, it can bring respect and even adulation from the many who see what's at stake. We can also get stressed out of our minds by nonstop crises, the constant search for funding, battles lost, and increasing violence against activists. When we assume point position, we take a lot of punishment, and when we step back to take a breather, we often feel guilty. But in truth we are not abandoning the cause; we are choosing to continue the work of the Great Turning in another form—the way the head goose, when she's tired, repositions herself to fly in the windstream of the others, and another flyer takes her place.

Work of this kind buys time. It serves to save some lives, and some ecosystems, species, and cultures, as well as some of the gene pool, for the sustainable society to come. It is, however, insufficient to bring that society about.

II. Analysis of structural causes and creation of alternative institutions

The second dimension of the Great Turning is equally crucial. To free ourselves and our planet from the damage being inflicted by the Industrial Growth Society, we must understand its dynamics. What are the tacit agreements that create obscene wealth for a few, while progressively impoverishing the rest of humanity? What interlocking causes indenture us to an insatiable economy that uses our larger body, Earth, as supply house and sewer? It is not a pretty picture. It takes courage and confidence in our own common sense to look at it with realism; the rewards are great when we do. As citizens are discovering in an upsurge of teach-ins and conferences on the subject, we can demystify the workings of the global economy. When we see how this system operates, we are less tempted to demonize the politicians and corporate CEOs who are in bondage to it. And, for all the apparent might of the Industrial Growth Society, we can also see its fragility—how dependent it is on our participation, and how doomed it is to devour itself.

In this second dimension of the Great Turning, we are not only studying the structural causes of the global crisis; we are also creating structural alternatives. These two efforts go hand in hand. They use the same mental muscles, the same kind of knowledge, the same itch for practicality. In countless localities, like green shoots pushing up through the rubble, new social and economic arrangements are sprouting. They may be hard to see at first, because they are seldom featured in the media, but if you keep your eyes open and fiddle with the focal length, they come into view—like a faint green haze over things, intensifying here and there in pockets of grass, cress, clover. Not waiting for our national or state politicos to catch up with us, we are banding together, taking action in our own communities. The actions that burgeon from our hands and minds may *look* marginal, but they hold the seeds for the future.

Here are just a few examples of the many diverse initiatives underway:

- Face to face teach-ins and study groups on the nature of the Industrial Growth Society, to expose the workings of the global economy—such as those offered by the International Forum on Globalization (active in North America and Europe) and the Boston-based United for a Fair Economy.

- Educational services on the ecological and human costs of a consumer society, such as those provided by the Worldwatch Institute (Washington, D.C.), the Positive Futures Network (Seattle), the

Northwest Earth Institute (Portland, Oregon), the Natural Step (Sweden), the Schweisfurth Institute (Germany), and think-tanks like the Club of Rome and the Balaton groups launched by Donella Meadows and company, as well as countless groundbreaking university courses on the economics of sustainability.

- Creation of new, more accurate measures of wealth and prosperity, to replace the monetary indices of growth and development (such as the Gross Domestic Product) which have been driving the Industrial Growth Society and ignoring its effects on living systems.

- Community-based services for conflict resolution and mediation, to replace litigation.

- Strategies and programs for nonviolent, citizen-based defense, to replace reliance on military preparedness and retaliation.

- Reduction of reliance on fossil and nuclear fuels and conversion to renewable, cost-effective energy based on wind, solar, photovoltaic, biomass and tidal technologies, such as is occurring in California, Minnesota, Denmark, and Germany.

- The spread of land trusts and conservancies, as nonindividualized forms of land ownership with built-in allegiance to Earth's needs and abundance.

- Collaborative living arrangments such as co-housing and ecovillages which, in a broad variety of legal forms, allow singles, families, and generations to care for each other and the land, while respecting their distinctive needs.

- Local initiatives creating community gardens; consumer and marketing cooperatives; tool-sharing and skills banks; Community-Supported Agriculture; restoration projects reclaiming streams, watersheds, wetlands, and arable land.

- Community and municipal composting and recycling programs.

- Holistic health and wellness methods supplementing medical models of diagnosis and treatment, and enlisting the self-healing capacities of body and mind.

- Local currencies, like the Ithaca Dollar in New York, based on the exchange of goods and services, so that the resources of citizens are cycled within their own communities (instead of being drained away by franchise outlets and multinational corporations).

- Countless new ventures in education, replacing the lockstep model of schooling created to serve industrialism, opening to children their natural world and the intellectual capital of their community, and encouraging adults to engage in lifelong learning.

- Electronic communication systems enabling activists worldwide to rapidly share information, evolve strategies, and coordinate actions outside of bureaucracies and corporate-controlled mass media.

III. Shift in perceptions of reality, both cognitively and spiritually

These nascent institutions cannot take root and survive without deeply ingrained values to sustain them. They must mirror what we want and how we relate to Earth and each other. They require, in other words, a profound shift in our perception of reality—and that shift is happening now, both as cognitive revolution and spiritual awakening. It is the third, most basic dimension of the Great Turning.

The insights and experiences that enable us to make this shift are like the hub of the wheel: they enable its turning. Profoundly generative, they are present now. In our consciousness and in our lives, they come in many forms. They arise as grief for our world, giving the lie to old paradigm notions of the essential separateness of the isolated, competitive ego. Or they may arise from our glad response to breakthroughs in scientific thought, to the new lens on reality provided by quantum theory, astrophysics, and general living systems theory—as we see, with a sigh of relief, that the reductionism and materialism which shaped the worldview of the Industrial Growth Society are about as useful as the abacus in understanding the nature of the universe. Or we may find ourselves moved by the wisdom traditions of native peoples and mystical voices in our own religions, hearkening to their teachings as to some half-forgotten song that reminds us again that our world is a sacred whole in which we have a sacred mission.

Now, in our time, these three rivers—anguish for our world, scientific breakthroughs, and ancestral teachings—flow together. From the confluence of these rivers we drink. We awaken to what we once knew: we are alive in a living Earth, source of all we are and can achieve. Despite our conditioning by the industrial society of the last two centuries, we want to name, once again, this world as holy.

These insights and experiences are absolutely necessary to free us from the grip of the Industrial Growth Society. They offer us nobler goals and deeper pleasures. They help us redefine our wealth and our worth. The reorganization of our perceptions liberates us from illusions about what we need to own and what our place is in the order of things.

Taking us beyond the tired old notions of competitive individualism, they bring us home to each other and our mutual belonging in the living body of Earth. The ingredients and forms of this awakening are many, including:

- General living systems theory, revealing the self-organizing nature of reality and the presence of mind in nature.

- Gaia theory, showing our planet to be a living system and our larger body.

- Deep ecology and the deep, long-range ecology movement, retrieving us from anthropocentrism and calling us home to community with all beings.

- Creation Spirituality and Liberation Theology, which break through the dichotomies erected by hierarchical religious thought, and invoke the sanctity of all life.

- Engaged Buddhism and similar currents in Hindu, Hasidic, Sufi, Taoist, and other traditions, coming forth now with teachings of respect for Earth and the "interbeing" of all life-forms, as grounds for both spiritual practice and social action.

- The resurgence of shamanic traditions and their enlivening means for knowing our identity with Earth and other species.

- Ecofeminism, blending political critique with the women's spirituality movement, reanchoring us in the natural world, and refiguring reality and the self in radically relational terms.

- Ecopsychology, lifting the aims and means of psychotherapy into larger concerns of social pathology, and helping us to question our acquiescence to the destruction of our world.

- The simple living, or voluntary simplicity, movement which liberates people from patterns of consumption that do not reflect their needs, enabling them to find more frugal and satisfying ways of connecting with their world.

- Music and art expressing our interconnectedness, and incorporating sounds and images from nature.

Though we hardly have words for it, this cognitive, spiritual, and perceptual revolution is occurring at a stunning rate of speed. These lines from the late California poet Robinson Jeffers[3] capture the flavor of this awakening:

...I entered the life of the brown forest,
And the great life of the ancient peaks, the patience of stone, I felt the
*   changes in the veins*
In the throat of the mountain, a grain in many centuries, we have our own
*   time, not yours; and, I was the stream*
Draining the mountain wood; and I the stag drinking; and I was the stars
Boiling with light, wandering alone, each one the lord of his own summit;
*   and I was the darkness*
Outside the stars, I included them, they were a part of me. I was mankind
*   also, a moving lichen*
On the cheek of the round stone...
*   ...how can I express the excellence I have found,*
*   that has no color but clearness;*
No honey but ecstasy ...

This shift in our sense of identity will be life-saving in the sociopolitical and ecological traumas that lie before us. All honest forecasts are for rough weather ahead. Because the Industrial Growth Society depends on accelerating consumption of resources, it is unsustainable. It cannot last, for the simple reason that it is inexorably and exponentially destroying itself. In system terms, it is on "runaway." As its distant markets and supplies dry up, and its interlocked financial institutions collapse, the shock waves wash over us all, tumbling us into fear of chaos.

The realizations we make in the third dimension of the Great Turning save us from succumbing to either panic or paralysis. They help us resist the temptation to stick our heads in the sand. They also help us withstand the temptation to turn on each other, finding scapegoats on whom to vent our fear and rage. But when we know and revere the wholeness of life, we can stay alert and steady. We know there is no private salvation. We join hands to find the ways the world self-heals—and see the chaos as seedbed for the future.

Though we can discern the Great Turning and take courage from its manifold activity, we have no assurance that it will happen in time. We cannot tell which will happen first: the point of no return, when we cannot stop the unraveling of the systems supporting complex life-forms, or the moment when the elements of a sustainable society cohere and catch hold.

If the Great Turning should fail, it will not be for lack of technology or relevant data so much as for lack of political will. When we're distracted and fearful, and the odds are running against us, it is easy to let the heart and mind go numb. The dangers now facing us are so pervasive and yet often so hard to see—and painful to see, when we manage to look at them—that this numbing touches us all. No one is unaffected by it. No one is immune to doubt, denial, or disbelief about the severity of our situation—and about our power to change it. Yet of all the dangers we face, from climatic change to nuclear wars, none is so great as the deadening of our response.

That numbing of mind and heart is already upon us—in the diversions we create for ourselves as individuals and nations, in the fights we pick, the aims we pursue, the stuff we buy. So let us look at it. Let's see what this deadening is and how it happens. For the work this book describes helps us wake up from that sleep and come back to life. Then, reconnected with our deepest desire, we will be able to take part in the Great Turning. We will choose life.

Chapter 2

THE GREATEST DANGER: APATHEIA, THE DEADENING OF MIND AND HEART

It is the destruction of the world
in our own lives that drives us
half insane, and more than half.
To destroy that which we were given
in trust: how will we bear it?
—Wendell Berry[4]

T HE GREAT TURNING ARISES in response to what we know and feel is happening to our world. It entails both the perception of danger and the means to act. As conscious, embodied beings endowed with multiple senses, we are geared to respond: instantly we leap from the path of an oncoming truck, dash to douse a fire, dive into a pool to save a child. This response-ability has been an essential feature of life throughout our evolution; it allows us to adapt to new challenges and generate new capacities. It enables whole groups and societies to survive, so long as their members have sufficient information and freedom to act. In systems terms, response to danger is a function of feedback—the information circuit that connects perception to action. Appropriate response depends on an unblocked feedback loop.

But in our present situation, things don't seem that simple. The perils facing life on Earth are so massive and unprecedented that they are hard to believe. The very danger signals that should rivet our attention, summon up the blood, and bond us in collective action, tend to have the opposite effect. They make us want to pull down the blinds and busy ourselves with other things. Our desire for distraction supports billion-dollar industries which tell us everything will be all right so long as we buy this car or that deodorant. We eat meat from factory-farmed animals and produce grown by agribusiness, knowing of the pesticides and hormones they contain, but preferring not to think they'll cause harm. We buy clothes without noticing where they are made, preferring not to think of the sweatshops they may have come from. We don't bother voting, or if we do, we vote for candidates we may not believe will address the real problems, hoping against all previous experience that they will suddenly awaken and act boldly to save us. Have we become callous, nihilistic? Have we ceased to care what happens to life on Earth?

It can look that way. Many reformers and activists decry public apathy. To rouse us, they deliver yet more terrifying information, as if we didn't already know that our world is in trouble. They scold and preach about moral duties, as if we didn't already care. Their alarms and sermons tend to make us pull the shades down tighter, stiffening our resistance to what appears to be too overwhelming, too complicated, too out of our control.

So it's good to look at what this apathy is, to understand it with respect and compassion. *Apatheia* is a Greek word that means, literally, nonsuffering. Given its etymology, apathy is the inability or refusal to experience pain. What is the pain we feel—and desperately try not to feel—in this planet-time? It is of another order altogether than what the ancient Greeks could have known; it pertains not just to privations of wealth, health, reputation, or loved ones, but also to losses so vast we can hardly name them. It is pain for the world.

PAIN FOR THE WORLD

From news reports and life around us, we are bombarded with signals of distress—of job layoffs and homeless families, of nearby toxic wastes and distant famines, of arms sales and wars and preparations for wars. These stir within us feelings of fear, anger, and sorrow, even though we may never express them to others. By virtue of our humanity we share these deep responses. To be conscious in our world today is to be aware of vast suffering and unprecedented peril.

Even the words—fear, anger, sorrow—are inadequate to convey the feelings we experience, for these connote emotions long familiar to our species. The feelings that assail us now cannot be equated with ancient dreads of mortality and "the heartache and the thousand natural shocks that flesh is heir to." Their source lies less in concerns for the personal self than in apprehensions of collective suffering—of what happens to our own and other species, to the legacy of our ancestors, to unborn generations, and to the living body of Earth.

What we are dealing with here is akin to the original meaning of compassion: "suffering with." It is the distress we feel on behalf of the larger whole of which we are a part. It is the pain of the world itself, experienced in each of us.

No one is exempt from that pain, any more than one could exist alone and self-sufficient in empty space. It is as natural to us as the food and air we draw upon to fashion who we are. It is inseparable from the currents of matter, energy, and information that flow through us and sustain us as interconnected open systems. We are not closed off from the world, but integral components of it, like cells in a larger body. When that body is traumatized, we sense that trauma, too. When it falters and sickens, we feel its pain, whether we pay attention to it or not.

That pain is the price of consciousness in a threatened and suffering world. It is not only natural, it is an absolutely necessary component of our collective healing. As in all organisms, pain has a purpose: it is a warning signal, designed to trigger remedial action.

The problem, therefore, lies not with our pain for the world, but in our repression of it. Our efforts to dodge or dull it surrender us to futility—or in systems' terms, cut the feedback loop and block effective response.

PSYCHOLOGICAL SOURCES OF REPRESSION

No outside authority is silencing us—yet, at least in North America. No physical force is restraining us from devoting our courage and creativity to the protection of life on Earth. What then is stifling our responses, as individuals and as a society? Let's look first at the psychological reasons why we repress our pain for the world, and then at those that derive from economic and social forces.

Fear of pain

Our culture conditions us to view pain as dysfunctional. There are pills for headache, backache, neuralgia and premenstrual tension—but no pills, capsules or tablets for this pain for our world. Not even a stiff drink really helps. To permit ourselves to entertain anguish for the world is not only painful, but frightening; it appears to threaten our capacity to cope with daily life. We are afraid that if we were to let ourselves fully experience these feelings, we might fall apart, lose control, or be mired in them permanently.

Fear of despair

A sense of some overarching meaning to our lives is as necessary as oxygen. We can face and endure tremendous hardships with heroic courage, so long as we believe there is some purpose to our existence, some value to our actions—whether we define them in terms of personal character-building, like the Stoics, or of nation-building, like the pioneers. But the present crisis, if we dare to look at what it forebodes, presents vistas of such unprecedented loss as to threaten with absurdity all that we have believed in. So, lest we drain our lives of meaning, we look away. We fear that once we admit our despair, even to ourselves—once we let ourselves feel it—we'll be paralyzed.

For people of religious faith, the prospect of losing hope is particularly challenging. "God won't let this happen," many of us think, or try to think, when images of vast destruction surface in our minds. Even to entertain these images can seem to contradict our belief in a loving and powerful deity, and in the goodness of creation itself. Are feelings of despair a sign of inadequate faith?

Every major religion calls us to open to the suffering we see around us. The prophets of Judaism, Jesus Christ, the Buddhist bodhisattva, and the brotherhood at the heart of Islam, as well as countless other sacred teachings, command such compassion. Yet we tend to forget those summons to take within ourselves the travail of our world. Assuming, perhaps, that our God is too fragile or too limited to encompass that pain, unsure whether God will meet us in the midst of such darkness, we hesitate to let ourselves experience it, lest our faith be shattered or revealed as inadequate.

Fear of appearing morbid

"Be sociable." "Keep smiling," our society tells us with its cult of optimism. "If you can't say something nice, don't say anything at all," many of us were admonished as children.

A sanguine confidence in the future has been a hallmark of the American character and a source of national pride. A desire to emulate it spreads now in the global monoculture fostered by multinational corporations. The successful person, as we conclude from commercials and electoral campaigns, brims with optimism. In such a setting, feelings of anguish and despair for our world can appear to be a failure of maintaining confidence and even competence.

Distrust of our own intelligence

Many of us are reluctant to express our concerns for fear of exposing our ignorance, or of getting embroiled in a debate requiring facts and figures beyond our command. The conditions we face are complexly interwoven and hard to understand. The global economy encourages us to rely on "experts"—like the scientists and economists and politicians who tell us that there is no link between nuclear plants and breast cancer, pesticide spraying and asthma, trade agreements and joblessness. It is easy to distrust our own judgment, especially when others around us seem to agree with the way things are. This intellectual timidity, so useful to the power holders, can override our own legitimate experience of distress.

Fear of guilt

Few, if any, of us in the Industrial Growth Society are exempt from the suspicion that we are accomplices to far-reaching abuses of other beings and of the living body of Earth. It is hard to participate in social and economic life without feeding, clothing, and transporting ourselves at the expense of the natural world and other people's well-being. As Peter Marin writes in an essay on moral pain,

> Many of us suffer a vague, inchoate sense of betrayal, of having somehow taken the wrong turning, of having somehow said yes or no at the wrong time and to the wrong things, of having somehow taken upon ourselves a general kind of guilt, having two coats while others have none, or just having too much while others have too little—yet proceeding, nonetheless, with our lives as they are.

We also carry an inchoate sense of accountability for the massive acts of violence perpetrated by our governments. Americans have a huge burden to bear in this respect: the decimation of our native peoples, the enslavement of Africans and the oppression of their descendants, the nuclear bombing of Hiroshima and Nagasaki, the Vietnam and Gulf Wars, suppression of liberation movements in Central America, spiraling arms sales around the world, and CIA-abetted drug traffic—the painful list could go on. We prefer to sweep it under the rug, because we hate feeling guilty—it flies in the face of all we like to think we are and represent. We have neither patience nor practice for dealing with collective guilt, but we can learn. Other governments—Canada, South Africa, Japan, Germany, England—are showing us today that it is possible to acknowledge moral shame, with strength and dignity—and that it is healing. Meanwhile, until we all learn what to do with our feelings of guilt, we'll be likely to lock them away—and in so doing, lock up our pain for the world.

Fear of causing distress

Pain for the world is repressed not only out of embarrassment and guilt, but out of compassion, as well. We are reluctant to burden our loved ones; we would shield them from the distress we carry. Not wanting them to worry, we focus our attention on business-as-usual. For parents this psychological burden is especially heavy. We don't want our children to be troubled or fearful as they face the already challenging tasks of learning and growing. Our deep desire to protect them from harm can make us try to protect them from knowing and feeling what's happening to our world.

Fear of being unpatriotic

Love of country lies deep within most of us, often deeper than our criticisms and disappointments about national policies. It is woven of pride and gratitude for our history and heroes and for the land itself. In America, built as it was on utopian expectations, this love of country seems to require an almost religious belief in our manifest destiny as a fulfillment of human dreams. To entertain feelings of despair over our country's present condition and role in the world seems almost un-American. If we express such feelings, do we sap the confidence we need as a nation to survive in a competitive world? Many politicians would have us silence our fears and doubts, lest they erode our sense of national virtue, and our determination to prevail.

In paying heed to these voices, we overlook an essential element in the American character—the capacity to speak out, to "tell it like it is." From the time of the pilgrims, there have been those who refused to be silent, who rang alarms with Paul Revere, who called for defiance with Patrick Henry, who with Sojourner Truth, Emma Goldman, Martin Luther King and countless others gave voice to the future by speaking out. Most of these people were criticized by their contemporaries and attacked as unpatriotic, but we now can see the vital role they played in history.

Fear of appearing weak and emotional

Many of us refrain from expressing our deep concerns for the world, lest we give the impression that we are prey to our feelings. For centuries the dominant white male culture divorced reason from emotion. Thinking that reality can be apprehended in an "objective" fashion, it placed greater value on the analytic operations of intellect than on the "subjective" realm of feelings and intuitions. Though depth psychology and systems theory have long since revealed the fallacy of "objectivity," old habits die slowly. Emotion-tinged responses are taken as a sign of weakness, impassivity as evidence of strength. Many of us who grew up in the dominant society or operate within it, hide our pain for the world, even from ourselves. We often fear that if we express it, or even allude to it, we will be considered unstable and unreliable, especially in work situations. Given the way they are socialized, men suffer more than women from the fear of appearing weak and emotional, but women experience it, too. They often withhold their expression of concerns lest these be treated condescendingly, as "just like a woman."

Belief in the separate self

It is hard to credit our pain for the world, if we believe that we are essentially separate from it. The individualistic bias of Western culture conditions us to think so. And so does mainstream analytic psychology, with its assumptions that we are driven by competitive impulses and that our sufferings stem from intrapsychic conflict. Psychology has been the study of the individual psyche. Though in the last decades attention has broadened to include family dynamics, the family system is generally seen as the sole source of its own dysfunction, while the social, economic, political, and ecological systems in which that family lives have been largely ignored.

So people have come to assume that feelings of fear, anger, or despair about the world are merely a reflection of personal inner conflict. If all our drives are egocentered, then our distress over the state of the world indicates an abnormality; it must manifest some private neurosis—rooted perhaps in early trauma, or unresolved distress with a parental figure that we're projecting on society at large. Thus we are tempted to discredit feelings that arise from solidarity with our fellow-beings, dismissing them as some kind of personal morbidity. "Even in my therapy group," writes a teacher, "I stopped mentioning my fears of nuclear war. The others kept saying, 'What are you running from in your life by creating these worries for yourself?'"

Conditioned to take seriously only those feelings that pertain to our individual needs and wants, we find it hard to believe that we can suffer on behalf of society itself, and on behalf of our planet, and that such suffering is real and valid and healthy.

Fear of powerlessness

Probably the most frequent response to the mention of any global threat is to the effect that "I don't think about that because there is nothing I can do about it." Logically, this is a non sequitur, confusing what can be thought and felt with what can be done. And it is a tragic one, for when forces are seen as so vast that they cannot be consciously contemplated or seriously discussed, we are doubly victimized—impeded in thought as well as action.

Resistance to painful information on the grounds that we cannot "do anything about it" springs less from powerlessness—as measured by our capacity to effect change—than from the fear of *experiencing* powerlessness. The model of self which predominates in Western culture is "I am the master of my fate and the captain of my soul." That discourages us from confronting issues which remind us that we do not exert ultimate control over our lives. We feel that we ought to be in charge of our existence and emotions, to have all the answers. And so we tend to shrink the sphere of our attention to those areas in which we believe we can exercise some direct control. This becomes a self-fulfilling prophecy: the smaller our sphere of attention, the smaller our sphere of influence. We become as powerless as we fear to be.

SOCIOECONOMIC SOURCES OF REPRESSION

When Joanna first wrote about our pain for the world in 1978, the causes which she explored and enumerated were largely psychological. By now, given the accelerated and hypertrophied state of the Industrial Growth Society, additional factors emerge. The corporate global economy, with the increasing pressures it exerts on individuals, families, and communities, and its spreading control of information channels, makes it yet more difficult for people to respond to the world's cries of distress, or even to hear them. How is this so?

The mass media

Information about what is happening to our world is far more restricted now than twenty years ago. With the rapid corporate monopolization of the media, less information comes through to convey the abuses being inflicted on other humans and on the natural world. Censorship increases, blocking reports that would inform the public of corporate misdeeds, and the collusion of politicians. So does "misinformation," outright deception, lest the public question the nature of the system in which it lives. This control of the mass media makes it much easier for individuals to avoid feeling pain for their world, by staying ignorant of its true plight.

Instead of informing people about the condition of the world, the corporate-controlled media serve predominately as distraction, soporific, and goad to consume. As the economy globalizes, and corporations sink their teeth into every society they can reach, the monoculture they purvey infects even subsistence farmers with dreams of unobtainable and unsustainable affluence. Australian activist Benny Sable dramatizes the pervasive message of this monoculture in many a demonstration against clearcutting or uranium mining or massive hydroelectric projects. He stands motionless, often high atop a pile of casks marked radioactive, in a black wetsuit painted with a skeleton and these words:

CONSUME

OBEY

BE SILENT

DIE

Job and time pressures

The corporate mergers characterizing the advanced state of the Industrial Growth Society rob people of employment, make them scramble for jobs, and feel highly insecure in those they still manage to hang on to. Moonlighting, they rush from one job to another, to piece together a living wage. Most young families, in order to pay the bills, need both parents to work for pay, or try to. The pace accelerates, taking its toll on every spare moment, every relationship. As employment benefits are cut, and social health and welfare programs decimated, economic anxiety mounts. The world narrows down to one's own and one's family's immediate needs. There's little time to learn about the fate of the world, or let it sink in. If a free hour is left at the end of the day, one prefers to zone out with a beer in front of the television—and the packaged fantasies of the Industrial Growth Society.

Social violence

The economic hardships generated by the Industrial Growth Society tear the fabric of our society and breed violence. Jobless youth act out their hopelessness, inflamed by the greed and brutality constantly portrayed by the media, and embittered by the cynicism modeled by the power holders. We fear our own city streets, barricade ourselves behind locked doors, take refuge in gated enclaves. Politicians and demagogues direct our frustrations against each other—especially against those most victimized by the global economy. For the failures of capitalism, we start scapegoating each other.

Whether or not we directly experience the violence of our society, it impinges on us all. It colors our common life. It erects a defensive armor around the heart that impedes us from opening to the pain of our world. It blocks us from knowing that this pain is inside us, too.

CONSEQUENCES OF REPRESSION

Repression takes a mammoth toll on our energy, and also on our sensitivity to the world around us. Repression is not a local anesthetic. If we won't feel pain, we won't feel much else, either—both loves and losses are less intense, the sky less vivid, pleasures muted. As a doctor working with Vietnam veterans observed, "The mind pays for its deadening to the state of our world by giving up its capacity for joy and flexibility." [5]

This dulling of response to the condition of our world is called *psychic numbing*. Robert J. Lifton, who coined the term in his study of Hiroshima survivors, now applies it to us all—recognizing how widely we are affected by the massive threats to life on Earth. Because psychic numbing operates on the collective level as well as within the individual, it gives rise to a whole laundry list of common ailments in our culture: fragmentation and alienation, escapist pursuits, addiction, random violence, political passivity, blaming and scapegoating, suppression of vital information, diminished intellectual performance, a sense of powerlessness, and burnout. These effects in turn create more to exclude from our consciousness. The process is reciprocal. Here cause and effect compound each other in a vicious circle, or in systems terms, a positive feedback loop.

Sages through the years have warned us about this. "The truth that many people never understand until it is too late is that the more you try to avoid suffering, the more you suffer" (Thomas Merton). "You can hold yourself back from the suffering of the world: this is something you are free to do... but perhaps precisely this holding back is the only suffering you might be able to avoid" (Franz Kafka).

Let's examine the effects of repression more closely, recognizing that each in turn can function as a cause.

Fragmentation and alienation

We all tend to lead a double life. While on the surface we focus on business as usual, underneath there is a vague awareness of impending doom. As with any form of dishonesty, this creates an internal split, engendering self-doubt and leading us to distrust our inner knowing, our deep source of creativity and insight. Cut off from our own authority, we become more susceptible to manipulation by advertising and propaganda.

This inner split gives rise to a sense of isolation. Inhibitions against speaking of our deep concerns distance us from others. Even when, on a cognitive level, these concerns seem valid, it is hard to relate them to the tenor of life around us. They produce such psychic dissonance that we begin to question our own perceptions, even our own sanity.

So we seal off an authentic part of ourselves and we are cut off as well from deeper connections with others. "Given the social taboo against crying out [over the state of the world], people distance themselves from each other as do the families and friends of the terminally ill," says theologian Harvey Cox. And so many of us suffer alone and apart, unaware of our common struggles, deprived of the mutual support we all need.

Displacement activities

Rats in the laboratory, when threatened, are observed to busy themselves in frenzied, irrelevant activities. So apparently do we. Our society has turned increasingly through this century to a desperate pursuit of pleasure and short-term gratification. A new hedonism is evident in the consumption of goods, sex, entertainment, alcohol and drugs—and the obsessive pursuit of money as an end in itself. This hedonism derives from more than sheer appetite. Its frantic quality does not convey a healthy lust for life so much as the contrary: we doubt the possibility of real happiness and the continuance of life. We try to grab all we can while it lasts. Helen Caldicott calls this "manic denial."

Feelings of despair over the world and our future may be pushed below conscious awareness, but they surface again in other guises. They may be expressed outwardly against society in acts of violence and vandalism, and inwardly in self-destruction—as the rising rates of drug abuse and suicide among children attest. These problems cannot all be traced to idiosyncratic disorders and drug use; to an unmeasurable extent they relate to rage about what is happening to our world.

Blaming and scapegoating

When feelings of pain for our world remain unnamed and unacknowledged, the vague, free-floating sense of being threatened by something intolerable often turns us against others. We seek scapegoats to blame for our inchoate sense of alarm. Carl Jung called this kind of phenomenon "the projection of the shadow."

For many years Americans demonized the Russians and the

Communists, and now deprived of those foes, we cast about for new enemies within our own borders on whom to vent our suspicions and anger. We blame illegal immigrants, welfare recipients, jobless and homeless people, and other more or less disenfranchised groups for our troubles. The upsurge of racist and sexist resentments, the recent spates of church burnings and painted swastikas, hate crimes, and diatribes on radio talk shows against gays, feminists, and other "deviant" minorities all evidence an unacknowledged and misdirected dread of the future.

Political passivity

To silence our suppressed fears, we comfort ourselves with the thought that we can and should trust our leaders. "There are profound, powerful and unconscious needs to see the government as powerful, protective, and wise," reads a report to the New York Psychiatric Association. "People use fantasies about the government to allay their anxiety. Even though its efficacy to prevent war is acknowledged to be faulty, the government becomes the fantasized repository of war-preventing expertise. There is also an emotional payoff in having a strong, aggressive government, so that the citizen can feel less aggressive."[6]

Repression of our pain for the world disempowers us politically. Separated from one another as well as from our own deepest wisdom, we become more docile, obedient.

Avoidance of painful information

To the extent that we fear feeling despair for the world, we tend to screen out the data that provoke it. People admit with increasing frequency, "I don't read the paper anymore...I tune out the news...I can't take it anymore, it bums me out." We often tune out even the news that is available to us, cutting ourselves off from vital feedback.

Diminished intellectual performance

The repression of strong emotion impairs our capacity to think, according to psychologist Thomas Scheff. It clouds both perception and thought, rigidifies mental responses and results in a loss of intellectual clarity. Even when we pay attention to information about the state of our world, we do not process it well if we are in a condition of psychic numbing.

Burnout

When we are courageous enough to study the available data, they turn out to be more alarming than most of us had assumed. Many peace and environmental advocates, exposed to terrifying information in the course of their work, carry a heavy burden of knowledge. It is compounded by feelings of frustration, as they fight an uphill battle to arouse the public. Yet they view their own despair as counterproductive to their efforts. They take no time to mourn. In their role as mobilizers of the public will, they don't feel they can "let their hair down" and expose the extent of their own distress. The consequent and continual repression of feelings takes a toll on their energies that leaves them vulnerable to bitterness, depression, exhaustion, and illness.

Sense of powerlessness

Silence concerning our deepest feelings about the world and the future of our species along with the fragmentation, isolation, burnout, and cognitive confusion that result from that silence—all converge to produce a sense of futility. Each act of denial, conscious or unconscious, is an abdication of our power to respond. It relegates us to the role of victim, before we even engage and try to change the situation.

BREAKING FREE

Our pain for the world, including the fear, anger, sorrow, and guilt we feel on behalf of life on Earth, is not only pervasive. It is natural and healthy. It is dysfunctional only to the extent that it is misunderstood and repressed. We have seen in this chapter how easily that repression happens in today's culture, and what it costs us.

We don't break free from denial and repression by gritting our teeth and trying to be nobler, braver citizens. We don't retrieve our passion for life, our wild, innate creativity, by scolding ourselves and soldiering on with a stiff upper lip. That model of heroic behavior belongs to the worldview that gave us the Industrial Growth Society.

The most remarkable feature of this historical moment on Earth is not that we are on the way to destroying our world—we've actually been on the way for quite a while. It is that we are beginning to wake up, as from a millennia-long sleep, to a whole new relationship to our world, to ourselves and each other. This new take on reality makes the Great Turning possible. We described it in Chapter 1 as the third and most basic level of that revolution. It is so central to the arising of the Life-sustaining Society that it is like the hub of a turning wheel.

The worldview now emerging—if we are bold to experience its implications—lets us behold anew and experience afresh the web of life in which we exist. It opens us to the vast intelligence of life's self-organizing powers, which have brought us forth from interstellar gases and primordial seas. It brings us to a larger identity in which to cradle and transcend our ego-identified fears. It lets us honor our pain for the world as a gateway into deep participation in the world's self-healing. The group work of the last twenty years, which this book describes, is based on this worldview.

More basic to the Great Turning than any ideas we have about it is the act of courage and love we make when we dare to see our world as it is.

And I would travel with you
to the places of our shame

The hills stripped of trees, the marsh grasses
oil-slicked, steeped in sewage;

The blackened shoreline, the chemical-poisoned water;

I would stand with you in the desolate places, the charred places,
soil where nothing will ever grow, pitted desert;

fields that burn slowly for months; roots of cholla & chaparral
writhing with underground explosions

I would put my hand
there with yours, I would take your hand, I would walk with you

through carefully planted fields, rows of leafy vegetables
drifting with radioactive dust; through the dark
of uranium mines hidden in the sacred gold-red mountains;

I would listen with you in drafty hospital corridors
as the miner cried out in the first language

of pain; as he cried out
the forgotten names of his mother I would stand
next to you in the forest's

final hour, in the wind
of helicopter blades, police

sirens shrieking, the delicate
tremor of light between

leaves for the last
time Oh I would touch with this love each

wounded place

—Anita Barrows [7]

Chapter 3

THE BASIC MIRACLE:
OUR TRUE NATURE AND POWER

Qum Qum Ya Habibi Kam Tanam
Arise, arise my beloved, how you sleep
The sun and the moon do not sleep
The stars and the trees do not sleep
The lover and the beloved do not sleep
Arise, my beloved, do not sleep.
—Sufi chant

TO THOSE OF US WHO HAVE GROWN UP in the Industrial Growth Society, the view of reality that breaks upon us now is breathtakingly new. It comes from contemporary science and finds support in ancient spiritual traditions. It helps us understand our relationship to the world and awaken to powers within us for its healing. Liberating us from constricted notions of who we are and what we need, it brings us home to our true nature—in league with the stars and trees of our thrumming universe. It is basic to the Great Turning—and fundamental to the work this book presents.

We people of "Western Civilization" have struggled to master the natural world around us. We have studied the Earth and the cosmos, attempting to discover the essential building blocks of life that we might manipulate them into more efficient mechanisms to provide for our wants and needs. We have acted as if we could know and control the world from the outside, as if we were separate from it. We came to think of ourselves as made of better stuff than the animals and plants and rocks and water around us. And our technologies of the last centuries amplified disastrously the ecological effects of that assumption.

Perhaps we made our biggest error in thinking of the world as made of "stuff" to begin with. Fortunately—and paradoxically—our very search for mastery and knowledge through science has itself brought us to the dawning realization that the world, indeed the universe, seems not to be composed of "stuff" at all. Each time we have grasped what appeared to be a "basic building block," it has dissolved into a dance of energy and relationship, with no real substance at all! And so we awaken today to a new kind of knowledge, a developing comprehension of our radical interrelatedness to everything in the universe.

LIVING SYSTEMS THEORY

Modern science and the Industrial Growth Society grew up together. With the help of René Descartes and Francis Bacon, classical science veered away from a holistic, organic view of the world to an analytical and mechanical one. The machines we made, to extend our senses and capacities, became our model for the universe. Separating mechanism from operator, object from observer, this view of reality assumed that everything could be described objectively and controlled externally. It has permitted extraordinary technological gains and fueled the engines of industrial progress. But, as twentieth century biologists realized with increasing frustration, it cannot explain the self-renewing processes of life.

Instead of looking for basic building blocks, these life scientists took a new tack: they began to look at wholes instead of parts, at processes instead of substances. They discovered that these wholes—be they cells, bodies, ecosystems, or even the planet itself—are not just a heap of disjunct parts, but are dynamically organized and intricately balanced "systems," interdependent in every movement, every function, every exchange of energy and information. They saw that each element is part of a vaster pattern, a pattern that connects and evolves by discernible principles. The discernment of these principles gave rise to general living systems theory.

Austrian biologist Ludwig von Bertalanffy, known as the father of general systems theory, called it a "way of seeing." And while its insights have spread throughout the physical and social sciences, spawning groundbreaking derivative theories, the systems perspective has remained just that—a way of seeing. Anthropologist Gregory

Bateson called it "the biggest bite out of the Tree of Knowledge in two thousand years."[8]

How life self-organizes

By shifting their focus to relationships instead of separate entities, scientists made an amazing discovery—amazing at least to the mainstream western mind. They discovered that nature is self-organizing. Or rather, assuming that to be the case, they set about discerning the principles by which this self-organizing occurs. They found these principles or system properties to be awesomely elegant in their simplicity and constancy throughout the observable universe, from suborganic to biological and ecological systems, and mental and social systems, as well. The properties of open systems which permit the variety and intelligence of life-forms to arise from interactive currents of matter and energy are four in number.

1. Each system, from atom to galaxy, is a whole. That means that it is not reducible to its components. Its distinctive nature and capacities derive from the interactive relationships between its parts. This interplay is synergistic, generating "emergent properties" and new possibilities, which are not predictable from the character of the separate parts—just as the wetness of water could not be predicted from oxygen and hydrogen before they combined, or just as the tensile strength of steel far exceeds the combined strengths of iron and nickel. This property of open systems challenges the universal applicability of the Second Law of Thermodynamics, that cornerstone of classical science on which rest notions of entropy, the running down of all life.

2. Despite continual flow-through of matter-energy and information, and indeed thanks to that flow-through, open systems are able to maintain their balance; they self-stabilize. By virtue of this capacity, which von Bertalanffy called *fliessgleichgewicht* (flux-equilibrium), systems can self-regulate to compensate for changing conditions in their environment. This homeostatic function is performed by registering /monitoring the effects of their own behavior and matching it with their norms, like a thermostat. It is understood as a function of feedback—negative or deviation-reducing feedback, to be precise (also called "cybernetics one"). This is how we maintain our body temperature, heal from a cut, or ride a bicycle.

3. Open systems not only maintain their balance amidst the flux, but also evolve in complexity. When challenges from their environment persist, they can fall apart or adapt by reorganizing themselves around new,

more responsive norms. This, too, is a function of feedback—positive or deviation-amplifying feedback (also called "cybernetics two"). It is how we learn and how we evolved from the amoeba. But if our changing behaviors are not compatible with the challenges we face, and do not achieve a new balance with them, the positive feedback loop gets out of control and goes into "runaway," leading eventually to systems breakdown.

4. Every system is a "holon"—that is, it is both a whole in its own right, comprised of subsystems, *and* simultaneously an integral part of a larger system. Thus holons form "nested hierarchies," systems within systems, circuits within circuits, fields within fields. Each new holonic level—say from atom to molecule, cell to organ, person to family—generates emergent properties that are nonreducible to the capacities of the separate components. Far different than the hierarchies of control familiar to societies where rule is imposed from above, in nested hierarchies (sometimes called holonarchies) order tends to arise from the bottom up; the system self-generates from spontaneously adaptive cooperation between the parts, in mutual benefit. Order and differentiation go hand and hand, components diversifying as they coordinate roles and invent new responses.

Fire, water, and web

The mechanistic view of reality separated substance from process, self from other, thought from feeling. In the systems perspective, these dichotomies no longer hold. What appeared to be separate and self-existent entities are now seen to be interdependent. What had appeared to be "other" can be equally construed as a concomitant of "self," like a fellow-cell in a larger body. What we had been taught to dismiss as mere feelings are responses to our world no less valid than rational constructs. Sensations, emotions, intuitions, concepts, all condition each other, each a way of apprehending the relationships which weave our world.

As systems we participate in the evolving web of life, giving and receiving the feedback necessary for its sustenance, and maintaining integrity and balance by virtue of constant flow-through. To convey this dynamic process, theorists have used a variety of images. Fire and water are prominent among them. "We are not stuff that abides," says Norbert Wiener, "we are patterns that perpetuate themselves; we are whirlpools in a river of everflowing water."[9] Or we are like a flame, says Leon Brillouin; as a flame keeps its shape by transforming the stuff that flows through it, so do we in the constant processes of metabolism.[10] To convey the nature of the relationship between open systems, a frequent image is that of nerve cells in a neural net. Systems political scientist Karl Deutsch took it as a model for social as well as biological systems, arguing that free circulation of information is essential to health and survival.[11] By their synergistic interactions neurons differentiate and enhance each other in their diversity. Weaving an ever more responsive and intricate net, they give rise to intelligence.

The holonic shift in consciousness

The image of the neural net conveys a major systems insight: mind is not separate from nature; it is in nature. Mind pervades the natural world as the subjective dimension within every open system, however primitive, says systems philosopher Ervin Laszlo.[12] It is ubiquitous in the circuits of information, or feedback loops, guiding every relationship, says Gregory Bateson.[13]

In humans, and some other big-brained mammals, mind is endowed with a remarkable feature: self-reflexive consciousness. It emerged by necessity, when the system's internal complexity grew so great that it could no longer survive by instinct or trial and error. It needed to evolve another level of awareness in order to weigh different courses of action; it needed, in other words, to make choices. A new level of self-monitoring emerged—feedback about feedback, in ever-complexifying assemblies of loops. The self-observant "I" arose. It arose by virtue of decision-making.

Self-reflexive consciousness, which requires a high degree of integration and differentiation, does *not* characterize the next holonic level, the level of social systems. Though an "esprit de corps" can be sensed in organizations with strong allegiances, it is too diffuse to register and respond to all the feedback necessary for its survival. The locus of decision-making remains within the individual, susceptible to all the vagaries of what that individual considers to be of self-interest. And our present modes of decision-making seem simply too slow and too corruptible to respond adequately to the survival crisis produced by our Industrial Growth Society and its technologies.

Could this very crisis, confronting us as it does with destruction of the bases of complex life forms on Earth, engender a collective level of self-interest in choice-making—in other words, self-reflexivity on the next holonic level?

Fearful of fascism, we might well reject any idea of collective consciousness. It is important to remember that genuine, systemic self-organizing requires diversity of parts in spontaneous, unconstricted play. A monolith of uniformity has no internal intelligence.

The holonic shift in consciousness would not sacrifice, but instead require, the uniqueness of each part and its point of view. It would begin, almost imperceptibly, with a sense of common fate, and a shared intention to meet it together. It would start to emerge in unexpected behaviors, as individuals in countless settings meet to speak and reflect on what is happening to their lives, their world. It would manifest in an unpredictable array of spontaneous actions, as people step out from their private comforts, giving time and taking risks on behalf of Earth and their brother-sister beings. It would include all the hopes and changes that give reality to each dimension of the Great Turning. And given the dynamics of self-organizing systems, it is likely that as we reflect and act together, we will soon find ourselves responding to the present crisis with far greater confidence and precision than we imagined possible.

Gaia theory

Insights from systems theory soon revolutionized the way we saw our planet home. James Lovelock and Lynn Margulis studied the chemical balances of our atmosphere and discovered that they are maintained within the narrow limits necessary for life, by self-regulating processes. These are the hallmark of a living system.

Thankfully, Lovelock did not call this hypothesis, soon to become a theory, the "hypothesis of self-regulative processes of the biosphere" or something which would have made it much more respectable to his fellow scientists. Instead he listened to his friend, novelist William Golding, who suggested he call it Gaia for the early Greek goddess of the earth, thereby catching people's poetic imagination. Like the Apollo photo of Earth from space, this image of Earth as a whole living being has transformed the way many of us now think of our planetary home. No longer a dead rock we live upon, the Earth is a living process in which we participate. Earth, as a home for life, is a being that we can both harm and help to heal. Earth takes on a presence in our consciousness, not unlike the presence of gods and goddesses in the lives of our early ancestors.

Positive disintegration

Dangers to their survival move living systems to evolve. When feedback tells them—and continues to tell them—that their old forms and behaviors have become dysfunctional, they respond by changing. They adapt to such challenges, as we saw in the third property of systems, by seeking and incorporating more appropriate norms. They search for values and goals which allow them to navigate in more varied conditions, with wider connections. Since its norms are the system's internal code or organizing principle, this process—which Ervin Laszlo calls "exploratory self-reorganization"—is a kind of temporary limbo. To the mind it can be very disorienting. Psychiatrist Kazimierz Dabrowski names it "positive disintegration."[14] It can feel like dying.

In periods of major cultural transition, the experience of positive disintegration is widespread. Such is the case now for us in this time of Great Turning. Everywhere anomalies appear: developments that don't fit our expectations, or in systems terms, that don't match previously programmed codes and constructs. Bereft of self-confidence and old coping strategies, we may feel that we and our world are falling apart. Sometimes we panic or shut down; sometimes in desperation we get mean and turn on each other.

It helps to recall that in the course of our planetary journey we have gone through positive disintegration countless times. The life living through us repeatedly died to old forms and old ways. We know this dying in the splitting of the stars, the cracking open of seeds in the soil, the relinquishment of gills and fins as we crawled onto dry land. Our evolution attests to this, and so does our present lifetime, as we learned to move beyond the safeties and dependencies of childhood. It is never easy. Some of the uglier aspects of human behavior today arise from fear of the wholesale changes we must now undergo.

To let ourselves feel anguish and disorientation as we open our awareness to global suffering is a part of our spiritual ripening. Mystics speak of the "dark night of the soul." Brave enough to let go of accustomed assurances and allow old mental comforts and conformities to fall away, they stand naked to the unknown. They let processes which their minds could not encompass work through them. Out of darkness, the new is born.

DEEP ECOLOGY

Our interdependence with all life of Earth has profound implications for our attitudes and actions. To clarify these implications and free us from behaviors based on outmoded notions of our separateness from nature, deep ecology arose, both as a philosophy and a movement. The term was coined in the 1970s by Norwegian philosopher Arne Naess, a mountain climber and scholar of Gandhi.

In contrast to reform environmentalism, which treats the *symptoms* of ecological degradation—clean up a river here or a dump there for human well-being—deep ecology questions fundamental premises of the

Industrial Growth Society. It challenges the assumptions, embedded in much Judeo-Christian and Marxist thought, that humans are the crown of creation and the ultimate measure of value. It offers us a broader and more sustainable sense of our own worth, as viable members of the great evolving community of Earth. It holds that we can break free from the species arrogance which threatens not only ourselves but all complex life-forms within reach.

Beyond anthropocentrism

We cannot genuinely experience our interrelatedness with all life if we are blind to our own human-centeredness, and how deeply embedded it is in our culture and consciousness. Deep ecologist John Seed, an Australian rainforest activist, describes both the ways it constricts us, and the rewards we find in moving beyond it.

Anthropocentrism means human chauvinism. Similar to sexism, but substitute "human race" for man and "all other species" for woman...

When humans investigate and see through their layers of anthropocentric self-cherishing, a most profound change in consciousness begins to take place. Alienation subsides. The human is no longer a stranger, apart. Your humanness is then recognized as merely the most recent stage of your existence, and as you stop identifying exclusively with this chapter, you start to get in touch with yourself as mammal, as vertebrate, as a species only recently emerged from the rainforest. As the fog of amnesia disperses, there is a transformation in your relationship to other species, and in your commitment to them.

John Seed points out that this liberation is more than an intellectual process. For him, as for many other people, it has been engendered and deepened by taking part in actions on behalf of Earth.

"I am protecting the rainforest" develops to "I am part of the rainforest protecting myself. I am that part of the rainforest recently emerged into thinking." What a relief then! The thousands of years of imagined separation are over and we begin to recall our true nature. That is, the change is a spiritual one, sometimes referred to as deep ecology. [15]

The ecological self

Arne Naess has a term for the wider sense of identity that John Seed describes. He calls it the *ecological self*, and presents it as the fruit of a natural maturation process. We underestimate ourselves, he says, when we identify self with the narrow, competitive ego. "With sufficient all-sided maturity" we not only move on from ego to a social self and a metaphysical self, but an ecological self as well. Through widening circles of identification, we vastly extend the boundaries of our self-interest, and enhance our joy and meaning in life.

A welcome and significant feature of this concept is the way it transcends the need to sermonize about our moral responsibilities to other beings. When we assumed that we were essentially separate, we preached altruism—the Latin term *alter* being the opposite of *ego*. This is not only philosophically unsound, from the perspective of deep ecology and other nondualistic teachings, but also ineffective.

> What humankind is capable of loving from mere duty or moral exhortation is, unfortunately, very limited.... The extensive moralizing within the ecological movement has given the public the false impression that they are primarily asked to sacrifice, to show more responsibility, more concern, and better morals.... [But] the requisite care flows naturally if the self is widened and deepened so that protection of free nature is felt and conceived of as protection of our very selves. [16]

Asking deeper questions

Naess and his activist colleagues called for a "deep, long-range ecology movement." Whether or not it is yet discernible as a movement, certainly its ideas have circulated widely, providing a powerful impetus to both green activists and academic debates.

While these ideas have evolved into a deep ecology platform—including such principles as the recognition that life-forms have an intrinsic right to exist, and that human population is excessive in relation to the carrying capacity of Earth—deep ecology is neither an ideology nor a dogma. Of an essentially exploratory character, it seeks to motivate people to ask, as Naess puts it, "deeper questions" about their *real* wants and needs, about their relation to life on Earth and their vision for the future. As parts of a larger living whole—be it a society, an ecosystem, or a planet—our comprehension of it is necessarily partial; we cannot stand aloof, blueprints in hand, and deliver final answers. But the questions we ask of ourselves and each other act as a solvent, loosening up encrusted mental structures, and freeing us to think and see in fresh ways.

Related movements: ecofeminism, ecojustice, ecopsychology

This kind of basic inquiry has fostered movements and modes of thought that do not necessarily link themselves with deep ecology, though they share many of its philosophical premises as well as much of its critique of the Industrial Growth Society. Many activists and thinkers (including the authors) identify themselves with more than one of these overlapping movements, each of which brings distinctive concerns and perspectives.

Obvious parallels exist between the ways that entrenched power structures treat nature and the ways they treat women. *Ecofeminism* emerged in the 1970s, as scholars, writers, and organizers illumined these parallels and explored their common cultural roots. Many incisive voices argue that the war against nature waged by the Industrial Growth Society arises from more ancient patterns of domination. They question deep ecologists' focus on anthropocentrism as the source of our pathology, and challenge them to discern the *andro*centricism (patriarchy) which underlies it. Their insights help us recognize the mindset bred by centuries of male rule—the dualism and objectification, the divorce of mind from body, of logic from experience; and they offer more holistic ways of knowing. Defender of the redwoods, the late Judy Bari was an ecofeminist who personified the deepest values of the movement. Despite assaults that shortened her life, she persisted in her commitment to nonviolence, her compassionate concern for the loggers' future, and her penetrating analysis of the corporate forces destroying their livelihood and the land itself.

As ecofeminism brings the issue of gender to our understanding of the environmental crisis, the *ecojustice* movement brings issues of race, class, and poverty. The old divide between activists in defense of social and economic rights and those in defense of nature no longer holds. It is increasingly evident that their goals are inseparably linked and mutually reinforcing. The wreckage and contamination caused by the Industrial Growth Society degrade humans and habitats alike: polluting industries are located and toxic wastes are dumped where poor people and people of color live. The farm workers sprayed by pesticides, the miners poisoned by uranium, the forest dwellers whose homes are clearcut... all are largely people of color. Their race and poverty make them easier for a prejudiced society to overlook. The ecojustice movement has effectively challenged environmentalists to broaden their awareness to the suffering of humans as well as trees and dolphins. Through its outreach to larger sections of society, it holds promise for a vastly wider participation in the work of the Great Turning.

Western psychology has virtually ignored our relationship to the natural world. Our connection to the source of life does not figure in its definition of mental health, nor is our destruction of our life-support system included in its list of pathologies. It has failed to ask Paul Shepard's rather obvious and haunting question: "Why does society persist in destroying its habitat?" Now the new discipline of *ecopsychology* addresses this failure and studies the human psyche within the larger systems of which it is a part. It explores how our cultural alienation from nature engenders not only careless and destructive behavior toward our environment, but also many common disorders such as depression and addiction. Psychotherapists within the movement recognize how their profession has blinded itself to the larger context of their clients' lives and pathologized their pain for the world. These pioneers break new ground as they help clients find strength and meaning through experiencing their interconnectedness with all life, and acting on its behalf.

> Ecopsychology invites psychotherapy practice to expand its focus beyond the inner landscape, to explore and foster the development of community, contact with land and place, and ecological identity.... It invites us to hear the Earth speaking through our pain and distress, and listen to ourselves as if we were listening to a message from the universe. [17]

ANCIENT TEACHINGS

The view of reality afforded us now by systems science and ecological thought is remarkable in its convergence with ancient teachings of our planet's people. At the same time that we are discovering the process nature of our world as a dynamically interrelated whole, we rediscover this understanding in spiritual traditions from East and West, North and South. We find it not only in Taoist, Hindu, and Buddhist sages and scriptures, and not only among indigenous peoples who still know and live this truth. We also find this vision expressed in the most mystical teachings of Christianity, Judaism, and Islam. Perhaps only we, who shaped and are shaped by the Industrial Growth Society—blinded as we have been by our prowess in manipulating tools and producing goods—have forgotten our embeddedness in a larger, living whole.

The meeting of these spiritual traditions with the Westernized, modern mind may well be, as Arnold Toynbee asserted in relation to Buddhism, the most significant occurrence of our planet-time. These traditions not only contribute to our philosophical understandings, but also serve to embody and enliven these understandings—so that they become real to our experience and efficacious in our lives. We do not live by conceptual abstractions. We are not brains on the end of a stick. We are vital, juicy, flesh-and-blood beings, and ideas become truly real for us through our senses and imagination—through stories, images, rituals that enlist our capacity for devotion, our tears and laughter. Entertained solely by the intellect, ideas lack power to lift us into new perspectives and new meanings for our lives. Our ancestors knew this, hence their ritual celebrations to honor Earth and their yogas to open body and mind.

The Abrahamic religions

Spiritual lineages resurfacing today are helping us internalize the vision of reality offered by systems science and deep ecology. Each points beyond narrow confines of orthodoxy, as they present for our rejoicing the basic miracle of our existence.

From Islam comes a resurgence of mystical Sufism. The best-selling poetry of Rumi, the fables of Nasrudin, and the teachings of many contemporary emissaries offer a devotional response to the essential mystery at the source of our interdependent lives.

Within Christianity, clerics and theologians alike break through superstructures of dogma to find at the core of their faith a celebratory vision of our true nature and calling, consonant with the latest findings of science. This vision is not new: Nicholas da Cusa, a fifteenth century mathematician and cardinal, perceived God as "an infinite circle, whose circumference is nowhere, and whose center is everywhere."

From Judaism, too, comes a plethora of fresh, arresting voices recalling their religion's ancient reverence for the living body of Earth. They remind their brother-sister Jews that the call to justice includes *all* life-forms, and summon them to drink once again from the ecological currents of their faith.

Earth-centered religions

Meanwhile, yet more ancient wellsprings of Earth wisdom open. Shamanic traditions of the indigenous peoples of America, Africa, Australia, Old Europe, Siberia and Arctic regions resurface in our day with the same message. Their voices find a hearing because they tell us— as the natives *we* are of the late Industrial Growth Society—what we want to know once again: that as kin to the animals and plants, rocks and airs of this sacred world, we can tap its powers, take part in its healing.

Simultaneously, fresh archeological evidence brings us knowledge of the Goddess of pre-patriarchal cultures. Embodying not only the abundance of Earth, but also the reverence and fairness this abundance requires, she guided gathering and hunting societies, gave rise to agriculture and ancient arts over warless millennia. Despite persecutions and inquisitions, remnants of this earth-based wisdom still survive on the margins of the major religions, in practices of Wicca or witchcraft, and today's neopaganism. Through a host of fine scholars and teachers, its subtle understanding of life's interlinked processes now reemerges. As systems theory does in relation to classical science, goddess wisdom breaks down the mind-matter dichotomy erected by patriarchal structures of thought, and points to Earth's self-organizing powers. Many see the women's spirituality movement, spreading like leaven even within traditionally male-identified religions, calling to justice and serving to resacralize life, as a "return to the goddess."

Buddhist teachings

Of the Asian traditions now breaking upon the Western mind, Buddhism especially helps us understand the new ecological paradigm, and work with it in the healing of our world. The core doctrine of the Buddha Dharma, basic to its psychology and ethics, is the "dependent co-arising" of all phenomena—arguably the clearest conceptualization of mutual causality prior to general systems theory. It comes not only from empirical observation and subtle nonlinear logic, but also from a resolve to relieve suffering. It is meant to free us from the prison cell of egocentricity and possessiveness, and usher us into the gladness of harmonious, responsible relationship with all that is.

In the Buddha Dharma we find practices and imageries to help us realize our profound interexistence. Mental disciplines based on a sophisticated understanding of the mind help us relate to reality in terms of process, or impermanence, rather than in terms of solid, self-existing objects to grasp or reject. They school us to confront in our own psyches the fears, greeds, hatreds at the root of human suffering; to experience how these "fetters" or "poisons" arise from fictive notions of a permanent, separate self; and to progressively let them go. Meditations—such as loving kindness, compassion, and joy in the joy of others—further decondition old patterns of fears and competitiveness and serve as ground and compass in a fluidly interdependent world. (Adaptations of some of these meditations appear in Chapter 12.)

The Buddha Dharma also provides images for the mind's eye and models for a life of action. From Mahayana Buddhism comes the Jewel Net of Indra, a polycentric vision of reality that presents a total contrast to the hierarchical view. Each being occupying a node in the vast net of everything is a gem whose many facets reflect all the other gems and their reflections, too, back and forth infinitely. The world is interwoven in such a way that each node of its living net contains all mysteries; no need to climb to heaven to find the sacred, when at each spot is Buddha nature—and there the intelligence and compassion at the core of life can ignite entire. As in the hologram of modern science, each part contains the whole.

The bodhisattva, the Buddhist hero figure, is one who knows and takes seriously the dependent co-arising of all things. That is why he also knows that there is no private salvation, and that is why she turns back from the gates of nirvana to reenter samsara, the world of suffering, again and again to minister to all beings until each, to every blade of grass, is enlightened. Here is revealed the compassion that blooms naturally when we open to our condition of profound mutuality. Since that condition pertains to us all, whether or not we acknowledge it yet, we are all, in a sense—the Scripture tells us—bodhisattvas.

These teachings, practices, and images have, like systems theory, inspired and shaped "the work that reconnects" presented in this book. For the Buddha's core teaching of dependent co-arising, we sometimes use a new word, coined by a Vietnamese Zen master of today. It recalls the term "interexistence" used by some systems theorists to characterize the relationship of open systems, but is less of a mouthful. The word made popular and potent by Thich Nhat Hanh is "interbeing."

THE NATURE OF OUR POWER

As our pain for the world arises from our systemic interexistence, so does our power. Yet the generative creativity operating in and through open systems is very different from our customary notions of power.

Power-over

The old concept of power, in which most of us have been socialized, originated in the worldview which assumed reality to be composed of discrete and separate entities—rocks, plants, atoms, people. An Aristotle classifying these entities into categories or a Newton or Galileo studying their vectors and velocities all worked with that assumption. Power came to be seen as a property of those separate substances, inferred from the way they could appear to push each other around. It became identified with domination. It was equated with the exertion of one's will over others, limiting their choices. This is a linear, unidirectional view of causality, in which power is a zero-sum game: "the more of it you have, the less of it I have"; "if you win, I lose." It fosters the idea, furthermore, that power correlates with invulnerability. To keep from being pushed around, defenses are needed. Armor and rigidity make one more powerful, less likely to be influenced or changed, i.e. dominated by the other.

From the systems perspective this notion of power is both inaccurate and dysfunctional. The exertion of greater force can certainly serve to defend oneself and others, but that function is one of protection, not to be confused with the generation of new forms, behaviors, and potentials. That capacity operates more organically and reliably from the bottom up, as "power-with." Systems scientists call it *synergy*.

Power-with

Living systems evolve in variety, resilience, and intelligence; they do this not by erecting walls of defense and closing off from their environment, but by opening more widely to the currents of matter-energy and information. They integrate and differentiate through constant interaction, spinning more intricate connections and more flexible strategies. For this they require not invulnerability, but increasing responsiveness. Such is the direction of evolution. As life forms evolve in complexity and intelligence, they shed their armor, grow sensitive, vulnerable protuberances—like lips, tongues, ears, eyeballs, noses, fingertips—the better to sense and respond, the better to connect in the web of life and weave it further.

We may wonder why power as domination, which we see enacted around us and on top of us, seems so effective. Many who wield it seem to get what they want—money, fame, control over others' lives. Yes, they do, but always at a cost to the larger system and to their own well-being within it. To the social system, power-over is dysfunctional because it inhibits diversity and feedback; by obstructing self-organizing processes, it fosters entropy—systemic disintegration. To the power holder himself, it is like a suit of armor: it restricts vision and movement. Narrowing awareness and maneuverability, it cuts him off from fuller and freer participation in life; he has far fewer options for response.

Power and feedback

Power-with or synergy is not a property one can own, but a process one engages in. Efficacy is transactional. Take the neuron in the neural net. If it were, hypothetically, to suppose that its powers were a personal property to be preserved and protected from other nerve cells, and isolated itself behind defensive walls, it would atrophy, or die. Its health and its power lie in opening itself to the charge, letting the signals through. Only then can the larger systems of which it is a part learn to respond and think.

The body-politic is much like a neural net, as Karl Deutsch asserts. Like the brain,

> Something inside me has reached to the place where the world is breathing.
> —Kabir [18]

society is a cybernetic system which only functions well with unhampered flows of information. That is how our mind-bodies work. When you put your hand on a hot stove, you rapidly withdraw it, because feedback tells you your fingers are burning. You wouldn't know that if you began censoring your body's reports.

Self-governance requires the free circulation of information necessary to public decision-making. In the present hypertrophied stage of the Industrial Growth Society, however, even governments that call themselves democracies suppress information unwelcome to corporate interests. We learn daily of high-level cover-ups, a scientific panel's findings officially rejected, a report censored. We have become accustomed to misinformation and deception about an enormous array of dangers, such as the relationship of cancer and other diseases to radioactivity, food additives, or household products. We hear little about the effects and causes of thinning ozone and the greenhouse effect, even when we're awash in record-breaking floods and hurricanes, and global food reserves are at an all-time low. This institutionalized secrecy is understandable in terms of protecting vested interests, but it comes at a high price. For any system that consistently suppresses feedback—closing its perceptions to the results of its behavior—is suicidal.

The power of disclosure and refusal

While the concept of power-with summons us to develop empathy, it also calls for vigilance and assertiveness in responding to the self-organizing needs of the larger system. It is our systemic responsibility to give feedback to our body politic, and unblock that feedback which has been suppressed. This is essential to the Great Turning from the Industrial Growth Society to a Life-sustaining Society. Many of its unsung heroes are women and men who, often at considerable personal risk, unearth and disclose important information held from the public.

Our interexistence with others in the web of life does not mean that we should tolerate destructive behavior. On the contrary, it means we should step in when our collective health and survival are at stake. That can involve lobbying for laws, or intervening in a more direct fashion, nonviolently, to remove authority from those who misuse it. This is not a struggle to "seize" power so much as to release it for efficient self-governance. Thus we act, not only for ourselves and our own group or party, but also on behalf of all the other "neurons in the net." Then we are sustained by the myriad resources of that net, which include all our differences and diversities.

Acting on behalf of the larger system, for the common good, is becoming alien to the mores of the Industrial Growth Society. Corporations, by their very financial structure, must maximize their own short-term profits, regardless of the impact. Within this increasingly competitive system, individuals perceive their own self-interest to be in conflict with the interests of others. Many are so deeply entrenched in this point of view that they assume activists must be similarly motivated, and label them as "special interest groups." To act on behalf of the common good can serve overlapping purposes: it brings needed feedback to the system about challenges it faces, and transforms the premises under which that system operates. It helps to change the norms from individual, competitive self-interest to collective, systemic self-interest.

Synergy and grace

When we make common cause on behalf of the Earth community, we open not only to the needs of others, but also to their abilities and gifts. It is a good thing that power-with is not a personal property, because, frankly, none of us possesses all the courage and intelligence, strength and endurance required for the Great Turning. And none of us *needs* to possess them, or dredge them up out of some private storehouse. All the resources we will need arise out of our interactions, as we commit ourselves to a common intent for our common fate.

This is the nature of synergy, the first property of living systems. As parts self-organize into a larger whole, capacities emerge which could never have been predicted, and which the individual parts did not possess. The weaving of new connections brings new responses and new possibilities into play. In the process, one can feel sustained—and *is* sustained—by currents of power larger than one's own.

This phenomenon is similar to the religious concept of grace, but distinct from the traditional understanding of grace, as it does not require belief in a God. Whether restoring a garden or cooking in a soup kitchen, there is a sense sometimes of being supported by something beyond one's individual strength, a sense of being "acted through." This empowerment often seems to come through those for whose sake one acts. In the last unprotected groves of redwoods, young activists weather the cold rainy winter and police violence, as they perch in the trees to save them from illegal logging. Their valor and endurance is not their own, they say, but bestowed upon them by the the great beings they seek to save. "They know we're here; they give us strength." This kind of empowerment is familiar to many today who work for their own threatened communities, or for distant peasants ripped from land and livelihood, or for children imprisoned in sweatshops and brothels. Those who risk their lives to protect marine mammals, and those who risk jail to stop paying taxes for weapons, and those who risk their jobs to "blow the whistle" on corruption and deception—they also draw on vaster powers of life. These people, whose numbers are countless, show us what can happen through us when we break free of the old hierarchical notions of power. Grace happens when we act with others on behalf of our world.

Chapter 4

THE WORK THAT RECONNECTS

You, sent out beyond your recall,
go to the limits of your longing.
—Rainer Maria Rilke[19]

INSIGHTS INTO THE BASIC MIRACLE OF OUR EXISTENCE—be they from general living systems theory, Buddhist teachings, or other ancient voices—have broken upon us in the very century that has brought us to the brink of destroying our planet as a home for conscious life. They are fundamental and far-reaching enough to help us liberate ourselves from the Industrial Growth Society and create together a Life-sustaining Society. If we can let these insights shape our own life purposes, they can enable the Great Turning.

That is a big "if." For while the new paradigm is the stuff of countless lectures and books, it is purveyed mainly on the intellectual level. As a plaything of the mind, it is fascinating—even hopeful—but we urgently need ways to let it transform our lives for the healing of our world.

Over the last twenty years, since the late 1970s, a form of personal and group work has grown up to help us do just that. Arising first in North America, it spread to Eastern and Western Europe, Australia, and Japan through articles circulating from hand to hand, and through workshops that have engaged some hundreds of thousands of people, within and beyond movements for peace, justice, and a healthy environment. First it was called "Despair and Empowerment" work, then after a few years "Deep Ecology" work. Sometimes we call it "Awakening as Earth" or "Our Life as Gaia," sometimes "Being Bodhisattvas" or "All Beings in the Mind of God." Now, as those of us involved in this work see its universality and practicality—how it calls people of all persuasions and backgrounds to engage their energies on behalf of life—we are uncertain what to call it. We are shy of labels, knowing how they can limit and confuse. Yet the work demands to be shared, for its premises in the new paradigm are clear, its principles precise, its methods efficacious. So for now, in this book, we simply call it "the Work that Reconnects."

THE GOALS OF THE WORK

The central purpose of the Work that Reconnects is to help people uncover and experience their innate connections with each other and with the systemic, self-healing powers in the web of life, so that they may be enlivened and motivated to play their part in creating a sustainable civilization.

In order to do this, we pursue these contributing goals:

- to provide people the opportunity to experience and share with others their innermost responses to the present condition of our world
- to reframe their pain for the world as evidence of their interconnectedness in the web of life, and hence of their power to take part in its healing
- to provide people with concepts—from systems science, deep ecology, or spiritual traditions—which illumine this power, along with exercises which reveal its play in their own lives
- to provide methods by which people can experience their interdependence with, their responsibility to, and the inspiration they can draw from past and future generations, and other life-forms
- to enable people to embrace the Great Turning as a challenge which they are fully capable of meeting in a variety of ways, and as a privilege in which they can take joy
- to enable people to support each other in clarifying their intention, and affirming their commitment to the healing of the world

THEORETICAL FOUNDATIONS

The theory underlying this work is implicit in the preceding chapters: it derives from the present challenge to choose life, from recognition of what stops us, and from understandings of the self-organizing powers of the universe, the basic miracle. The following statements make more explicit the principles on which we base the Work that Reconnects.

1. This world, in which we are born and take our being, is *alive*.
It is not our supply house and sewer; it is our larger body. The intelligence that evolved us from star dust and interconnects us with all beings is sufficient for the healing of our Earth community, if we but align with that purpose.

2. Our true nature is far more ancient and encompassing than the separate self defined by habit and society.
We are as intrinsic to our living world as the rivers and trees, woven of the same intricate flows of matter/energy and mind. Having evolved us into self-reflexive consciousness, the world can now know itself through us, behold its own majesty, tell its own stories—and also respond to its own suffering.

3. Our experience of pain for the world springs from our interconnectedness with all beings, from which also arise our powers to act on their behalf.
When we deny or repress our pain for the world, or treat it as a private pathology, our power to take part in the healing of our world is diminished. This apatheia need not become a terminal condition. Our capacity to respond to our own and others' suffering—that is, the feedback loops that weave us into life—can be unblocked.

4. Unblocking occurs when our pain for the world is not only intellectually validated, but experienced.
Cognitive information about the crises we face, or even about our psychological responses to them, is insufficient. We can only free ourselves from our fears of the pain—including the fear of getting permanently mired in despair or shattered by grief—when we allow ourselves to experience these feelings. Only then can we discover their fluid, dynamic character. Only then can they reveal on a visceral level our mutual belonging to the web of life.

5. When we reconnect with life, by willingly enduring our pain for it, the mind retrieves its natural clarity.
Not only do we experience our interconnectedness in the community of Earth, but also mental eagerness arises to match this experience with new paradigm thinking. Concepts which bring relatedness into focus become vivid. Significant learnings occur, for the individual system is reorganizing and reorienting, grounding itself in wider reaches of iden-

tity and self-interest.

6. The experience of reconnection with the Earth community arouses desire to act on its behalf.
As Earth's self-healing powers take hold within us, we feel called to participate in the Great Turning. For these self-healing powers to operate effectively, they must be trusted and acted on. The steps we take can be modest undertakings, but they should involve some risk to our mental comfort, lest we remain caught in old, "safe" limits. Courage is a great teacher and bringer of joy.

THE SHAMBHALA PROPHECY

Coming to us across twelve centuries, the prophecy about the coming of the Shambhala warriors illustrates the challenges we face in the Great Turning and the strengths we can bring to it. Joanna learned it in 1980 from Tibetan friends in India, who were coming to believe that this ancient prophecy referred to this very planet-time. She often recounts it in workshops, for the signs it foretold are recognizable now, signs of great danger.

There are varying interpretations of this prophecy. Some portray the coming of the kingdom of Shambhala as an internal event, a metaphor for one's inner spiritual journey independent of the world around us. Others present it as an entirely external event that will unfold independent of what we may choose to do or what our participation may be in the healing of our world. A third version of the prophecy was given to Joanna by her friend and teacher Choegyal Rinpoche of the Tashi Jong community in northern India.

There comes a time when all life on Earth is in danger. Great barbarian powers have arisen. Although these powers spend their wealth in preparations to annihilate one another, they have much in common: weapons of unfathomable destructive power, and technologies that lay waste our world. In this era, when the future of sentient life hangs by the frailest of threads, the kingdom of Shambhala emerges.

You cannot go there, for it is not a place; it is not a geopolitical entity. It exists in the hearts and minds of the Shambhala warriors—that is the term Choegyal used, "warriors." Nor can you recognize a Shambhala warrior when you see her or him, for they wear no uniforms or insignia, and they carry no banners. They have no barricades on which to climb to threaten the enemy, or behind which they can hide to rest or regroup. They do not even have any home turf. Always they must move on the terrain of the barbarians themselves.

Now the time comes when great courage—moral and physical courage—is required of the Shambhala warriors, for they must go into the very heart of the barbarian power, into the pits and pockets and citadels where the weapons are kept, to dismantle them. To dismantle weapons, in every sense of the word, they must go into the corridors of power where decisions are made.

The Shambhala warriors have the courage to do this because they know that these weapons are *manomaya*. They are "mind-made." Made by the human mind, they can be unmade by the human mind. The Shambhala warriors know that the dangers threatening life on Earth are not visited upon us by any extraterrestrial power, satanic deities, or pre-ordained evil fate. They arise from our own decisions, our own lifestyles, and our own relationships.

So in this time, the Shambhala warriors go into training. When Choegyal said this, Joanna asked, "How do they train?" They train, he said, in the use of two weapons. "What weapons?" And he held up his hands in the way the lamas hold the ritual objects of dorje and bell in the lama dance.

The weapons are compassion and insight. Both are necessary, he said. You have to have compassion because it gives you the juice, the power, the passion to move. It means not to be afraid of the pain of the world. Then you can open to it, step forward, act. But that weapon by itself is not enough. It can burn you out, so you need the other—you need insight into the radical interdependence of all phenomena. With that wisdom you know that it is not a battle between "good guys" and "bad guys," because the line between good and evil runs through the landscape of every human heart. With insight into our profound inter-relatedness—our deep ecology—you know that actions undertaken with pure intent have repercussions throughout the web of life, beyond what you can measure or discern. By itself, that insight may appear too cool, too conceptual, to sustain you and keep you moving, so you need the heat of compassion. Together these two can sustain us as agents of wholesome change. They are gifts for us to claim now in the healing of our world.

These two weapons of the Shambhala warrior represent two essential aspects of the Work that Reconnects. One is the recognition and experience of our pain for the world. The other is the recognition and experience of our radical, empowering interconnectedness with all life.

The Work that Reconnects belongs to a much larger cycle of time than our fragmented attention spans, so it is very important to just keep on going. Listen to how Rilke puts it, in a poem in which he lets God speak:

> You, sent out beyond your recall,
> go to the limits of your longing.
> Embody me.
>
> Flare up like flame
> and make big shadows I can move in.
>
> Let everything happen to you: beauty and terror.
> Just keep going. No feeling is final.
> Don't let yourself lose me.
>
> Nearby is the country they call life.
> You will know it by its seriousness.
>
> Give me your hand. [20]

Chapter 5

GUIDING GROUP WORK

THE DETERIORATING CONDITIONS OF OUR WORLD and the plight of other beings impinge on us all. We are in this together. Never before have our destinies been so intertwined. The fact that our fate is a common fate has tremendous implications. It means that in facing it together openly and humbly, we rediscover our interconnectedness in the web of life. From that rediscovery spring courage, a deeper sense of community, and insights into our power and creativity.

This is the experience of people who come together in the Work that Reconnects. The affirmations in this book can be explained in terms of systems theory, psychology, and spiritual teachings, but their truth for us who engage in the work comes from what we experience together.

PART I
Why Work in Groups?

Workshops provide focus and duration.
In the daily run of life the global dangers facing us can appear too pervasive, too remote, too appalling to discuss in a personal fashion without soon shifting the topic. A workshop is an island in time where, removed from other distractions and demands, we can focus together long enough to reach and explore our deep responses to these dangers. The group serves as a lens which helps us to sustain the gaze.

Group work provides support.
The natural emotions evoked in us by the growing threats to life on Earth

> The roots of my personal agony and despair lie in having spent months at a time in close proximity to weapons of unfathomable destructive force. That experience led to a pattern of repressing my deepest feelings about the existence and possible use of nuclear weapons. The workshop provided a safe haven and highly relevant content, and for the first time allowed me to squarely face my feelings—without running. I am deeply grateful for that opportunity to begin to resensitize a part of myself which had become numbed, and to take that pain as the basis for real spiritual growth and new direction in my life.
> —Commander of a Nuclear Submarine

are hard to deal with alone. By its nature the workshop serves as a haven and laboratory for exploring these responses together. We need each other to discover that our responses are not isolated, and that sharing them brings a deep sense of community and collective power.

Workshops offer safe structures.

The group exercises allow us to practice some behaviors uncommon in our daily life. We learn to hear each other's deepest feelings about this planet-time, without taking responsibility for them or contradicting them. We can express our dreads without trying to shield others, and our dreams without having to explain them. We learn deeply rewarding ways of connecting with people.

Group work is synergistic.

What occurs in the life of a group, even over a short period of time, is creative in unpredictable ways. From the interactions, connections are woven that are unique to each particular mix of people. The synergy of a group reveals the profoundly collaborative nature of life itself. Group members often express a sense of coming home to genuine community, if only for a day. The power of the work comes from the group itself, and does not depend on the charisma of the leader, who is just a member of the group with a particular and important role to play.

Group work creates momentum.

A group provides a setting for initiating ongoing relationships and joint endeavors. Participants in workshops often continue to meet afterwards, for mutual support and collaboration.

The Role of the Guide

One person can be the guide, or a team of guides can plan and facilitate together, or group members can share leadership by taking turns leading discussion and exercises.

Each of us has our own style of working, as distinctive as the ways we walk or laugh. Trust it. Our naturalness and genuineness in the work is our gift to workshop participants. If you are a singer, your workshop will probably draw on the power of sound and music. If you dance or do yoga, you may encourage people to use their bodies to explore and express their responses to the conditions of our world. Some guides work in a fairly structured way, moving from one exercise to another. Others prefer a less directive approach, giving people more leeway in setting their own agenda and following their needs as they arise.

The guide's tasks

So how do we facilitate? What are our responsibilities as guides? Essentially, our task is to provide processes which help people know their pain for the world, their interconnectedness with all life, and their power to take part in the Great Turning. For this to happen, our responsibilities include:

1. creating a safe setting in which people can come to trust themselves and each other;

2. presenting the goals of the workshop and eliciting agreement on them;

3. formally dedicating the work to the healing of the world (or the welfare of all beings, or the Great Turning, as you wish);

4. helping the group stay focused on the work at hand;

5. offering exercises appropriate to the occasion, arranging them in sequence, and explaining them clearly;

6. working within time constraints, in a manner that does not rush or drag things out;

7. helping the group enjoy itself.

Cofacilitating with one or more other guides

Two or more guides working together provide support for one another, and training as well, if one is less experienced. The combination of talents, style, and life experience enriches the work. Seeing a variety of guides with different styles and levels of experience helps participants realize that they too might guide this work. Obviously, cofacilitation requires a carefully designed plan for the workshop, and ongoing communication among the guides, including check-ins during breaks and "debriefings" at the end of each day.

Working with Strong Emotions

This work brings powerful emotions to the surface. Most of us are unaccustomed to dealing with strong feelings among relative strangers. Here are some pointers:

1. Be sure you have done a good measure of your own despair work before attempting to facilitate others'.
Only through experiencing such feelings firsthand can you genuinely validate them in others as natural and normal; only then can you know them to be strengthening and integrating. If you have not allowed yourself to "touch bottom" in owning your pain for the world, you run two risks. One is fear of these emotions. The other is voyeurism. A guide who has not plumbed his or her own feelings risks using others' expression of feelings as a vicarious outlet.

2. Respect people's emotions.
Remember that anger, sorrow, fear, and guilt are natural responses to the suffering of other beings and the deterioration of our world. Do not rush in to comfort when these responses well up. Your very presence, acceptance, and matter-of-fact bearing are reassurance enough.

Keep in mind the distinction between our pain for the world and its emotional discharge. Tears indicate release of tension; they are healing. As we learn from Reevaluation Counseling, laughing and yawning are also forms of discharge, and should not be taken as signs of indifference or boredom.

3. Respect people's defenses and resistance.
Let no one in the workshop feel pressure to register or display emotion. Catharsis is healthy, but the outward expression of emotion is no measure of its inner intensity, or of a person's capacity to care.

In a workshop Joanna led in New York, Tom, a university student declared, "The despair I feel is that I don't feel despair. My heart feels like a rock. I'm afraid I don't care the way the rest of you do." In response, Joanna reflected on how, in a way, he spoke for us all. In each of us, alongside whatever else we feel, are desires to shut out and shut down. She encouraged the group to get in touch with this resistance to feeling, and to express it with appropriate vehemence—"I don't care. Don't talk to me about dying whales or hungry children; I really don't give a damn. Leave me alone." That impromptu exercise invigorated everyone, including Tom, and the group work proceeded with greater intensity.

4. Engage in the process.
If you direct the proceedings without engaging in them personally, people

are likely to feel manipulated. To act as guide and simultaneously partic-ipate in the work requires a "bifocal" attention. This is tricky, but not difficult. You will grow in your ability to stay alert to the group as a whole and, at the same time, to join in a given exercise.

5. Trust the process.
It is not up to you as guide to resolve the emotions of the workshop par-ticipants, or to rescue them by convincing them that "there is hope" or "life is worth living." If you fully realize that pain for our world is proof of our interconnectedness—that it can open us to the knowledge of the web of life—then you will be able to stay grounded in the midst of emo-tional turbulence.

6. Trust the compassion and community arising in the group.
From war veterans to street youth to middle-class professionals, people are remarkably available to each other when they are dealing with com-mon anguish. As people recognize their shared plight—and behold each other expressing it openly—unsuspected reserves of caring and empathy are summoned forth. Stay open to the play of this mutual support, and expect that you will not give so much as you will receive.

Personal Despair and Social Despair

"How does all this connect with the despair I feel about my personal life?"

"My anger over corporate despoiling of the environment—is it really just my rage against the father who abused me?"

"How do I know if I'm weeping for the planet or my lost lover (lost child, failed career, etc.)?"

Such questions often surface in a workshop. Whether or not expressed, they are present in the minds of participants and need to be addressed.

Our culture, including mainstream Western psychology, tends to reduce our pain for the world to personal maladjustments. This leads people to suppose that feelings of personal despair must be resolved and eradicated before feelings of social despair can be considered legitimate. "First I've got to work through my relationship with my mother...or with my addiction...." The notion that one must find enlightenment, undergo transformation, or get one's head straight *first*, before dealing with social despair, keeps many otherwise intelligent people in a state of moral infantilism.

In any case, most people come to workshops with a good measure of personal as well as social causes for despair. They wonder about the relationship between the two and sometimes feel they cannot credit or validate their pain for the world unless this relationship is clarified. In responding, the following points are helpful:

1. It is neither possible nor necessary to draw crystal-clear distinctions between the personal and social roots of our pain for the world. Because we are all interconnected, suffering in our personal lives always has roots in our collective lives, and the suffering of each of us compounds in turn our collective pain.

2. Our experience of personal suffering can serve to sensitize us to the sufferings of our world. The poets and visionaries who saw into the nature of our time—the Kafkas and Orwells, the Kierkegaards and Virginia Woolfs—were hardly robust, "well-adjusted" specimens of mental health. They are like the ghost-trap which Tibetan Buddhists weave of sticks and wool, and erect near funeral sites to catch wandering restless spirits. Some of us seem to be woven by life's fortunes to serve a similar purpose, to be ghost-traps catching the invisible currents of pain that haunt our planet-time. It is an essential function, for it lets us bring needed feedback into the larger system.

3. Therefore, by virtue of our very infirmities, we can serve our world. Mahatma Gandhi himself was assailed by many inner, psychological contradictions, but he did not devote his life to their resolution on a personal level. As psychohistorian Erik Erikson observed, Gandhi was able to "lift his private patienthood to the level of the universal one, and to try to solve for all what he could not solve for himself alone."[21] This is the role of the "wounded healer."

> Strength of heart comes from knowing that the pain that we each must bear is part of the greater pain shared by all that lives. It is not just "our" pain but *the* pain, and realizing this awakens our universal compassion.
> —Jack Kornfield[22]

If persons in the workshop need counseling or therapy in dealing with personal distress, encourage them to obtain it. Meanwhile the workshop's focus on the pain of our world may help them momentarily release their private preoccupations into the larger arena of concern that they share with others.

Stresses in Guiding Group Work

To guide a workshop can be profoundly rewarding. Such a privilege is not without its pressures—and it is well to recognize them.

A sense of inadequacy can arise at the outset in informing others about the workshop we are planning. Because it is still a novel venture in the eyes of many, it is easy to feel awkward in explaining it, or doubtful of our own capacities to lead it. When the workshop takes place, the responses of the participants relieve these qualms. The release and empowerment they experience validate our efforts. Yet even so, in continuing to facilitate such groups, fears can assail us now and again. The grief and horror people share in the workshops from the depths of their being, stay in our awareness, fill us at times with a great sadness. We may begin to feel like lightning rods for people's anguish. Some nights after a workshop, we may be haunted by the vivid images of doom that people have shared, and weighted with sorrow that such fears should impinge on their lives.

We may also have expectations about how people will respond to the workshop, and feel discouraged when these expectations are not met. We may envision dramatic breakthroughs and insights while the participants in a particular workshop do not immediately reflect the inner changes they experience. We may blame ourselves for our lack of skill.

Once in a while, about halfway through a workshop, people desperate for solutions look to the guide for answers. These subliminal expectations of the guide may be tinged with resentment. "Why aren't you telling us what to do? Why are you getting us all upset if you don't have a solution to the problems?" What causes the resentment here is not a person's pain for the world, but his fear and anger about the pain.

How do we deal with these stresses? When we embark on the work as a guide, we find our own strengths. Here are some pointers to help us find them:

- Stay clear and grounded in your true intention. Remember why you are doing this work.

- Remember that what people say and do in a workshop is not a measure of its long-term effect on their lives.

- Be patient with yourself and stay centered. Keep breathing.

- A support group can give you encouragement and constructive criticism. This can be the group you trained with, or with whom you studied this book.

- Trust the interconnectedness of open systems. Let the knowledge of the living web guide and sustain your work, like grace.

PART II
The Workshop Setting

The settings in which we meet to engage in this group work are as varied as our lives. Workshops have been held in churches, schools, clinics, town halls, livingrooms, in armories, and beside nuclear testing sites. They have varied in length from an hour and a half in the midst of a larger conference to a week in a rural retreat. They can be held just once, or they can form a series, with the group meeting regularly over a period of time. Workshops have ranged in size from a half-dozen people to a hundred or more.

A time and a space should be set aside where participants can engage in the work without being distracted or interrupted by the demands of their daily lives. You will want a space that can be closed to outside disturbance, and spacious enough to permit people to move around easily. However, work has been done in cramped quarters like a crowded church basement, and in noisy public settings such as parks or the corner of a high school cafeteria. Wherever the gathering place, remember that the real context or setting of the work is the threatened planet, our larger body and home.

Access to nature, for some of the exercises and for breaks, helps participants reconnect with the more-than-human world. And although we may have limited choice in the matter, the relative environmental health of the setting affects the experience people have. As more and more of us succumb to environmental sensitivities, we try to arrange for a minimally toxic setting, without fumes from new carpeting, cleaning chemicals, or paint. We also request in our advertising and registration mailings that participants refrain from using scent, and insist that smoking be limited to outside areas well away from entrances. If possible, we find space that is wheelchair accessible. And for residential workshops, we make sure that healthy vegetarian food is at least an option.

The design of the workshop space itself helps support the work. Some guides like to create an altar in the room, inviting people to bring special objects and photos for it. Distracting posters and signs may be covered or removed. If possible, chairs and floor cushions are set up in a circle, or concentric arcs for larger groups. Flowers and plants always beautify a room and remind us of the natural world outside the walls. Anything we can do to create an attractive space helps, but the work itself carries its own focus, and can take place in almost any setting.

Sequencing

When people meet together in a workshop, what do they find? They find a safe setting and structures which allow them to acknowledge and to explore their deep responses to planetary dangers. Breaking out of isolation and self-distrust, they experience the validity of these felt responses and find them to be rooted in caring and interconnectedness. Over time, we have discerned a sequencing of the work which facilitates this process.

The work generally unfolds in four successive movements: 1) affirmation; 2) despair work; 3) a perceptual shift; and 4) preparing for action. As we plan and conduct a workshop, we attend to this dynamic flow, and order the group's activities in ways which invite it. Our awareness and attention to this spiral is more important than the particular methods we employ.

1. Affirmation: coming from gratitude.
To begin with simple, ordinary thankfulness for our existence grounds all the work that will follow. To take time to express our love for life on Earth, in brief and concrete terms, opens the mind and heart—and serves as context for the pain we will also acknowledge and share.

2. Despair work: owning and honoring our pain for the world.
Here we confront the realities of our planet-time, including the degradation and suffering of Earth and her beings, and let ourselves experience our responses to these realities.

3. The shift: seeing with new eyes.
Here we trace our pain for the world to its source, the larger matrix of our lives. At this turning point of the work, we see our pain and our power as rooted in our interconnectedness. We explore our connectedness to past and future generations, and to the more-than-human world, drawing upon them for strength and guidance.

4. Going forth.
In the last stage, we explore the synergistic power available to us as open systems and apply these understandings to our work for social change. We develop visions and plans that will help each participant take concrete steps appropriate to his or her situation.

The following chapters correspond to these movements. To distinguish them in any categorical way can be misleading, for the process is too fluid and dynamic to be put into separate boxes. Furthermore, this four-part movement is not completed once and for all, but tends to turn back on itself. Despair work may reemerge at any point in a workshop. Workshop facilitators learn to be comfortable with this, and are prepared to change planned activities if needed to make room for it. At the same time, deliberately or randomly reintroducing despair work late in the workshop disrupts the flow and may send participants off without adequate closure.

The sequence of a workshop does not need to be made explicit to participants; it's a judgment call as to when this might be appropriate. Some groups are reassured by a sense of overall structure and want to know that they won't be "stuck in despair." But to others, knowing about the sequence can impede their sense of spontaneity and make the work seem contrived. So it is a question of art, of touch.

Opening the Workshop

Openings set the tone for what follows. This is the time when participants listen most closely, to learn the "ground rules" and decide how they will approach the work. The following steps help create an atmosphere of openness, safety, and mutual respect.

1. Greet participants individually, if only for a moment.
Joanna has a practice of making brief physical contact with each person as she introduces herself and hears their names. This puts everyone on the same level, dissolving any imagined barrier between leader and participant with genuine connection. It lets them know that their presence is appreciated. Joanna finds that this practice reminds her of whom she has come to serve and moves her away from self-concern.

2. Help participants to relax.
If people are new to the work, they usually come with mixed feelings and an initial measure of awkwardness and tension. Some bodily movement—standing, stretching, and deep breathing —eases these tensions, and helps people feel more alert and involved. Singing is excellent, too.

3. Clarify logistics.
Tell people when breaks will occur and the location of the bathrooms. Limit food and drink to breaks, and note taking and audio taping to lecture sections of the workshop. Specify that full-time attendance is expected and that only active participants are allowed in the workshop.

4. Secure agreements.
Affirm your commitment and ask specifically for their agreement to: full participation, punctual beginning and ending of sessions, and confidentiality for anything personal shared during the workshop.

5. Dedicate the work.
Formally verbalize a group intention that the work people are about to do

serve the healing of our world and the creation of a sustainable society. Joanna finds it useful to repeat this before each exercise. This helps both the guide and the participants to not let the value of the work depend on how they happen to feel about it in the moment.

6. Help participants to focus.
The workshop requires full attention, so we often begin with an invitation like this:

> *We are here to use this time and space together. It is a unique opportunity. Our bodies are here; let us allow our minds to arrive also.... Many of us hurried to get here, perhaps leaving some chores undone and some calls we needed to make. Let's look at these bits of unfinished business in our mind's eye...and now let's put them up on a shelf and leave them there until five o'clock .*

7. Clarify the purpose of the workshop.
Make sure people understand that our purpose here is to explore our inner responses to the condition of our world and prepare to take part in its healing. It is not to discuss or debate the causes of the global crisis, nor to agree on collective actions. Let people know that this will be an active workshop, with a range of experiential exercises.

8. Affirm presence and power of feelings.
Acknowledge from the outset that our responses to the plight of our world are inevitably charged with emotion. To feel grief, fear and anger is natural, indeed appropriate, and this is a safe place to express them.

9. Have people introduce themselves.
After your initial comments, which should be as brief as clarity allows—ten minutes should do it—let people hear from each other. Even as they introduce themselves, they can move directly to a level of deep personal sharing; ways to let this happen are suggested in the next chapter.

Helping People Speak and Listen

A good workshop is a highly participative venture; therein lies its power to connect, inform, invigorate. The greatest gift that a guide can offer to participants is the opportunity to listen to themselves and each other. And when they really do that, so much caring and wisdom emerge that the participants become each other's teachers.

In the whole group
In a typical conversation, some individuals tend to dominate and some stay quiet, while others wait impatiently to get a word in edgewise. This

pattern does not encourage full participation and attention. A "talking object," passed around the circle or taken from the center by the person who wishes to speak, helps people take turns and slows the pace for better listening. You can use a stone, a plain or decorated stick, a feather, a conch shell, or a ritual object that has special meaning for you. A meditation bell can be passed around the circle, each person sounding it once after speaking, allowing the tone to carry the group into silence for a moment before the next speaker begins.

Joanna has a special stone which she carries from workshop to workshop. She introduces it to the group in this way:

> *This is a powerful stone, because when you hold it, you have everyone's attention. And when you hold it, you can only tell the truth. People in many places from American campuses to Japanese hill towns have held this stone while speaking the truth of what is happening to their world. Imagine you can feel their hands on it.*

Encourage spontaneity. Rehearsing what one is going to say interferes with listening to others. If you ask people to respond to a specific question, give them a few minutes at the outset to think about what they want to say, so they will be able to listen better to the others. Then as each person speaks, his or her words are received in attentive silence, without verbal response.

Anyone who has facilitated a group of ten or more people knows the quandary of time. We want to respect each speaker, but all too often as we go around the circle, each statement grows a little longer, and the time for other activities slips away. To counteract this tendency, ask for brevity—clearly—at the outset, reminding people that brief expressions are often the most evocative, like haiku. Molly sometimes warns the group that she will break in about a third of the way around with a reminder about brevity. She may even specify the point in the circle, so when the reminder comes, the previous speaker doesn't feel criticized.

Another time-minding method utilizes a watch which is silently passed to the one who is speaking when his time is up—one minute, say, or two. He finishes his sentence and then holds it while the next person speaks, passing it to her after the allotted time, and she in turn does the same for the following speaker. This quiet and easy method shares the responsibility with everyone in the group.

In small groups and pairs

People can speak more fully, of course, when you divide them into small groups or pairs. Encourage groups to share the time and listen respectfully. Sometimes free conversation with lots of give and take is appropriate, but it can go off on tangents and deprive people of equal time. Taking turns lets people speak without interruption, have time to think or even go into silence. This approach fosters better listening, too. If you choose that mode, say how much time is available (e.g. five minutes per person) and signal when each interval has elapsed. You can always allow a few minutes at the end for general conversation if time permits. Groups can also keep their own time, passing a watch as in the large group.

In dyads and small groups when people are given an allotted time to express themselves, encourage them to use it for silence as well. In stillness, they can listen to their body, or what is underneath the words they spoke, or what is still out of reach, awaiting articulation. Many times in these structured listening situations, people hear themselves saying something for the first time. They need time to hear it and absorb it, before anything else happens. To jump in with words right after people have shared their deepest feelings can trivialize or dissipate the intensity of the moment. Sheer presence—steady, alert, and caring—is the most appropriate response.

Teaching how to listen
Many people have never really learned to listen, especially in a group setting. A Russian workshop participant once said, "We all like to talk, but nobody likes to listen." There seems to be more prestige and power in talking, more gratification, and this tends to reinforce habits of talking lots and listening seldom.

Sometimes it is appropriate at the outset to give guidelines for listening. Here are some examples:

• In the large group, respect the person talking by giving your full attention, without interruption or side conversations.

• In dyads, sit facing each other, looking into the other person's eyes as much as you can, with your arms relaxed.

• In dyads, give your partner your full attention and remember you don't have to solve the problem or give advice.

• Listen to yourself when you are speaking.

• Let silence happen.

After laying out these guidelines, two colleagues of ours often demonstrate what *not* to do in three brief role-plays. In the first, the listener interrupts, contradicts, and denies the validity of the feelings the person expresses. In the second, the listener diagnoses the problem, gives advice, praises the speaker inappropriately, and makes comparisons to other situations. In the third the listener distracts himself by looking away, studying his watch or his nails, etc. These caricatures usually evoke hooting laughter as people recognize common experiences.

Sustaining Group Energy and Participation

The quality of the work correlates directly to the quality of attention that the participants bring to it. To help them stay alert and engaged, here are some approaches we have found useful.

1. Use different modalities, vary them, and change the pace.
Maintain a balance between verbal and nonverbal activities, between sitting and moving, between working in the large group and in smaller constellations. Such alternations enliven people and allow for a variety of learning styles.

After a period of talking, activities which move beyond words deepen the work. Imaging with colors on paper or with clay lets feelings and intuitions surface, and enriches communication among members of the group. So does touch, through the simple holding of hands, or more fully and eloquently in exercises such as "the Cradling" (see Chapter 8). Guided meditations help move from concepts to experience, as do periods of silent reflection, indoors and out.

> The turning point for me was when I stopped talking and just looked, when I studied someone's hand and realized—for the first time in my life—the sheer miracle of a human being.
> —Engineer & workshop participant

To balance periods of sitting, bring in movement: games, circle dances, free dance to strong music, stretching, and singing. "The Cradling" also works here, with a gentler kind of movement. You may want to teach a circle dance and return to it throughout the workshop. Joanna's sudden introduction of a movement activity often comes as a delightful surprise to workshop participants, adding zest to the experience, getting people moving before they have a chance to feel self-conscious about it.

After a lunch break, a ten-minute group nap, introduced with relaxation suggestions and soothing music, helps participants rest and digest their food, honors the natural drowsiness which often occurs after eating, and builds a sense of group trust. People return to waking feeling refreshed and respected as physical beings.

2. Go outside for contact with the wider world.
Send participants out on a mission, such as finding an object for use in an exercise, or for a silent walk, or do a group exercise outside. The "Mirror Walk" (see Chapter 6) is particularly effective outside, whether in a city or a rural setting.

3. Take the pulse.
As guide, you want to know what is happening with the people in your workshop—are they feeling restless, anxious, isolated? If it's not clear to you, find out by asking. Invite participants to "check-in" with a phrase, sentence, sound, or gesture expressing what they are feeling at that moment, either randomly or by going around the circle. Remember you cannot meet everyone's needs at the same time and no one really expects you to, but the very act of checking in helps people feel more engaged and responsible.

4. Brainstorm.
When she introduced brainstorming to village organizers in Sri Lanka, Joanna translated it as "thinking out loud together" and described it as "pretending we are one collective brain." Indeed, by its nature, it can let us feel that we are nerve cells interacting in a neural net. Brainstorming is familiar to many, but even so, it is important to review the groundrules (laid out in Chapter 6).

5. Use a "fishbowl."
This process allows a large group to engage in a discussion without too many people trying to speak at once. Place five or six cushions in the middle of the room in a circle, within a larger circle of chairs. Volunteers sit on the cushions, leaving one empty, and begin a dialogue on a selected topic (usually something that has come up spontaneously in the workshop which the group wants to explore). After about five minutes, when the conversation is well underway, the empty cushion becomes available for anyone from the outer circle who wants to join in. When this happens, someone in the center—who has already spoken—moves back to the outer circle, vacating a cushion for someone else. People continue to join the inner circle, and leave it after speaking, until a sense of resolution is reached, or the alloted time is up.

6. Remember the wider circle.
In this work, people gain a sense of participation not only in each other's lives, but also in those of other beings. This larger context of the work can be made explicit quite simply in a number of ways. For example, in a circle, invite people to imagine the vaster dimensions of the circle and all

those whom it includes, an invisible circle linking everyone around the globe, and through time to our ancestors and the beings of the future. Have them close their eyes, join hands, and feel that the hand they are holding could be that of an enemy soldier, or a politician, or a hungry child. Invite them to speak aloud the names of those they invite into the circle, loved ones, people with whom they are in conflict, national and world leaders, teachers who have gone before, and beings not yet born. Sometimes people mention various endangered animals, or a grove of trees.

Closing the Workshop

A focused completion process respects the depth of experience and communication that has occurred. People have taken risks, and trusted each other with disclosures they may never have shared before. They need a transition back to the tenor of ordinary life; they need to say good-bye to the community they have created and enjoyed.

Take care to end on time so that people with engagements do not leave before the others are finished; make it a part of your commitment to the group. If people still want to talk, go through the formal ending on time and invite them to finish up on their own afterwards.

Closing Circle

Coming together in a full circle at the end of the workshop honors the mutuality the participants have experienced. Speeches are unnecessary: simple words of acknowledgment suffice. As guides, you might acknowledge the courage and caring of those in the circle, and the fact that the workshop is but one step in our collective journey. You can say that the deep responses we have uncovered here together are likely to well up in the days ahead more powerfully than ever before, and that is all right, for we are strong and resilient and not alone. Even though this particular circle may not meet again physically, it will remain part of our lives. You can ask participants to take some moments of silence to look around the circle, reflecting on what they have learned from each other and what they wish for each other in the time ahead. Then you can invite brief words of closing from the group, and end with a song, a sounding, or silence.

Other ways to use a closing circle are described at the end of Chapter 11.

Follow-up

People will want to be able to maintain contact with each other after the close of the workshop. Such contact honors the sense of community they built together and provides support for the visions and plans they hatched. You can encourage this in a number of ways:

1. List of participants.

Have people sign in (with addresses, phone numbers, fax, and e-mail) when they arrive. Make photocopies to be given out at the end of the workshop, or sent soon after by mail.

2. Information on local resources and actions.

The end of a workshop is a good time to share information about organizations and projects in which people can become involved. Participants want and need this, the wider the variety the better. So, collect and provide materials—but don't recruit. Put up some sheets of newsprint where participants can write up further resources and actions; this is preferable to a lot of announcements.

3. Intentions and plans.

Many of the exercises in Chapter 11 help people to realize what they have to offer and to make concrete plans for action. To let these plans be briefly shared with the whole group enhances commitment and allows other participants to offer suggestions and support. When time permits, an exercise like "Receiving Blessings" can be part of the closing circle. People can also write brief descriptions of their projects, to be copied and distributed by mail.

4. Follow-up session.

An evening gathering within a week or so after the workshop allows participants to continue their learning and plans for action. If the workshop guide is not available, someone else in the group can facilitate. Such follow-up sessions have generated ongoing groups that last for years.

Evaluation

In workshops longer than two or three hours, it is good to let people give feedback on the experience. This should occur prior to the closing circle. Participant evaluation is helpful in several fairly obvious ways.

1. It lets you see the workshop through participants' eyes. It affirms strengths you may have doubted and indicates skill areas you will want to work on. People's reactions are often different from what their behavior suggested.

2. Your openness to this feedback models light humility and unselfconsciousness, which is how people best work together.

3. Evaluation offers participants an immediate opportunity to contribute to the work, building a sense of mutual respect, belonging and responsibility.

Evaluation can be done in either individual written form or as a group activity. If it is to be written, give the participants open-ended questions (orally, posted on newsprint, or on a prepared form) such as "What did you find most useful?... Least useful?" Handing out evaluation forms to be mailed later provides more time for reflection, but brings a smaller return.

Evaluations done collectively and orally are quicker (ten minutes can be sufficient). As enjoyable, high-energy brainstorms, they generate more items of response. An effective form is three wide columns on newsprint or blackboard, the first headed by a plus sign (for what the participants liked), the second by a minus sign (for what they liked less, or what didn't work for them), and the third by an arrow (for suggestions for improvement). In true brainstorm fashion, these are not to be argued, discussed, or defended—just noted—and thus a rich blend of contrasting reactions often appears. The same activity might appear in both the plus and minus column, according to different people's evaluations. In this approach, participants can note the variety of responses and are less likely to generalize from their individual experience.

You may have little experience in guiding group work. Even now with years of experience, both of us often feel that we've made mistakes and sometimes scold ourselves afterwards for having not done better. Reading this book will help you, but the best teacher is the actual doing of the work. Give yourself that experience, remembering that the work evolves through our collective practice, mistakes and all.

Chapter 6

AFFIRMATION:
COMING FROM GRATITUDE

Just to live is holy,
to be is a blessing.
—Rabbi Abraham Heschel

W E HAVE RECEIVED AN INESTIMABLE GIFT. To be alive in this beautiful, self-organizing universe—to participate in the dance of life with senses to perceive it, lungs that breathe it, organs that draw nourishment from it—is a wonder beyond words. And it is, moreover, an extraordinary privilege to be accorded a human life, with this self-reflexive consciousness which brings awareness of our own actions and the ability to make choices. It lets us choose to take part in the healing of our world.

THE VALUE OF GRATITUDE

Gratitude for the gift of life is the primary wellspring of all religions, the hallmark of the mystic, the source of all true art. Yet we so easily take this gift for granted. That is why so many spiritual traditions begin with thanksgiving, to remind us that for all our woes and worries, our existence itself is an unearned benefaction, which we could never of ourselves create.

In the Tibetan Buddhist path we are asked to pause before any period of meditative practice and precede it with reflection on the preciousness of a human life. This is not because we as humans are superior to other beings, but because we can "change the karma." In other words, graced with self-reflexive consciousness, we are endowed with the capacity for choice—to take stock of what we are doing and change directions. We may have endured for eons of lifetimes as other life-forms, under the heavy hand of fate and the blind play of instinct, but now at last we are granted the ability to consider and judge and choose. Weaving our ever-complexifying neural circuits into the miracle of self-awareness, life yearned through us for the ability to know and act and speak on behalf of the larger whole. Now that time has come, when by our own decision we can consciously enter the dance.

In Buddhist practice, that first reflection is followed by a second, on the brevity of this precious human life: "Death is certain; the time of death is uncertain." And that reflection, too, awakens in us the precious gift of the present moment—to seize this chance to be alive right now on Planet Earth.

That our world is in crisis—to the point where survival of conscious life on Earth is in question—in no way diminishes the value of this gift. On the contrary. To us is granted the extraordinary privilege of being on hand: to take part, if we choose, in the Great Turning to a sustainable society. We can let life work through us, enlisting all our strength, wisdom, and courage, so that life itself can continue.

There is so much to be done, and the time is so short. We can proceed, of course, out of grim and angry desperation. But the tasks proceed more easily and productively from an attitude of thankfulness for life; it links us to our deeper powers and lets us rest in them. That is true as well for the Work that Reconnects, as described in this book.

Affirmation begins with a warm, personal greeting, welcoming each person to the workshop. When you see each comer as a gift, it helps them feel gladness. Then we take some moments to evoke the love we share for life on Earth, without labeling the process as "affirmation." This relaxes and enlivens us, and serves as wholesome, generative ground for all that follows. It also brings to the surface our pain for the world, because knowing what we treasure triggers the knowing of how threatened it is.

EXERCISES

Warm-ups: Opening through Breath, Body, Sound, and Silence

(3 to 5 minutes each)

Purpose

Most of us are braced, psychically and physically, against the signals of distress that continually barrage us in the news, on our streets, in our environment. As if to reduce their impact on us, we contract, like a turtle into its shell. At the outset of a workshop, therefore, we turn to the breath, the body, the senses—for they can help us to relax, and open out and tune in to the wider currents of knowing and feeling.

Breath

The breath is a helpful friend in this work, for it connects the inside with the outside, revealing our intimate and total dependence on the world around us. It connects mind with body, lending attention to that ever-flowing stream of air, stilling the chatter and evasions, and making us more present to life. The breath also reminds us that we as open systems are in constant flow, not stuck within any given feeling or response, but dynamic and changing as we let it pass through us.

Begin by having everyone pay attention to their breathing for a few moments, or for the next three breaths. Remind them how precious the breath is, and how lucky we are in each moment to be able to inhale and exhale. You can lead the group in a brief breathing practice, to be done standing.

Breathe deep. Feel the air flow through the body like a blessing, the oxygen quickening each cell awake. Draw in that air that connects you with all being, for there is no one alive in this world now who is not breathing like you, in and out...in a vast exchange of energy with the living body of our planet, with seas and plants. Stretch high and wide to let more air in. Then fall forward from the waist with a forceful exhalation, expelling the tensions and toxins of the day. Let the breath cleanse and open us.

In the course of the work, as we let ourselves experience our pain for the world, the breath continues to serve us, much as it serves a woman in childbirth. It helps us stay loose and open to the knowings that need to happen and the changes that want to occur. (See "Breathing Through" in Chapter 12.)

Body

All the threats facing us in this planet-time—be they toxic wastes, world hunger, or global warming—come down in the final analysis to threats to the body. Our bodies pick up signals that our minds may refuse to register. Our unexpressed and unacknowledged dreads are locked into our very tissues along with known and unknown toxins—in our muscles, in our throats and guts, in our ovaries and gonads. Essential joys come through the body as well: the tastes, sights, sounds, textures, and movement which connect us tangibly to our world. Our faithful "Brother Ass," as St. Francis called it, is our most basic connection to our planet and our future.

To bring attention to the body, continue the guidance you began with the breath, using your own words to suggest something like the following:

> *Stretch. Stretch all muscles, then release. Slowly rotate the head, easing the neck with all its nerve centers. Rotate the shoulders, releasing the burdens and tensions they carry. Behold your hand, feel the skin. Feel the textures of the world around you, clothing, arm of chair, tabletop, floor. Your senses are real; they connect you with your world; they tell you what it is like. You can trust them. Come to your senses. Come back to life.*

In the midst of a conference on the nuclear threat, Joanna led a session on despair work. The group was polite and dutifully attentive, though a bit tired after a morning of terrifying films, facts, and figures. She began by inviting people to breathe deeply, close their eyes, and simply listen to their bodies. *We have been trying to handle this information with our heads alone—as if we were a brain on the end of a stick—now let's hear what our bodies have to say...* In the quiet that followed, many began to weep, and within minutes this group of relative strangers was sharing fears and sorrows they had seldom, if ever, expressed.

Sound

To open up and tune in, we also turn to sound—sounds we make, sounds we hear. The physical universe, say the ancient Hindus and modern physicists, is woven of vibrations, and so are we. Releasing our attention into sound moves us beyond the self's cramped quarters into wider apprehensions of reality. Nonmelodic music can weave our awareness into those larger patterns. So can sounding—letting the air flow through us in open vowels, letting our voices interweave in *ah's* and *oh's*, in *Oms* or *Shaloms*.

Sounding together we feel our capacity for community vibrate within and among us. Sounding also clears the throat, helping us feel more present to each other and ready to speak.

Silence

Many traditions, like that of the Quakers, know the power of "gathered silence," where together in stillness we attune to inner, deeper knowings. In this planet-time, when we face dangers too

> This is a time to be still no longer ... a time for crying out—as Hebrews cried out in bondage and Jesus on the cross.... We need to give vent to our massive pain and fear. A people must move from muteness to outcry if it is ever going to take the next step.
> —Harvey Cox, theologian

great for the mind to embrace or words to convey, silence serves. It can be as rich as sounding, while serving a complementary purpose: sounding helps us to release the planetary anguish; silence helps us to listen to it. So, later in the workshop, once we have had opportunities to specify our concerns and apprehensions, we take moments to be with each other in silence.

Some guides like to begin every session with a period of silence, eyes closed, just to settle in. Sometimes they pose a question before the silence, to stir reflection for a dialogue to follow, suggesting that when people feel ready to speak out of the silence, they may do so. This can move us to a deeper level, while closing the eyes builds trust and helps people relax and reflect.

Group Introductions

(30 - 45 minutes, depending on size of group)

Purpose

To uncover our deepest concerns about what is happening to our world, people need to hear both from each other and from themselves. Such sharing begins right away with introductions.

At best, introductions are concrete and brief (say, a minute or two per person). Brevity has the virtue of letting everyone speak, of encouraging those who are initially shy, and of requiring the more verbose to distill their thoughts. Concreteness makes sharing more potent and engaging to the listeners, because it avoids rambling generalizations and focuses on a particular personal experience.

Description

1. Start on a positive note, by asking participants to share in one of these ways:

> As you tell us your name and where you're from, tell us also something particular that you love about being alive. (Or)...share something you did or saw today that made you glad to be alive. (Or)...tell us about a place you love. (Or)...tell us what makes your heart sing.

2. We can move then to our personal responses to the plight of the world. We need to get to this soon, because many people come to the workshop just for the opportunity to express out loud and at last their feelings of apprehension without fear of being seen as morbid, sick, or unpatriotic. To keep that initial sharing vivid, immediate, and concrete, we can say:

> Let's go around the circle again and each briefly share an experience of the last week or so that caused you pain for the world. It can be an incident, a news item, a dream.... If tears should come, please share them, too...

Remember to model the sharing first, including stating your name even though participants know it. Before you begin, allow some moments of silence. This lets participants tune into their own experience and choose what they want to share, so they can listen more attentively to others. See Chapter 5 for ideas on monitoring time.

At the conclusion of these introductions, you can point out to the

"My name is Mark. I work on contract to the Navy, consulting on weapons systems. This week my little boy was sorting books for a school sale, and asked if he should keep some of his favorites to pass on to his own children. I could hardly answer because I realized that I doubted he would live that long...."
—Workshop participant in Maryland

participants that, in each case, the deep concerns that they have just shared have something in common: they extend beyond the separate ego, beyond personal needs and wants. Whether experienced with fear, anger, or grief, they are rooted in caring, and they are to be honored as evidence of our interconnectedness. You might introduce the practice of "breathing through" (Chapter 12) for participants to use in the workshop as well as in their lives, to handle pain in a way that grounds them in the realization of their interexistence.

This kind of initial sharing is useful in other settings as well, in any meeting or classroom setting on issues of collective concern. It engages people on a deep level, cuts through unnecessary verbiage and competition, and builds solidarity.

Brainstorm on the Great Turning

(30 minutes)

Purpose
The epochal transition from the Industrial Growth Society to a Life-sustaining Society, which we described in Chapter One as the "Great Turning," constitutes the political, economic, social, and spiritual challenge of this planet-time. By virtue of its necessity and scope, it impinges on all of us, and offers a meaningful context for the workshop. To present the Great Turning at the outset, briefly defining its nature and delineating its dimensions, starts people off on an affirming note; it puts wind in their sails and imbues their individual work with collective significance.

Description
For liveliness and better learning, let the group itself fill in the features of the Great Turning. A brainstorm is good for this. After the guide has given the central idea and the three main dimensions, she invites the group to unpack them—to cite from *their* own experience and information the evidence *they* see of the Great Turning. The guide may choose to focus the brainstorm on one of the dimensions—such as alternative social and economic structures, that are appearing now as harbingers of the Life-sustaining Society. Or he may choose a topic as broad as the Great Turning in its entirety. If the group is sizeable, say over twenty, several sheets of newsprint on the wall and several scribes will be needed, for the contributions come thick and fast. These sheets can be left up, or brought out again later, to feed the thinking and planning the group will do in the final "Going Forth" portion of the workshop.

The beauty of a brainstorm is that it gets out as many ideas as possible in a limited amount of time. A high-energy process, it loosens up the mind, frees the imagination, and ignites appreciation for the breadth of others' ideas and experience. For this to happen, remind the group of the three rules of effective brainstorming: 1) Do not censor, explain, or defend your ideas. 2) Do not evaluate or criticize the ideas of others. 3) Save the discussion until afterwards.

The Mirror Walk

(40 minutes)

Purpose

The Mirror Walk, adapted from the familiar Trust or Blind Walk, provides a deepening of sensory awareness, a fresh sense of gratitude for life, and a change of pace and focus. It makes vivid the perspective of deep ecology —that is, our interbeing with the rest of creation—and breaks through the mental screen that objectifies and separates. It can help people experience the world as their larger body—and even, when they use their eyes at specified moments, to imagine that they are looking in a mirror. Hence the name. Suitable at any point in the workshop, it is excellent near the beginning, since it develops trust among participants and moves beyond words and concepts to immediacy of contact with the outside world.

Description

An outdoor setting with growing things is most rewarding, but even city streets have served well. Forming pairs, people take turns being guided with eyes closed, in silence. Deprived of sight, they have the chance now to use their other senses with more curiosity and wonder than usual, and to experience trusting another person with their safety. Their, partners, guiding them by the hand or arm, offer them various sensory experiences—a flower or leaf to smell, the texture of grass or tree trunk, the sound of birds or children playing—all the while without words. The tempo is relaxed, allowing time to fully register each encounter. Every so often, the guide adjusts his partner's head, as if aiming a camera, and says, "Open your eyes and look in the mirror." The ones being guided open their eyes for a moment or two, and take in the sight.

Demonstrate with a volunteer as you give instructions. Remind participants to maintain silence, except for the occasional invitation to look in the mirror.

After a predetermined length of time, roles are changed. Provide an audible signal when it is time to switch, using a bell or drum or call.

At the end of the second shift, each pair forms a foursome with another pair and takes time now to speak of the experience. After ten minutes or so, bring their attention to the larger group and invite a general sharing. "What did you notice?" "What surprised you?" "What feelings came up, in guiding or being guided?" Many will be eager to respond, often with distinctive insights.

THE PRESENCE OF GRATITUDE THROUGHOUT THE WORK

The affirmative note we strike at the outset of the workshop will continue to reverberate. In the stages of the work and the exercises that follow, notice how consistently gratitude is summoned. Even in the despair work, we are reminded to be thankful—for the chance to speak the suffering, and for each other. In the Open Sentences exercise in the next chapter, Joanna increasingly uses the fourth variation: after people have expressed what is hard for them, living in this time of crisis, they say what they appreciate about it, and the ways they can take part in the Great Turning. Gratitude for the miracle of life, for each other, and for the motivation that brings us to this work are explicitly evoked and nurtured in the Milling, the Cradling, My Choices for This Life, and the Remembering, described in the following chapters. The Deep Time work fosters thankfulness for the ancestors and for the inspiration offered by future generations, just as the exercises surrounding the Council of All Beings bring gladness for our bonds to other life-forms. The individual visioning and planning we do as we prepare to "Go Forth" help us to be aware of the vast resources we can draw upon, and to take grateful note of our own strengths, too. The sense of how blessed we are by the life we share, in this amazing universe, can be nourished in an ongoing way by the meditations offered in the last chapter for us to take with us into our days.

Chapter 7

DESPAIR WORK: OWNING AND HONORING OUR PAIN FOR THE WORLD

Overcome any bitterness that may have come
because you were not up to the magnitude of the pain
that was entrusted to you.
Like the Mother of the world,
who carries the pain of the world in her heart,
each one of us is part of her heart,
and therefore endowed
with a certain measure of cosmic pain.
You are sharing in the totality of that pain.
You are called upon to meet it in joy
instead of self-pity.
—Sufi saying[23]

ZEN POET THICH NHAT HANH WAS ASKED, "What do we need to do to save our world?" His questioners expected him to identify the best strategies to pursue in social and environmental action, but Thich Nhat Hanh's answer was this: "What we most need to do is to hear within us the sounds of the Earth crying."

In despair work, that is what we do: we uncover our pain for the world, and honor it. We bring to awareness our deep inner responses to

> In despair work you discover that others aren't afraid of your pain for the world, and you witness theirs. Then you can dare to hope something for humanity and for what we can do together. When we unblock our despair, everything else follows—the respect and awe, the love. That's why I never state the case for despair in my workshops, but just let people hear it from themselves and each other.
>
> —John Seed, rainforest activist

the suffering of our fellow beings and the progressive destruction of the natural world, our larger body. These responses include dread, rage, sorrow, and guilt. They are healthy and inevitable—and usually blocked by the pressures of daily life and fear of being overwhelmed by despair. Now, in this first stage of the Work that Reconnects, they are allowed to surface without shame or apology.

Note the term "allowed to surface." We do NOT try to instill these knowings and feelings in people; for compassion—the capacity to suffer-with—already inheres in us all, like an underground river. All we do here is help that river come into the light of day, where its currents mingle and gain momentum. We need not scold or manipulate people into what we think they "should" be feeling if they were moral or noble; we simply help each other uncover what is already there. Only honesty is needed. Then we discover, as Thich Nhat Hanh puts it, that "the pain and joy are one."

For each person this process entails:

- acknowledging our pain for the world (verbally or silently)

- validating it as a wholesome response to the present crisis

- letting ourselves experience this pain

- being able to express it to others

- recognizing how widely it is shared by others

- and recognizing that it is not "crazy" but that it springs from our caring and connectedness.

NOTES ON GUIDING THESE EXERCISES

Fear of "negative thinking"
Sometimes people are reluctant to acknowledge their distress about the situation we are in, for fear of reinforcing negativity and making things

worse. This concern seems to come from a misunderstanding of the New Age view that "we create our own reality" and it results in a refusal or incapacity to see what is actually going on. Creating a false dualism between "negative" and "positive" thoughts, it operates in the service of totalitarianism. It diverts attention from the very real world we all participate in, and cuts off the feedback necessary for the system's healing. If a workshop participant expresses this fear of "negativity," listen respectfully, then help the person see where it can lead. Often people only need reassurance that it is all right to feel how they feel, and that they will not be punished for it.

Using the quoted passages in the exercises
These are included for illustrative purposes only. Translate them into your own words and images. Reading them like a script sounds artificial, even boring. It distances you from the participants, making it hard for you to intuitively and creatively respond to the needs of the moment. In preparing to lead an exercise you have not yet experienced, read the instructions and quoted versions over several times to get a clear feel for its structure and tenor. Either mentally or on a slip of paper, record the main points and key phrases you want to use. Practice until you feel comfortable and authentic.

EXERCISES

Small Group Sharing

(25 to 45 minutes)

Purpose
Following initial introductions, small group sharing gives participants an early opportunity to express and listen to the central concerns that brought them to the workshop. This is not a conversation, with give and take among the group's members. Rather, each participant in turn has a period of time to explore thoughts and feelings without interruption.

Description and timing
Have people gather in groups of about four (at least three and no more than five). Each person speaks for the same period of time (between five to ten minutes) while the others listen without verbal response. If the speaker finishes early, or pauses for a while, the group should sit in silence until the time period is up. Often the speaker will find more to say. Be sure to review

the guidelines on listening in Chapter 5, and introduce them to the group.

Themes for the sharing are open-ended and general, such as a recent experience of the condition of the world—when suffering and uncertainty has impinged on your personal life, or a time when you felt pain for the world particularly acutely. Later in the workshop, group sharing might be about people's experiences in a particular exercise. During the Shift (next chapter), people talk about their recent experiences of power and connection. Midway through a day-long or weekend workshop, invite people to share their responses to what has occurred to that point. Small group sharing can be used at any point to good effect, and is particularly useful near the beginning and during transitions.

The Milling

(15 to 20 minutes)

Purpose

This exercise, which is active and nonverbal, provides a change of pace after people have been sitting and talking. Instead of letting the power of the shared images and experiences dissipate in a general discussion, the Milling lets them sink in.

Description

People move about the room, periodically pausing on cue for silent one-to-one encounters. Choose from the types of encounters suggested here or make up your own. Each of our colleagues has a different style in the Milling. We record one pattern here only to give the flavor and tenor of the exercise.

Moving back chairs and cushions to make a large open space in the room, invite people to "mill"—to circulate around the room at a fairly energetic pace, without talking. Model this by walking quickly around the room, weaving through the people. *Let your eyes go out of focus; you won't bump. Soft vision. Use the whole space so we don't get into a snarl in the middle. Soft vision and you won't collide. If you find us going in the same direction, turn around and go upstream.*

1. In the first part, participants move like people on busy city streets, parodying the all too familiar rush which disconnects one person from another and makes us feel that everyone else is just in the way. *Just pretend you're on your lunch hour in Times Square, rushing to get some*

important things done . Keep moving. No talking. Just circulate, pass each other. Embellish this a bit, reminding people how time is accelerating. *You are a very important person with important things to do. Feel in your body the tension of having to make your way through others, like so many obstacles to your own trajectory.*

2. Next, the pace slows and participants begin to pay attention to one another, recognizing each other's presence and humanity. *Now we slow down a bit. We see the faces around us. "Oh, I'm not alone in this planet-time." Our eyes engage as we pass. Look , there is life in there!*

3. Then begins a series of one-to-one encounters. The first draws attention to the sheer presence of the other, and their choice to be here. (We use the ungrammatical "they" instead of "his or her.") *And you find yourself in front of someone—and stop. Standing there before them, take their right hand in yours. And without speaking, let yourself register their presence. Here is someone alive on planet Earth at just this same moment, born into the same period of crisis, confusion and speed. But they're not speeding right now. They're right here. And they've chosen to be here. Don't think there weren't plenty of other things they could do on this day—catching up on work, hanging out with friends. But they've chosen to be here with us to confront this crisis together. Feel your gladness that they made that choice and express that in any way that feels right to you.*

4. In the next encounter, we focus on the other person's love of and connection with life. *And we move on, go back to milling.... Again, you find yourself in front of another person, and take their hand in yours. Behold this brother-sister being, who spoke just now of their love for this life. Here is someone who is unafraid to love the gift of being alive on this planet. It's like medicine. Experience your own gratitude for this, and let them know it by some gesture.*

5. Now the focus moves to the other person's knowledge of the present crises, and willingness to face them. *Again, we move on.... And again we stop in front of someone. You are looking into the face of someone who has a good clue what's going on in our world.* (Give one or two examples of what's going on, such as the following:) *They know what country developed nuclear bombs, and actually used them on two great cities in another land. They know that this country has been preparing to do it again with bombs thousands of times greater. They know of forests being clearcut and farms paved over. There's not a day in which this person isn't aware of that; yet they haven't closed their eyes, haven't turned away. Experience your respect for this courage and express that respect in any way that feels right to you.*

6. In this encounter, the sense of touch is used to heighten awareness and through it, imagination. (This is similar to the Cradling exercise in Chapter 9. If you plan to use the Cradling soon, abbreviate or leave out this section now.) *Again, we go back to our milling, letting ourselves move like kelp in the ocean, touching lightly as we pass. And again we find ourselves in front of another person, and again we take their right hand in ours, but this time we close our eyes as soon as we've connected. Close your eyes so that all your attention can go into the sensation of touch. What is this object you are holding? There is life in it. If you were anywhere in outer space, in intergalactic reaches, and you were to grasp that, you would know that you were home. It is only made here. This is a human hand of Planet Earth and it has taken five billion years of conditions particular to this planet to shape it. Take both your hands and turn it, feeling it, flexing it. Explore it with great curiosity as if you had never known one before, as if you were on a research mission from some other solar system. Please note the intricacy of the bone structure. Note the delicacy of the musculature, the soft, sensitive padding on palm and fingertips. No heavy shell or pelt encloses this hand. It is vulnerable; it is easy to break or burn or crush. It is an instrument of knowing as well as doing.*

 Open your awareness to its journey through time. This was a fin once in the primordial seas where life began, just as it was again in its mother's womb in this lifetime. Countless adventures since then have shaped it, shaped it in connection with the convolutions of the neocortex and frontal lobes of the brain. This hand connected with tree and wind as it refined its intelligence. This hand: the ancestors are in it, ancestors who learned to push up on dry land, to climb, to reach, to grasp, to chip rocks, to gather weeds and weave them into baskets, to gather seeds and harvest them and plant them again; to make fire and carry it, banked, on the long marches through the ages of ice. It's all in that hand from an unbroken succession of adventures.

 Similarly, open your awareness to this hand's journey through this particular lifetime, ever since it opened like a flower as it came out of its mother's womb. Clever hand that has learned so much: learned to reach for breast or bottle, learned to tie shoelaces, learned to write and draw, learned to wipe tears, learned to give pleasure. You know there are people living now who believe they are worthwhile and lovable, because of what that hand has told them. There are people living now whose last touch in life will come from this hand, and they will be able to go into their dying knowing they are not abandoned. You know there are people living now who will be healed in mind or body by the power that this hand allows to flow through it. So experience how much you want that hand to be strong and whole for this time, to serve its brother-sister beings and the planet of which it is a part. And before you part, learn it by heart so that you can remember it is always part of your world. Experience how much you want it to be strong and play its part in the building of a culture of sanity and decency and beauty. Without words, express your appreciation of this hand, and your blessings for it.

7. In this encounter, we acknowledge the danger each person faces by living in this planet-time. Keep your voice matter-of-fact: we are simply acknowledging the realities. This part of the milling is a form of "death meditation." It confronts us with the transiency of human life, especially under the environmental and social threats we face now. Depending on the group and your own inclinations, those threats can be made more explicit as people look at each other.

   Moving on, we come to our last encounter. Facing each other, put your hands together palm to palm at shoulder height. You see before you someone who has chosen to be alive now, in this demanding and fearful time. You know and they know that this is a risky venture. Open your awareness to the fact that in their body, as in yours, are toxins that can bring cancer and other diseases, and with them, an early death. This person, like you, could die from a nuclear accident or attack. Don't look away! We can face this together. We must not let this knowledge of our common danger separate us; let it bond us. Keep breathing.

   Now there's another thing to see in this face. Allow your awareness to open to the very real possibility that this person will play a decisive role in the healing of our world, that they are just at the right place, at the right moment, with the right gifts and motivation. Allow that possibility to enter your mind and let them know how you feel about it!

8. Since strong responses are evoked in the course of the milling, some guides like to let participants talk at the end of the exercise. People can sit down with their last partner for a few minutes of sharing.

Comments

Be sure, as the guide, that your comments are gentle and nonmanipulative. Never tell or command people what to think, see or imagine. Use language that is suggestive only, and is in keeping with present realities. Do not say: "See this person before you as a victim of nuclear war." Rather: "Let the possibility arise in your consciousness...allow, if you will, the notion to surface that this person might..."

   Our workshops reveal that the present realities strike us with greater impact when we see them reflected in the face and figure of another person, even a stranger. To confront their possible suffering and death seems to jolt our minds and hearts more than the imagination of our own death; it breaks open our capacity to care.

Variation

The following abbreviated form of the Milling was used at a university ecopsychology conference.[24]

Stand quietly for a moment, close your eyes and be aware of your body. Think of all you have to do—the homework, a meeting to go to, a paper to write. Imagine yourself moving through your day staying focused on all the tasks you need to accomplish. Now open your eyes and begin to move; keep your focus on what you have to do. Hurry, move fast; so much to do. Be aware of how many people are in your way. Hurry. If you notice there are many moving in the same direction, reverse because you are not all going to the same place or doing the same thing. Move faster. Keep your focus on all you must do.

Now begin to slow down. Become aware of others moving along. Continue to slow down even more and allow yourself to look around. Notice who you pass. Notice the colors others are wearing. Begin to look in each other's eyes. As you do that, silently ask yourself, "Who is on this journey with me? What experiences might we share? What might be the significance of our being here at this time? What possibilities exist because of our being here now? How might we assist and support each other?"

Now stop; return to your chair and make a circle. Make it possible for us to see each other. Reflect for a moment on the experience we just had and notice how you feel now.

Open Sentences

(30 to 50 minutes)

Purpose

This exercise provides a swift and easy way for people to voice their inner responses to the condition of our world. Its structure helps people both to listen with total receptivity and to express thoughts and feelings that are usually censored for fear of comment or adverse reaction. The sequence of the sentences generally moves *from* thoughts and views *to* feelings.

Description

People sit in pairs, face to face and close enough to attend to each other fully. They refrain from speaking until the exercise begins. One is Partner

A, the other Partner B—this can be determined quickly by asking them to tap each other on the knee; the one who tapped first is A. When the guide speaks each unfinished sentence, A repeats it, completes it in his own words, addressing Partner B, and keeps on talking spontaneously for the time allotted. The partners then switch roles. Depending on the material, they switch after each open sentence or, more usually, at the end of the series. The listening partner—and this is to be emphasized—keeps silent, saying absolutely nothing and hearkening as attentively and supportively as possible.

If the partners switch roles once, after a series of sentences, invite A to convey without speaking his appreciation to B for B's supportive listening, and invite B to express—again nonverbally—her respect for A's concerns and his courage in sharing in them.

For the completion of each open sentence allow a minute or two— or longer, if the momentum is strong. Give a brief warning each time before it is time to move on, saying "take a minute to finish up," or "thank you." A clap or small bell can then bring people to silence, where they rest a few seconds before the next open sentence.

Here is a sample series of open sentences that we have used a great deal. Feel free to make up your own to address the particular interests of the group, remembering to keep them as unbiased and nonleading as possible.

1. I think the condition of our society is becoming...

2. I think the condition of our environment is becoming...

3. What concerns me most about the world today is...

4. When I think of the world we will leave our children, it looks like...

5. Feelings about all this, that I carry around with me, are...

6. Ways I avoid these feelings are...

7. Ways I use feelings are...

Variations

The Open Sentence format adapts easily and effectively to different time spans and situations.

- With groups of organizational or professional colleagues, the sentences can help articulate difficulties without beating around the bush, as well as renew inspiration. For example:

  1. What first inspired me to work for the Environmental Protection Agency (or become a physician or canvasser...) was...

  2. What I find hard in this work is...

   3. What keeps me going in this work is...

   4. What I hope can happen for us in this work (or organization) is...

- In a workshop for couples, these sentences can be included:
  - I am sometimes reluctant to share with my partner my pain for the world because...
  - The effect of these feelings on my relationship with my partner is...
- Working with teachers or parents, this exercise can include:
  - If I hide my concerns for the future from the children, it is because I feel...
  - In talking with the children about the news, what I would like them to know and feel is...
- Instead of the seven-part series given above, Joanna often uses this shorter three sentence format, allowing more time for each response:
  1. To be alive now in this time of global crisis, what is particularly hard for me is...
  2. What I appreciate about living in this time of crisis is...
  3. As I look at my life, it seems that some of the ways I take part in the healing of my world (or the Great Turning) are...
- In working with teens, we face special challenges, for it seems even more difficult for them to talk about their feelings, due to social pressure and their strong need to fit in. When Molly used this exercise in a high school classroom, she had the students complete the sentences first in writing, and then share in groups of three. Writing first helped the students to reflect more deeply, before "going public" with their thoughts and feelings. The written work also provided feedback for the teacher in planning future lessons.

The Truth Mandala

(60 to 90 minutes)

Purpose and background

This ritual exercise provides a simple, respectful, whole group structure for owning and honoring our pain for the world, and for recognizing its authority and the solidarity it can bring. The practice emerged in 1992 amidst a large, tension-filled workshop in Frankfurt, on the day of reunification between East and West Germany; since then it has spread to many lands.

One participant described his experience with the Truth Mandala in a weekend college workshop as a "deeply connecting experience." He wrote afterwards:

> One by one we shared our fear, our grief, our anger, and our emptiness. I could feel reservoirs of untapped compassion and courage emerge that enabled me to open and truly suffer with each person the concerns that each revealed. To be able to embrace our suffering and not pull back in denial or defense is a gift and one that is transforming. It pushes us, stretching our hearts to be able to hold all of life experience, not just the good or the joyful, but the difficult and the painful. And in so doing, we get to experience the great paradox of opening to the suffering, which is the opening to more life and joy and love and compassion.

Description

People sit in a circle. They sit as closely packed as possible for they are, as we often put it, creating a containment vessel, for holding and cooking the truth. The circle they enclose is divided into four quadrants (visible demarcations are not needed), and in each quadrant is placed a symbolic object: a stone, dead leaves, a thick stick, and an empty bowl. Entering each quadrant, the guide holds the object it contains and explains its meaning. Here are some words we use.

This stone is for fear. It's how our heart feels when we're afraid: tight, contracted, hard. In this quadrant we can speak our fear.

These dry leaves represent our sorrow, our grief. There is great sadness within us for what we see happening to our world, our lives, and for what is passing from us.

This stick is for our anger. For there is anger and outrage in us that needs to be spoken for clarity of mind and purpose. This stick is not for hitting with or waving around, but for grasping hard with both hands—it's strong enough for that.

And in this fourth quadrant, this empty bowl stands for our sense of deprivation and need, our hunger for what's missing, our emptiness.

You may wonder where hope is. The very ground of this mandala is hope. If we didn't have hope, we wouldn't be here.

We will begin with a dedication and a chant because this becomes holy ground, for nothing makes a place more holy than truth-telling. Then we will step in one at a time, spontaneously. We will take a symbol in our hands and speak, or move from one to another. We may come in more than once or not at all; there is no pressure on us to enter. Even if you stay on the periphery, you will find that, as each person enters the mandala, you are in there with them. We will speak briefly. In brevity, words are powerful.

Now the guide, entering each quadrant, demonstrates how its symbol can be used for speaking the knowings and feelings we carry. For example, holding the stone of fear:

"I'm scared by the spread of cancer and AIDS. Will my lover be next? Will I? Where can I go from the poisons? They are everywhere, in our air, our water, our food."

"I feel sorrow for the fate of Tibet—and for the loss of the old indigenous cultures. Now when we most need the wisdom of their ancient traditions, we wipe them out. So I weep for us, too."

"Oh, the fury I feel for our war on the poor! I can't believe that welfare bill! What will happen to the women, the children? What kind of jobs can they get?"

"I don't know what to do. I recycle, I take the bus, I change my diet, but in truth I don't know what can save us. I am empty of ideas, strategies, confidence."

Since we are not used to talking like this in public, we need the support of the whole group. After each person has spoken, let us all say, "We hear you." That's enough. Your agreement or approval is not needed—just your hearing and respect. And let us pause for three breaths in silence between speakings.

Maybe there's something you'll want to say that doesn't fit one of these quadrants, so this cushion in the center of the mandala is a place you can stand or sit to give voice to it—be it a song or prayer or story.

In the Truth Mandala we speak not only for ourselves, but for others, too. It is the nature of all ritual that it allows us to speak archetypally—not just as separate individual selves, but on behalf of our people, our Earth.

Let the ritual object—stone or leaves or bowl—focus our mind. We don't enter the mandala to perform or explain or report to the rest of us, but to let that object help us voice the truth of our own experience.

Before the ritual's formal start, ask for the group's commitment to confidentiality: "what is said here, stays here." Indicate also the duration of time you are giving to the ritual; this helps people be comfortable with the silences that arise.

The ritual time begins with your formal dedication of the Truth Mandala to the welfare of all beings and the healing of our world. And its proceedings are initiated with a simple chant or sounding. The syllable "ah" stands in Sanskrit for all that has been unsaid—and all whose voices have been taken from them, or not yet heard.

Trust yourself to sense the moment to draw the ritual to a close. You will read clues in people's body language and the energy of the group, or from utterances that seem to provide an appropriate note to end on. As you prepare to close, tell people, so that those who have been holding back and waiting to speak can seize the chance to do so. We often say:

The truth-telling will continue in our lives, but this chapter of it will draw soon to a close. Let those who have been waiting to come in, enter now and speak.

The formal closing of the Truth Mandala is a key moment in which to enlarge the group's understanding of what has transpired. First the guide, speaking generally and on behalf of all, honors the truth that each has spoken and the respectful support that each has given. Truth-telling, as Joanna says, is like oxygen: it enlivens us. Without it we grow confused and numb. It is also a homecoming, bringing us back to powerful connection and basic authority.

Then the guide points out the deeper import of each quadrant in the mandala. Each symbolic object is like a coin with two sides; the courage to speak our fear, for example, is evidence of trust. Indicating one object after another, say in effect:

> *Please notice what you have been expressing and hearing. In hearing fear, you also heard the trust it takes to speak it.*

> *The sorrow spoken over the dead leaves was in equal measure love. We only mourn what we deeply care for. "Blessed are they that mourn." Blessed are those who weep for the desecration of life, because in them life still burns clear.*

> *And the anger we heard, what does it spring from but passion for justice?*

> *The empty bowl is to be honored, too. To be empty means there is space for the new.*

Timing and group size

We have never conducted the Truth Mandala with fewer than twelve people or more than a hundred. Even with large numbers we draw it to a close after an hour and a half, because the process is intense, and though people are riveted, they grow more tired than they are aware of.

Place the ritual near the middle of the day, with a break following it. Be sure participants have already had an opportunity to talk with each other in some depth (Open Sentences or Small Group Sharing) before doing the Truth Mandala, so these strong distilled utterances come out of some reflection. Afterwards, some time for rest or journaling helps people absorb the experience, and they should honor that need rather than taking off for home right away.

Advice

1. Participate. Don't remain aloof, but enter the ritual as honestly and openly as you can, while fulfilling your responsibilities as a guide. This is not hard to do.

2. Review the section in Chapter 5 on dealing with strong emotions.

3. Feel free to adapt the arrangements to people's needs. In workshops with the elderly, the mandala is set up on a table rather than the floor; to speak, each person rises from their chair and stands by a quadrant, sometimes using a cane as a talking stick. In a psychiatric ward, the stone and stick are replaced with other objects, like a vine and a picture.

The Despair Ritual

(60 to 90 minutes)

Purpose and background

The despair ritual serves much the same purpose as the Truth Mandala, but with greater intensity. Originated by Chellis Glendinning after the Three Mile Island nuclear accident, it is one of the oldest and bravest forms of despair work. Its structure came to Chellis in a dream, and its function was inspired by the practice of "speaking bitterness," which was used in China to alleviate apathy and paralysis from the suffering incurred in the revolution.

> People confessed not their sins, but their sorrows. This had the effect of creating emotional solidarity. For when people poured out their sorrows to each other, they realized they were all together on the same sad voyage through life, and from recognition of this they drew closer to one another, achieved common sentiments, took sustenance and hope.[25]

The despair ritual has a similar result: moreover, its form offers people the opportunity to "touch bottom," in experiencing and expressing their pain for the world. As they do, people lose their fear of it. And the bottom becomes common ground—the place of deep connection and commitment.

Description

The process unfolds in three concentric circles. At the outset everyone is standing and moving in the outer ring, which is the Circle of Reporting. The next is the Circle of Anger and Fear, and the innermost, a pile of pillows at the center, is the Circle of Sorrow. Behind the outer ring, a corner space is marked off, with a potted plant or two, to create the Sanctuary.

After initial explanations by the guide (see "Advice" below), the ritual begins like the Truth Mandala with a vow of intention ("that the work we are about to do serve the healing of our world"), and a long sonorous sounding (usually "ah"). People now move around the outer circle counterclockwise, and at their own pace. Spontaneously they begin to make short statements about what is in their hearts and minds about the condition of the world. They report both facts and feelings—simply, briefly, without explanation. "In my city the homeless are being arrested now, and the shelters are closing." "The air pollution is giving my daughter asthma." "I am terrified of getting cancer." After each statement the group responds, "Indeed it is so," or "We hear you."

When emotion wells up and people feel moved not only to report it, but also to express it, they enter one of the two inner circles. In the middle one they may stride, stomp, pound pillows, shout out their anger or fear. Or they may move directly to the Circle of Sorrow, kneel or sink down on the cushions to release their grief, crying and sometimes holding each other. People stay in any circle as long as they want and return as frequently as they want. At different moments, almost half the participants may find themselves in the inner rings; all the while the reporting continues. As emotions and noise escalate, individuals may want to take refuge from the turbulence—then they go and sit a while in the Sanctuary. There they can be quiet and a bit removed, while still following and supporting the process.

The great advantage of having the three circles and the Sanctuary is that people can participate simultaneously at different levels of emotional engagement and catharsis. As they move back and forth, they discover the fluidity, as well as the depth, of their feelings. And those who don't give free rein to their feelings still provide a supportive presence.

After painful information and feelings have been expressed at length, and may have reached a crescendo (or repeated crescendos), the tone and direction of the group usually shifts. The movement *down* into darkness and distress begins to turn of its own dynamic into a movement up toward affirmation, as people experience the profound commonality of their caring. Statements like "my brother is dying of AIDS" are increasingly interspersed with "I'm planting a garden," or "Folks in my neighborhood are organizing a cooperative." This shift cannot be programmed, but it virtually always occurs. The prevailing mood begins to change, even though some still weep in the Circle of Sorrow. Often people start clustering there, touching each other's hands and shoulders, meeting each other's eyes in compassion and gratitude. A humming or song may arise. In a recent workshop someone began singing "We are the ones we've been waiting for," and the rest of us joined in; the singing went on for a long time. The ritual was over.

Each ending is different. Sometimes the larger portion of the group needs to stay longer with their feelings of despair; but even then, after an hour and a half, the guide can sense an abatement of energy, a shift in mood, a temporary kind of completion. Then, in an appropriate pause in the process, the guide moves to close the ritual by acknowledging the significance of what has transpired and inviting people to honor each other for their participation. He helps them refocus on the group as a whole. He may wish to resume the sounding that began the ritual, or have people take hands and move in a circle or chain, regarding each other with respect and appreciation.

Sometimes the closing is less dignified. Hilarity can happen when deep emotions have been released—all the more so when they pertain to our shared world. Then the tremendous solidarity that has been discovered can explode in dancing and drumming.

Advice to the guide

The despair ritual is quite a challenge to facilitate, requiring a lot of alertness, trust, and authenticity. Anyone serving as guide—or "road person" as Chellis put it—should reread the section on "Working with Strong Emotions" in Chapter 5, and also attend to the following counsel.

1. It is best not to offer and lead this process before you have experienced it.

2. Do not attempt it with less than a dozen people or more than fifty. Thirty or so is optimal.

3. With over 20 people, allow a couple of hours. This includes time for preliminary instructions and time at the end to unwind.

4. In your preliminary instructions, emphasize the fact that everyone has different emotional styles and timing. No one should feel *any* pressure to behave in a particular way. Emphasize, furthermore, that each person always has a choice about the extent to which they let themselves experience and express their emotions.

5. Remind the group of the distinctive nature of the ritual, which is to allow people to speak archetypally and on behalf of the collective. Here the dread, rage, and grief we express are not necessarily ours alone; given our interconnections in the web of life, the tears we shed could also be those of an Iraqi mother, a street child, a hunted whale. If someone sees another in the ritual process expressing strong feelings that they also share, they may show their solidarity by quietly standing or kneeling beside them.

6. Participate. Never hold yourself aloof from the ritual, as if you were some observer or magus. Take part fully *and* with a split attention—maintaining a continuous overall sense of how people are doing and watching for moments when you may need to intervene.

7. Intervene if people reporting from the outer circle fall into dialogue or debate. This is less likely to happen if you have clarified the distinctive nature of ritual.

8. Intervene if a person begins to distract or disturb the others by "acting out" some private emotional agenda. This occurs *very* rarely—only twice in the countless rituals the authors have guided but if it does, you can handle it. Simply go to the person, make physical contact (with their arms or shoulders), have them meet your eyes and then look around the group—to "come back" to it—and invite them to rest a while on the sidelines with your cofacilitator.

9. You may choose to provide support to persons undergoing extremely heavy emotional discharge. You can do this by touch or your simple physical presence beside them.

10. If nothing seems to be happening, just breathe and wait. Let people take their time.

11. If everything seems to be happening at once, the storming and sobbing looks as if it could go on for days, and you wonder how you'll ever bring the group back to "normal," our advice is the same: just breathe and wait. Your job is not to rescue people but to allow them to take advantage of this rare opportunity to share so fully their pain for the world. Trust the process.

12. As with the Truth Mandala, hold the ritual near the middle of the day, and let it be followed by a break. People need time quietly to absorb the experience, preferably together—so don't let people leave right afterwards. The Cradling, Spontaneous Writing, or Imaging with Colors and Clay are good follow-ons, and it's excellent to have some time in nature. The ritual should never be the last process of the day.

13. Later on, let people meet in small groups to debrief their experiences of the ritual. Conclude that period with a general discussion to give people a chance to say things to the whole group.

14. Do we need to say, "Don't do both the Despair Ritual and the Truth Mandala in the same workshop"?

Spontaneous Writing

(20 to 30 minutes)

Purpose
Good at any point, this exercise works especially well closely following the Truth Mandala or the Despair Ritual. It encourages people to open to

the wisdom and clarity that can emerge from telling the truth about their feelings for the world.

Description

Choose a word, a theme or phrase—perhaps something that emerged in a previous process—and post it. Have everyone in the group relax as they read it; and have them then take pen or pencil and write—spilling out, pouring out whatever comes to mind. Help them by your suggestions to release themselves from the judge and censor in their mind, and playfully or prayerfully to let come what comes. There is no requirement to read it to others and no requirement for spelling, grammar, or even "making sense." Suggest that people continue moving their pen or pencil even when nothing comes, just repeating the last word, drawing circles or whatever.

"With this dark and painful stuff, our task is to..." This half-sentence from the poster artist Sister Carita has been especially powerful after other despair work processes. Coming after the evocation and sharing of our feelings of pain for the world, it lets the depths of the psyche speak its own knowings. It lets each person, still feeling the support of the group, move alone now to catch a fresh glimpse of his or her distinctive truth. After ten or fifteen minutes of writing, people are almost invariably eager to share it. Let them do this in twos or threes.

Imaging with Colors and Clay

(30 to 40 minutes)

Purpose

The verbal expression of our concerns for the world has its limits, for words can hide as well as reveal. We use language not only to communicate, but to protect ourselves, distracting others' and our own attention from what is painful. To connect with our deep responses to the condition of our world, it helps to go beyond words, or dive beneath them to that subliminal level where we register inchoately the anguish of our time. On that level we can tap our energy and the wellsprings of our creativity; images and art give us access to it.

When we use colors on paper or model with clay, images surface; the tactile, visual engagement releases them wordlessly. According to neuropsychologists, artistic engagement shifts the locus of mental activity to the right hemisphere of the brain, with its capacity for thinking spatially rather than consecutively. We open our awareness to the web of life, and its far-reaching reciprocities, beyond linear cause-and-effect. Workshop participants are often surprised by what their hands have portrayed: potencies of feelings and reaches of concern that they had supposed were peripheral to their lives. Unlike the words we speak, these images seem to have a reality of their own: we feel less need to apologize, explain, or defend. The images, once birthed, are just there— like a fact of life, self-existent—and viewing them we feel at the same time both revealed and protected.

Colors

As you lay out the materials (large drawing paper and oil pastels, crayons, or marking pens), briefly explain the purpose of the exercise. Suggest people use color and shape to express whatever they are feeling and thinking, or choose a theme that has come up in the workshop.

Or use natural objects. Participants bring in from outside some small object that attracts their attention: a leaf, a rock, a piece of bark. Placing it in the center of their paper, they allow a drawing to appear as an expression of that object—lines and shapes and colors extending out from it, as if that piece of nature were the artist.

Acknowledge people's hesitations. Many people, especially adults, feel dismay when asked to engage in any kind of artwork. Make clear that the point here is not to portray or create anything, or to measure up to any artistic standard. Encourage participants to trust whatever shapes and images arise and any changes that emerge, remaining open to new directions and using more paper or clay as needed.

Drawing with the dominant hand, as we usually do, allows us to express forcefully and without frustration the images that have arisen. For this, allow plenty of time (say, 15 to 20 minutes) because people become very engrossed and want time to complete what they envision. On occasion, however, try drawing with the nondominant hand; people find it frees them more completely from the control of the censoring mind, keeping the focus on color and movement and feelings.

Encourage participants to work in silence. To let images arise, we need to let our thinking, talking mind take a rest. Soothing, nonvocal music helps. Inform people of time limits and give them a warning two or three minutes before the time is up.

Allow time at the end for quiet discussion. Imaging work is incomplete without the opportunity to share and explore it together. Have people gather in small groups, or in the larger circle (if not too large), their drawings face down. Then one by one they turn their sheets over and describe what they saw and felt as the lines and colors emerged on the paper. Avoiding psychological interpretations, other participants ask clarifying questions and offer observations to help deepen discovery of what the drawings reveal. Sometimes two or three drawings seem to resonate together. At the close, people often like to tape the sheets to the walls and move around absorbing them.

Variation

In another form of imaging, people make a mural together, drawing on a long roll of newsprint placed on the floor or wall. In intergenerational gatherings, adults and children can each—in turn or simultaneously—draw something they love or something that makes them "feel sad about the world." To do this first and in silence, and only later tell about what they have drawn, encourages children to express themselves in the company of grown-ups. They feel readier then to share what is on their minds, especially since they are freer with color and images than many adults.

Clay work

In a workshop, imaging on paper is easier to arrange and less messy than working with clay. Yet clay work, being more tactile and involving larger muscles can release emotion and tap our subconscious wisdom. Joanna experienced this personally during the Vietnam war when she felt sapped by a sense of futility. Here is how she later described the experience which took place at a Quaker-sponsored workshop:

> To give form to feeling, and tired of words, I worked with clay. As I descended into the sorrow within me, I shaped that descent in the block of clay —cliffs and escarpments plunging into abysses, dropping off into downward-twisting gullies, down, down. Though I wept as I pushed at the clay with fingers and fists, it felt good to have my sense of hopelessness become palpable, visible. The twisted, plummeting clay landscape was like a silent scream, and also like a dare accepted in bitter defiance, the dare to descend into empty nothingness.
>
> Feeling spent and empty, the work done, my mind turned to go, but then noted what my fingers had, of themselves, begun to explore. Snaking and pushing up the clay cliffs were roots. As they came into focus, I saw how they joined, tough and tenacious, feed-

ing each other in an upsurge of ascent. The very journey down-
ward into my despair had shaped these roots, which now thrust
upward, unbidden and resilient.

Chapter 8

THE SHIFT: SEEING WITH NEW EYES

For the raindrop, joy is in entering the river—
Unbearable pain becomes its own cure...

It's the rose's unfolding, Ghalib, that creates the desire to see—
In every color and circumstance, may the eyes be open for what comes.
—Ghalib (of 19th century India)[26]

IN DESPAIR WORK WE LOOK FULL-FACE at what is happening to our world, and that means dropping our defenses against our own feelings of dread, anger, guilt, and grief. As we allow these emotions to surface, we can perceive their distinctive character. We find that the dread we experience is not the same as fear of our own individual death, and that the anger is on behalf of others as well as ourselves. We find the sense of guilt is not personal blame so much as collective accountability as a society and as a species. And underneath all these responses is a depthless well of sorrow for the suffering and losses inflicted on our brother-sister beings and those who will come after us.

This in itself is a remarkable discovery, for it flies in the face of what the Industrial Growth Society has conditioned us to believe about ourselves. It doesn't match with the assumption that we are separate, independent beings, whose happiness must often be secured at the expense of others. On the contrary, it reveals that, in the depths of our psyches, we suffer with them. That "suffering with," we now recall, is the literal meaning of compassion. Far from being a sign of personal craziness, it is the noblest of capacities in most spiritual traditions.

Now we can realize from actual experience that it is from our inter-connectedness that feelings of pain for the world arise. The very distress that, when we hid it, seemed to separate us from other people, now uncovers the connective tissue bonding us. This realization, whether it comes in a flash of insight or as a gradual dawning, is a turning point in our perceptions—or, more precisely, in the way we interpret our percep-tions. We shift to a new way of seeing ourselves and a new way of understanding our power.

NATURE OF THE SHIFT

Many metaphors come to mind for describing this shift. It is like a turn-ing of the tide, or the pause between breathing in and breathing out. As we allow the world's pain to flow in, it rearranges our internal structures. Then, on the outflow, our gifts of response release back into the world. Or it is like a fulcrum, letting us shift the weight of our despair, turn it and raise it into new understandings. The Chinese character for crisis is a combination of two forms: one means danger, the other opportunity. On this fulcrum danger turns to opportunity. Or it is like a hinge. This hinge can swing us from pain to power because it is anchored in their common source: our interexistence within the web of life.

Or, yet another metaphor: this shift is a gateway. The approach to many an ancient temple is guarded by ferocious figures. In facing them down, in moving through our dreads and griefs, we gain entry to the truth that awaits us. We discover our mutual belonging, our "deep ecology," and the promise that it holds for us. Now we can see in our anguish for the world the good news of a larger consciousness at work; it is the universe knowing itself through us. This wisdom is bought at the price of "positive disintegra-tion," the crumbling of the system's old codes and constructs. Carl Jung said, "There is no birth of consciousness without pain."

> The human being in whom the earth has become spiritually aware, has awakened into consciousness, has become self-aware and self-reflecting. In the human, the earth begins to reflect on itself. In our deepest definition and deepest subjectivity, we humans are the earth. Conscious.
> —Sister Miriam McGillis [27]

The new aware-ness comes like grace. As meditation teacher Stephen Levine says, "Grace is a sense of interconnectedness... it is the experience of our underlying nature, then we may see that what is often called tragedy holds the seeds of grace. We see that grace is not always pleasant, though it seems always to take us to something essential in ourselves."

This shift in perception is an inner revolution which religious traditions call *metanoia*—turning around. In Mahayana Buddhism, it is termed *parinamana*, turning over, and described as filled with jubilation and dedication to the welfare of all. We "turn around" or "turn over" into wider awareness of who and what we are—as jewels in the Net of Indra, as members of the body of Christ, or the beloved of Krishna, or synapses in the mind of God.

Joanna in her group work often calls it the "tantric flip." The tantric tradition in Buddhism sees that every aspect of life, however ordinary or even repulsive, can be a means to enlightenment. All that is required is fully to enter the present moment—a joining so radical that it eclipses our preconceived notions and reorganizes the way we see. Then everything appears as Dharma.

For individuals this turning point arrives in different ways at different times. It occurs again and again, at different levels of one's consciousness and in relation to different parts of one's life. In the Work that Reconnects, it usually happens, in some form, about midway through a workshop.

How do you program this? You can't. It is not the doing of the guide so much as a function of the psychological and spiritual dynamics of the work itself.

What, then, is your role as guide? You pause to name what is happening, and by naming, you evoke and validate it. You help the group turn a corner. At that corner, you can look two ways, getting perspective on where you have been and at the same time glimpsing a new vista. Looking back at participants' experience in the despair work, you name the interconnectedness that is intrinsic to their pain for the world. Looking ahead, you indicate what this interconnectedness can mean for their lives and work to heal our world.

Jerry, as you wept for your children's future... Jan, as you opened to the grief and confusion of your clients... Bill, the rage you feel over the dumping of toxic wastes ... Helen, your suffering with the people of Mexico ... do you see? These concerns extend far beyond your own personal safety and comfort. They are more than fear of your own death. They come out of the web of life in which you belong. What does this say? Does it say something about your power? What kind of power can we draw from this interconnectedness?

PART I: BRAIN FOOD

Key concepts

After despair work people's minds need nourishment. Catharsis frees the intellect to think more clearly, without the obfuscations of denial and rationalization. It is time for some brain food. To convey the implications of what we have been uncovering and to provide ground for our further work, we present concepts basic to the cognitive revolution, the paradigm shift of our time.

Please note that in some cultures this group work proceeds best when its theoretical foundations are set forth at the outset. This work arose in a society which is conditioned by Anglo-Saxon predispositions to empiricism and inductive reasoning—where interpretations and conclusions are more welcome *after* direct experience. However, in continental Europe, for example, participants are more ready to trust the work when they are provided with a cognitive framework from the start. In such settings, we briefly articulate the theoretical premises set forth in Chapter 4 and allude to some of the concepts which will be unpacked more fully after some despair work.

Each guide has a world of experiences to draw from, and distinctive concepts and images to offer, in conveying the astonishing interconnectedness of life. Some take examples from nature, others from spiritual traditions. Guides who are musicians may speak of a shared world of rippling, intersecting vibrations. Those with a philosophical bent may speak of the "hundredth monkey" concept and of Rupert Sheldrake's hypothesis of "morphogenetic fields." Lovers of systems theory may talk about coevolving systems and emergent properties; community organizers about the synergies unleashed as they help citizens take charge of their lives; anthropologists and storytellers about ancient myths of cocreation in the web of life. There is no limit to the illustrative material that is here for us to use.

Remember to include certain basic concepts, which are essential to the Great Turning from the Industrial Growth Society to a Life-sustaining Society. Whatever illustrative material we may use, we always endeavor to make some key points. We distill them here from their fuller presentation in Chapter 3.

- The worldview underlying the Industrial Growth Society perceives reality in terms of discrete and separate entities, which relate to each other in a hierarchical and competitive fashion. Hence power has been understood as domination—power over, win/lose.

- We now, in the Great Turning, reclaim an understanding of the interdependence of all phenomena. Power is understood as mutual and synergistic, arising from interaction and generating new possibilities and capacities.

- The shift in perception is a figure-ground reversal—from separate entities to flows of relationship, from substance to process, from noun to verb.

- In this shift each self is seen as both unique and inseparable from its matrix, the web of life; its genuine self-interest includes other beings and the living body of Earth.

- The assumption that selves are essentially separate, and thereby competitive, breeds insatiable wants. Hence the overriding goal of economic growth, to which our global system is increasingly addicted, and which is inherently suicidal.

- The global crisis is at root a crisis in perception. There is no technological fix.

Pointers for teaching these concepts

1. Make time for them. These ideas are implicit in the exercises and will be reflected in comments made in the course of doing them; still it is good to plan a specific time to focus on these concepts, perhaps presenting a mini-lecture. Visual aids, if only a "chalk talk," are helpful.

2. Choose your approach. Which interpretive path—or "hermeneutic" as scholars call it—do you want to take? Some guides, like the authors, use insights from systems theory and spiritual traditions. Others, as described above, draw from their own wide-ranging studies and experiences.

3. Keep it simple. Use only a few analogies to convey this shift in perception, as you have known it.

4. At the same time, don't talk down to your audience. Assume that they are interested, serious, and smart. Don't be fooled by appearances. The shy young mother, the blue-haired crone, the high school dropout— each can startle you with their incisive and illuminating comments.

5. Don't be intimidated. If your life experience has not made you comfortable directing intellectual discourse, you may want to assemble a series of quotes or short passages which have enriched your own understanding. Perhaps you'll choose some earlier sections from this book. Then, instead of your reading them out like a scripted lecture,

distribute copies and have participants take turns reading them aloud, with pauses for reflection and then times for comment.

6. Remember that you are not trying to convince people. The only questions you should try to answer are those seeking clarification of what you said. Your role as guide is not to resolve people's doubts, but to offer food for thought and make room for the sharing of insights.

7. When you contrast worldviews, keep the focus on their psychological and behavioral effects, instead of trying to disprove one theory and prove another. (When we view things through an atomistic, mechanical model of the universe, we tend to act in careless, destructive ways—as evident in the damage we have done in the Industrial Growth Society. When we see ourselves as interdependent parts of the web of life, we tend to behave with more harmony and responsibility.) Ask people to sense how the model resonates with their hearts as well as their minds.

8. Set a time limit. Intellectual discussion gets heady—and keeps us in our heads. When time is up, ask participants to stand and stretch, and then move them into an exercise that reflects these ideas and grounds them.

PART II: EXERCISES

Experiential work gives form to the key concepts and lets participants explore their implications. Guided meditations such as "The Great Ball of Merit" and "Learning to See Each Other" (Chapter 12) are excellent right after the conceptual talk. Aikido exercises are also appropriate, dramatically demonstrating the relational character of power, and the synergy that arises when the force of an adversary is accepted and used nondefensively.

The following interactive exercises serve the Shift by helping us see the larger context in which our individual lives arise—the web of life through space and time. They use our innate powers of imagination and empathy to shift from a perspective based on self-as-separate-entity to one arising from our interexistence. They include not only the practices described below, but also those set forth in the next two chapters. Those in Chapter 9, called "Deep Time," make vivid our connections with past and future generations. Those in Chapter 10, "The Council of All Beings," serve to expand our self-interest to include the more-than-human world and let us perceive things from that wider perspective.

Exercises which do not fit exclusively in either of those two categories are offered in this chapter. Select from them in any order.

The Systems Game
(30 minutes)

Purpose and background

This lively, engrossing process provides a direct experience of the dynamic nature of open systems. We are indebted to Alice Pitty, who shared this game at Schumacher College in 1994. We have found it very useful in dramatizing the new paradigm view of reality, especially these two features of it:

1) that life is composed not of separate entities so much as of the relations between them, and

2) that these relations are continually self-organizing.

During or after any presentation of these concepts, this exercise is an excellent "breather," offering physical activity and provoking fresh thought and discussion.

Description

People stand in a large open space, either indoors or out. The guide may introduce the game in terms of one or both of the above purposes. *"We've talked about viewing reality in terms of relationships rather than separate, independent entities; how do we make that figure-ground shift in perception?"* Or: *"We've said that systems self-organize; how can we experience that?"*

The guide then gives two instructions. The first is: *"Mentally select two other people in the group, without indicating whom you have chosen."* The second is: *"Move so as to keep at all times an equal distance between you and each of these two people."* This, as the guide makes clear, does not mean just staying at the midpoint *between* the two others.

To pursue this objective, people immediately begin to circulate, each movement triggering many others in an active, interdependent fashion. Participants find they are, by necessity, maintaining wide-angle vision and constant alacrity of response. The process is purposeful, suspenseful, laced with laughter. It speeds up for a while, then may abate, accelerate, and again slow down toward equilibrium, but it rarely comes to stasis. The guide lets it continue for four or five minutes, then, as activity lessens, invites people to pause where they are and reflect.

The simple question, *"What did you experience?"* evokes fruitful discussion.

- Participants' reflections usually bring out some key features of self-regulating systems, such as the interdependence of all parts, and their continual activity in seeking and maintaining balance.

- People may realize that they thought the point of the game was to achieve stasis; the guide can bring out and challenge that assumption. The self-regulation of open systems requires constant internal activity.

- People may articulate perceptual and psychological shifts they experienced in the game. These can include a radically widened sense of context, and a larger, more porous sense of self. A temporary eclipse of self-consciousness may be noted, as one's perceptions focused not on one's own actions so much as on others'—that is, not on separate entities so much as on relations among them.

- *"Is this a closed system or an open system?"*, the guide may ask. If people think it is a closed system because no one entered from outside, it should be pointed out that an influx of energy, originating from the sun, empowered all participants. We wouldn't last long without food or drink from outside the system we just created. Individually and collectively, we are open systems dependent on inputs of matter-energy and information. Closed systems do not exist in nature.

- *"What feedback enabled us to fulfill our function (that is, of staying equidistant from two others)?"* If there is no answer, the guide may ask, *"Could we have done it with our eyes closed?"* The ensuing discussion can feature how not only visual perceptions, but also feedback of all kinds, guide us in our daily lives in the systems we cocreate at home and at work.

- *"Would anyone volunteer to organize this process?"* the guide may ask. It is obvious that no party or person on the outside could direct the movements necessary to keep this system in balance.

Variations

1. Have two people stay out of the room or area during the instructions, then call them in at a certain point and ask them to try to detect what is happening. When the process halts, and they learn (or have discovered) the principle guiding people's movements, ask the observers if they could organize this complex process from the outside.

   The point of this question is obvious. Relations within systems are so complex, they can only *self*-regulate. That is why life scientists came to the discovery of self-organizing systems in their efforts to understand life-forms with more than one variable or moving part (i.e. anything more complex than a helium atom, which has only one electron).

2. The observers are invited to walk quietly through the game while it is in process. The observers and the players note that this pass-through does not affect or disrupt the game, for the players are moving solely in relation to each other. In this fashion, we humans can pass through a forest or a swamp and not disrupt its defining relations. Now let this pass-through recur several times, bumping into people or blocking others' movements. Let players comment on their experience of disturbance or, as it's called in systems terms, persisting perturbation.

3. Another variation, used as a follow-on to the original process, is to decide with the group to immobilize two or more players and then proceed with the game. In the discussion that follows, people may reflect on the diminished fluidity they sensed in the group as a whole, or on their own experience if one of their partners was motionless. The decreased responsiveness and activity is often experienced as a dysfunction within the system, and comments on this fact can bring fresh insights.

4. Yet another variation is this: as the group slows down and seems to be approaching equilibrium, the guide may upset the balance by moving to a new position. Unless no one has chosen him, the group will start moving again to find a new equilibrium. People rarely notice who started this change of events, but in the ensuing discussion, the guide may recall that flurry of activity. It is fruitful now to reflect on how wide the effects can be from one small, intentional change within the system.

Widening Circles
(60 to 90 minutes)

Note: This exercise can serve as the sole experiential component of a short workshop or evening gathering.

Purpose
Widening Circles helps people to see with new eyes an issue or situation which is of great concern to them. Thus they participate in widening circles of identity. It is excellent for environmental activists, bringing wisdom, patience, flexibility, and perseverance. The name of the exercise is taken from Rilke's poem in his *Book of Hours*, that begins: "I live my life in widening circles/ that reach out across the world" and ends with "And I still don't know/ Am I a falcon, a storm,/ or a great song."

Description
Participants sit in groups of four. Ask them to choose, mentally, a particular issue or situation that concerns them. After a moment of silence, invite them to take turns speaking and listening to each other. Each person will describe the issue from four perspectives in turn:

(1) from their own experience and point of view, including their feelings about the issue;

(2) from the perspective of a person whose views are very different and even adversarial on the issue, introducing themselves and speaking as this person, using the pronoun "I";

(3) from the viewpoint of a nonhuman being that is involved in or affected by that particular situation;

(4) and lastly, in the voice of a future human whose life will be directly affected by the choices made now on this issue.

The guide announces these perspectives when the time comes for each one—instead of all at once at the outset—and repeats them in that sequential fashion for the following speakers. Give at least three minutes for each perspective. Signal the time with a verbal cue ("take another minute to finish") and then with a clacker or bell to end that part. Allow for silence between each part and at the end of each series.

To speak on behalf of another, and identify even briefly with that being's experience and perspective, is an act of moral imagination. It is not difficult to do: as children we knew how to "play-act." Use an uncharged, almost casual tone in your instructions; you are not asking people to "channel" or be omniscient, but simply to imagine another point of view. Allow some silence as they choose for whom they will speak and imaginatively enter that other's experience, so they can respect it and not perform a caricature of it. It is a brave and generous act to make room in your mind for another's experience and to lend them your voice; let the participants appreciate that generosity in themselves and each other.

Allow time at the end for people to share in their small groups what they felt and learned.

Variation
For shorter versions, use only one or two of the four perspectives.

The Cradling
(20 to 60 minutes)

Purpose

A guided meditation on the body, the cradling exercise serves many purposes. It permits deep relaxation, all the more welcome after dealing straight on with fearsome issues. It builds trust among participants, and a kind of respectful cherishing. It widens our awareness of what is at stake in the global crisis, for the dangers we face—pollution, ecological collapse, famine, warfare—are dangers because of what they do to the body. The Cradling also taps deeper levels of knowing, stirring reverence for life and for its powers in us. Usually, in dealing with the deterioration of our world, we try to get our minds around it; we deal with it on the informational level, as if we were brains on the end of a stick. The Cradling stills for a while the chattering computing mind and opens it to the wordless wisdom of life.

Description

People work in pairs, taking turns. First you model with a volunteer how Partners A lie down and Partners B, following your verbal suggestions, will "cradle" them, which means lifting arms, lower legs, and head.

Now Partners A, removing glasses and shoes, loosening ties and belts, lie down on the floor, close their eyes and relax. Assist with a brief guided relaxation (stretching, feeling the breath, letting weight sink down, releasing tension from feet, legs, hands, etc.). Soft background music like flute sound is helpful, but not essential. Carpeting makes a large difference, but even on a hard floor, this exercise has worked well.

Caution: Proceed with care and respect. Touching another person's body is a sensitive and often problematic issue. In some cultures it is virtually taboo; don't offer this exercise in south Asia, for example. In the U.S., even in California, people can interpret touch as an invasion of their personal integrity, especially if they have suffered physical and sexual abuse. So inform people that the exercise involves their letting their arms, legs, and head be lifted and held; ask them to choose a partner with whom they will feel comfortable.

Respect the participants for their trust and stay matter-of-fact in your manner, avoiding a portentous or sugary tone. Interspersing your words with silence, remain casual and reflective, as if observing some constellation in the heavens or a conch shell on the beach.

The following transcript of Joanna guiding the Cradling is offered for illustrative purposes only. You will not be repeating this word for word when you are the guide; you have your own style, your own experience to use. Now, however, read it reflectively to get a feel for the process, its pace and unfolding.

Lift gently your partner's arm and hand.... Cradle it, feel the weight of it...flex the elbow and wrist, note how the joints are hinged to permit variety of movement.... Behold this arm as if you had never seen it before, as if you were a visitor from another world....Observe the articulation of bone and muscle.... Turning the palm and fingers, note the intricacy of structure....What you now hold is an object unique in our cosmos: a human hand of Planet Earth....In the primordial seas where once we swam, that hand was a fin —as it was again in its mother's womb.... Feel the energy and intelligence in that hand —that fruit of a long evolutionary journey, of efforts to swim, to push, to climb, to grasp.... Note the opposable thumb, how clever and adept it is...good for grasping a tool, a pen, a gun....Open your awareness to the journey it has made in this lifetime...how it opened like a flower when it emerged from the mother's womb...how it reached to explore and to do.... That hand learned to hold a spoon...to tie shoelaces...to throw a ball...to write its name...to give pleasure...to wipe tears.... There is nothing like it in all the universe.

Gently laying down that hand, move now to your partner's leg and slowly lift it.... Feel its weight, its sturdiness.... This species stands upright.... Bend the knee, the ankle, note the play of bone and muscle. It allows this being to walk, run, climb.... Holding the foot, feel the sole, no hoof or heavy padding.... It is this being's contact with the ground.... Feel that heel; when it kicked in the womb, that was what the parents first felt through the wall of the belly.... "See: there's its heel".... And such journeys that leg has been on since then...learning to take a step and then another...walking and falling and getting up again...then running, climbing, kicking a ball, pedaling a bike...a lot of adventures in that leg...and a lot of places it has taken your partner...into work places and sanctuaries, mountainsides and city streets...gotten tired...sore...still kept going.... Gently putting it down now, move around to the other leg and cradle that one, too.

Observe this companion leg and foot...which shared those journeys...and many yet to come.... For all its weight and sturdiness, it can be broken, crushed...no armor...just skin that can tear , bones that can fracture.... As you hold that leg, open your thought to all the places it will take your partner in the future...into places of suffering perhaps...of conflict and challenge...on missions that your partner doesn't know about yet.... As you lay it back down, extend your wishes for its strength and wholeness.

Lift now your partner's other hand and arm.... Observe the subtle differences from its twin.... This hand is unique, different from all other hands.... Turning it in yours, feel the life in it.... And note also its vulnerability...no shell encases it, for those fingertips, that palm, are instruments for sensing and knowing our world, as well as for doing.... Flexible, fragile hand, so easy to break or burn.... Be aware of how much you want it to stay whole, intact, in the time that is coming.... It has tasks to do, that your partner can't even guess at...reaching out to people in confusion and distress, helping, comforting, showing the way.... This hand may be the one that holds you in the moments of your own dying, giving you water or a last touch of reassurance.... The world of sanity and decency that lies ahead will be built by hands like this one. With gratitude for its existence, put it gently down; move now around behind your partner's head....

Placing a hand under the neck and another beneath the skull, slowly, gently lift your partner's head.... (Partner A keep your neck relaxed, your head heavy, loose.) Lift that head carefully, cradle it with reverence, for what you now hold in your two hands is the most intricate, complex object in the known universe...a human head of Planet Earth...a hundred billion neurons firing in there...vast potential for intelligence...only a portion has been tapped of that capacity to see, to know, to envision....

Your hands holding your partner's head—that is the first touch your partner knew in this life, coming out of the womb into hands, like yours, of a doctor or midwife.... Now within that skull is a whole world of experience—of memories of scenes and songs, beloved faces...some are gone now, but they live still in the mansions of that mind....It is a world of experience that is totally unique and that can never be fully shared.... In that head, too, are dreams of what could be, visions that could shape our world....

Closing your eyes for a moment, feel the weight of that head in your hands. It could be the head of a Chinese soldier or an Iraqi mother, of an American general or an African doctor.... Same size, same weight just about, same vulnerability, same capacity for dreams that could guide us through this time.

Looking down at it now, think of what this head may have to behold in the times that come...the choices it will make...the courage and endurance it will need.... Let your hands, of their own intelligence, express their desire that all be well with that head.... Perhaps there is something that you want your partner to keep in mind —something you want them not to forget in times of stress or anguish.... If there is, you can quietly tell them now, as you lay their head back down....

Allow time for the recumbent partner to stretch, look around, slowly sit up. Then A and B reverse roles, and the verbal cues are offered again with some variations. At the conclusion of the whole process, time to reorient is important. Let the pairs talk quietly or remain in silence for a while; then let them gather in foursomes to speak of their experience.

Whatever words or images are used, it is good to touch on certain themes. Interweaving through the spoken words, these motifs renew and sharpen awareness of what it means to be a living person. They include:

1) the uniqueness of the human species in the cosmos,

2) its long evolutionary journey,

3) the uniqueness of each individual, and of each personal history,

4) the intricacy and beauty of the human organism,

5) its universality, linking us to other humans around the globe,

6) and its vulnerability.

If the number of workshop participants is uneven, the guide pairs up with the extra person, then leads the exercise while acting as Partner B, but not reversing roles. The extra person can then join another pair as a second cradling partner, if desired.

When participants lie down, remember to have them place themselves so that there is adequate room for their partners to move around them to cradle arms, legs and head.

Timing and variation

Depending on the time and space available, the Cradling can take two forms: the fuller version (like the example above) lasts about 45 to 60 minutes. When time or floor space is inadequate to accommodate the full Cradling, a brief version (10 to 20 minutes) can be conducted with pairs sitting face to face. The meditation then focuses on the hands and arms, and if space permits one partner to move around behind the other, the shoulders and head, as well. In that case, attention is directed to the burdens we carry, the stresses we tend to lock into our shoulders and necks; and the meditation on the head is appropriately adapted. If that is impossible or awkward, don't worry. So long as there is touch and attention, even the briefest form of this exercise is evocative and powerful.

❧

"Who Are You?"*
(75 minutes)

Purpose and background

This process in pairs serves to move us beyond constricted notions of who we are and what can happen through us. Of a metaphysical bent, it was originally inspired by followers of the Hindu sage Sri Ramana Maharshi. In their "enlightenment intensives," persistent inquiry helps participants to free themselves from socially constructed self-definitions and attain a realization of the inherently unlimited nature of consciousness. In our workshop the process is condensed and less ambitious. We use it to remind ourselves that we are not our social roles or our "skin-encapsulated egos" so much as conduits for conscious life.

Description

Each pair sits close together, far enough from the others to avoid distraction. The partners take turns querying each other, for thirty minutes each way, without comment. Here are Joanna's instructions to Partner A, which are repeated to B later.

Partner A, you begin by asking Partner B, "Who are you?" You listen. You ask again, "Who are you?" Again you listen, then repeat the question, "Who are you?" Rest assured that the answers will be different. You can vary the question, if you wish, with "What are you?" but you say nothing else. This continues for about ten minutes, until I ring the bell.

Then you shift to the second question, "What do you do?" Now, in a similar fashion, you listen to those answers and then keep repeating the query, "What do you do?" You can also phrase it, "What happens through you?"

After ten minutes, when I ring the bell, you will revert to the first question, "Who (or what) are you?" The process will repeat itself once more, taking seven or eight minutes with each question, ending with "Who are you?" for a final five minutes. The bell will signal when to change questions.

This is a strenuous mental exercise. It can produce extraordinary insights, sometimes with bursts of laughter, but it feels relentless. It must be undertaken gently and with respect. Remember, you are not badgering your partner. You're not suggesting that his responses are wrong; you're helping him go deeper. You are in service to your partner. The tempo and tonality of your questions will vary; you'll know intuitively when to ask again quickly and when to pause in silence. Now before you begin, bow to your partner—and to the essential mystery at the core of this being.

* Thanks to Nikolaus Einhorn for adapting this process to Deep Ecology work.

Partner A bows to B once more when the cycle of questions is over. As the partners change roles, let them stand and stretch, without talking. At the end of the entire exercise, which takes an hour, allow plenty of time for people to digest what has happened for them. Let the pairs relax and chat; then if there is time, bring them back together in the large group so that people can share some of their insights if they wish—which they usually do.

The Dance to Dismember the Ego
(60 minutes or more)

Background

This fanciful process derives from a Tibetan lama dance. For three days every spring, the monks of Tashi Jong, a refugee community in northwest India, honor their ancient Buddhist tradition with majestic, masked rituals. One of the high points for Joanna, a long-time friend of Tashi Jong, is the Dance to Dismember the Ego. In the center of the dancing ground lies a small clay doll, enclosed in an open, three-sided box. The three sides symbolize the three fetters that hold the ego together: craving, hatred, and delusion. The costumed monks, moving and leaping about it with their various ritual implements, embody the innate powers of mind, which can free us from the grip of self-centeredness. At the climactic close, the doll is "eaten" by the dancers, who pull it apart, lift it to their mouths, scatter it to the winds.

Back in the States, a group of a dozen Buddhist and Quaker friends to whom Joanna described the dance, wanted to try it themselves. Not only that, they *each* wanted to make their *own* ego doll. They wished to enact in material form what they knew in principle: that the self-centeredness that creates our suffering is not substantially and permanently real, not innate to our true nature. It needs, however, to be seen clearly, recognized for what it is, along with the fears and ignorance that create it, before it can begin to dissolve. From that first impromptu enactment at Temenos retreat center in Massachusetts arose the version of the dance Joanna has taken into workshops and classrooms over the last decade.

Purpose

This process aims to free us from some of the attachments to self-image which inhibit our joy in life and our effectiveness in action. Although totally serious in intent, it does not employ weighty moral judgments, but lightheartedness—even gratitude for our habitual efforts to shield and promote ourselves. It helps us learn that we can release nothing without accepting and appreciating it first.

Description

After acknowledging the original Tibetan dance that gave rise to this process, hunks of clay are passed out—a third to a half a pound per person. "Self-centeredness is endemic to us all. What form does *yours* want to take? How in this moment does your particular form of pride or self-attachment wish to shape itself?" Everyone is encouraged to work their clay in silence and watch what happens. They may see emerging before their eyes one of the roles or personae they have assiduously nurtured and defended over the years. To behold it now, sitting in front of them objectified, can bring a great sense of relief.

When all are ready, after fifteen or twenty minutes, they gather in a circle with their work. Now comes the dance itself, or more precisely, a celebrative "show and tell." One at a time, spontaneously, each person stands and parades around the circle displaying their ego doll for the admiration of all the others. As they do, they present its qualities, extol its ingenuity, and the group responds with applause and extravagant expressions of appreciation. This adulation is important because egos *love* to be admired. Then each ego is placed solemnly in the very center of the circle.

"Ta-daa! Presenting in its first-ever public appearance, the incomparable, one and only...smart-ass ego of mine; many hands and mouths to hide the hollow heart."

"Feast your eyes on this sensitive soul, bent over by the woes of the world and afraid of getting her hands dirty."

"This brilliant know-it-all likes to sit real cool on the sidelines and pass judgments."

When all the little clay sculptures are amassed in the center, the group rises to walk ceremoniously and affectionately around them, perhaps chanting a ritual farewell. With groups familiar with Buddhism, Joanna has used the ancient mantra from the Heart Sutra, *"Gaté gaté, paragaté parasam gaté; bodhi swaha!"* ("Gone, gone, gone beyond, completely gone beyond, far out!") We say good-bye, or at least prepare to say good-bye, to mental fabrications that have outlived their usefulness.

The ritual may end there, or the dolls can be broken apart, or cast into a fire, or into a body of water to dissolve, accompanied by shouts of support and jubilation. If this kind of dramatic ending is used, the guide should suggest that people relinquish their ego doll only if they feel ready.

My Choices for This Life*
(60 to 90 minutes)

Purpose

This process focuses on our individual lives and helps us see how their basic features and conditions can serve the healing of the world—almost as if we had chosen them for that purpose. It brings fresh appreciation for the chance to be alive in this planet-time. Like climbing a mountain and looking back on the landscape below, this exercise provides a vantage point that lets us see new things. From that overarching perspective, we can see unsuspected connections and goodness; even our suffering and limitations reveal their value for the work we have come to do.

Another name for this exercise is "The Bodhisattva Check-in," because it is inspired by the Buddhist teaching of the bodhisattva. Embodying our motivation to serve, the bodhisattva does not seek enlightenment in order to exit from this world of woe, but turns back from the gates of nirvana, having vowed to return again and again to be of help to all beings. It is equally useful whether or not we believe in rebirth. The bodhisattva archetype is present in all religions and even all social movements, be it in the guise of suffering servant, worker-priest, shaman, prophet, idealistic revolutionary, or community organizer. [28]

Description

Two introductory stages precede the main body of the exercise. First, the group is invited to contemplate the long panoramic journey of life on Earth. Along with words from the guide, a tape of tonal sound helps open the mind to that journey's vast expanses of time. The guide asks partici-pants to imagine that they can remember how they chose to be alive as a human in this moment of history. (Joanna tells of bodhisattvas and their vow to keep returning to the world to relieve suffering.) Participants imagine they are all together in that time out of time which preceded their birth. They learn of the crisis facing life on Earth at the end of the second millennium.

The challenges take many forms—the making and using of nuclear weapons, industrial technologies that poison and waste whole ecosystems,

---

* Thanks to Carol Wolman for the original meditative form of this exercise, which we called "The Incarnation Committee." Thanks to Xeto Henning and Stephan Noethen for helping to inspire this adaptation.

billions of people sinking into poverty—but one thing is clear. A quantum leap in consciousness is required if life is to prevail on Earth. Hearing this, we decide to renew our commitment to life (our bodhisattva vow) and reenter the fray—to birth as humans in the twentieth century, bringing everything we've ever learned about courage and community. This is a major decision. We make it together and feel each other's support, but it's like going over a cliff; we know we probably won't even recognize each other once we've assumed different bodies and identities.

Each person reflects on their readiness to take birth in so challenging a planet-time. When each has decided that they are ready to do this, they stand up, one by one. Let a drum or gong be sounded when all have stood. If a drum is used, it can keep on beating into the next brief stage, as people start circulating around the room.

Now you have taken birth in this planet-time, and you're walking around this room, just as you've walked through your lives right up to this moment. Here, however, something unusual is about to happen. As you move about, glancing into each other's faces, there will be one that you imagine you recognize. Perhaps it's something in the eyes, or expression or bearing, that lets you suddenly recognize one of your old buddies from that company (of bodhisattvas) with whom you made the decision to come back. When that happens, just stop and connect without words. And then sit down together in silence.

These wordless encounters can be very moving, like a homecoming. Soon everyone is seated; if the number is uneven, the guide takes a partner also.

Now the main part of the exercise begins. The partners in each pair take turns telling each other about the particular life they assumed—the selves and situations they chose to inhabit for the world-healing work they have come to do. Here is how the guide can instruct them:

All you know about your partner is that you chose together to take birth in this planet-time for the healing of Earth. Neither of you has a clue about what that choice has actually entailed for the other. Now, meeting at last, you are eager to tell and to hear about all the other choices that followed on that principal decision. Here is how you will report to each other, one at a time. And remember that you are reporting on your actual life, not some fantasy life.

On a sheet of newsprint, the guide writes a list of topics, briefly explaining each one.

WHEN. Tell your partner when you chose to be born. The year, and what that timing allowed you to experience in terms of historical conditions and events. Perhaps the time of year, too—was the light increasing or decreasing? If your astrological sign has meaning for you, speak of that as well.

WHERE. In what country and nation did you choose to be born, what region of it? In a town, city, or on the land? Which aspects of the natural world first greeted your eyes?

SOCIAL CONDITIONS. Which socioeconomic class, which race and ethnicity did you select? Report to your buddy, knowing that both the privileges and the privations which ensued from these conditions have served to prepare you for the work you came to do.

RELIGION. Into what faith tradition—or lack of same—did you take birth this time? Tell each other, knowing that those early religious images and stories and attitudes—or lack of same—lent form to your purpose, your hopes, your capacities to align yourself or to rebel, or seek alternatives.

GENDER. Now, which gender did you adopt this time around? In the telling, it may become clearer why you chose as you did. Feel free to refer to your sexual preference, too, and to what that has helped you realize about your bodhisattva calling in this planet-time.

PARENTS. What kind of man did you choose to be your father? What kind of woman your mother? (This might mean both birth parents and adoptive parents for some of you.) What kinds of relationships did you have with them as a child? Tell your partner, knowing that both the strengths of your parents and their wounds, both the loving care you received from them and the abuse you suffered, all have helped to equip you for the mission you came to perform.

SIBLINGS. Did you choose to be an only child or to have siblings? If siblings, in what order, where did you fit in? Tell your bodhisattva partner how the companionship, competition, or loneliness which ensued from that choice helped build the unique blend of strengths you bring to your world.

DISABILITIES. Which weaknesses and incapacities of body or mind did you choose to accept this time? How do they help you know and connect with the planet and the beings you've come to serve?

APPETITES. Which mental, physical, spiritual appetites did you summon for yourself in this planet-time?

MISSION. How do you now, at this point in your lifetime, understand your mission?

The list of words serves as a rough guide for each person's report to the partner, which is allowed to flow spontaneously. The time provided for each report can range from twenty or thirty minutes or more, depending on the day's agenda and the group's energy. It is good to provide a signal halfway through the allotted time, and again shortly before the end.

If possible, schedule this exercise before a break; participants are usually so stimulated by the perspective they have gained that they are eager to keep talking, with their partner and with others, too.

Caution

The notion of having chosen one's life conditions may be problematic for some people. The idea of taking responsibility for situations that have oppressed them can smack of "blaming the victim." You as guide may acknowledge this at the outset. Point out that we are not using the verb in its ordinary sense, as in choosing a car or a job, but in the larger or even metaphysical sense, in which we let ourselves accept and see the value of all that has befallen us. Spiritual traditions affirm that true liberation arises when we can embrace the particulars of our lives, and see that they are as right for us as if we had indeed chosen them. In other words, we move in this exercise to a higher level of logical type or discourse.

Variations and further topics

As you become familiar with this exercise, you may wish to add or subtract topics for the bodhisattvas' reports to each other. Additional themes have been used to good effect, and generally in a separate session, after the basic ones listed above. In the follow-on session, after a break, people can stay with the same partners or pair off with different ones. A new listener can give fresh intensity and greater range to one's thoughts; in that case, tell people they do not need to repeat themselves by telling the second partner about their earlier choices.

A follow-on session can address choices we made in this lifetime, relating, for example, to educational endeavors, spiritual practices, central relationships, and vocational explorations and commitments. This can be very rewarding, helping people perceive a certain consistency or integrity in what might have appeared as a random patchwork of pursuits. It can, however, degenerate into a kind of curriculum vitae, so the guide helps the participants retain that larger, superordinate bodhisattva perspective.

Then there is the beautiful question: "How did you let your heart be broken?" This provides such substance that it can take a whole session. For Joanna and two colleagues it took three engrossing hours as they drove to the Milan airport. They had just invented the "Bodhisattva Check-in" at the close of a week-long workshop in Assisi. Now in the car this question came to them; they answered it in turn, at length, returning to childhood memory, as if assuming that the question meant, "How did you first let your heart be broken?" They were deeply moved to discover how much that query let them understand about their lives, their mind-sets, and goals.

A recent participant wrote: "I have been thinking a lot about 'The Bodhisattva's Choices for this Life.' I found it very empowering. I consider myself an accountable person. I think of my life in terms of choices I've made. Yet I'd never before systematically reviewed all the major choices in my life, and celebrated them for bringing me to this time and place."

Chapter 9

DEEP TIME:
RECONNECTING WITH PAST AND
FUTURE GENERATIONS

It was the custom of my tribe
to speak and sing;
not only to share the present breath and sight,
but to the unborn.
Still, even now, we reach out
toward survivors. It is a covenant
of desire.
—Denise Levertov [29]

EOPLE OF TODAY RELATE TO TIME in a way that is surely unique in our history. The technologies and economic forces unleashed by the Industrial Growth Society radically alter our experience of time. It is like being trapped in an ever-shrinking box, in which we race on a treadmill. The economy and its technologies depend on decisions made at lightning speed for short-term goals, cutting us off from nature's rhythms and from the past and the future, as well. Marooned in the present, we are progressively blinded to the sheer ongoingness of time. Both the company of our ancestors and the claims of our descendants become less and less real to us.

This peculiar relation to time is inherently destructive of the quality and value of our lives, and of the living body of Earth. And it will intensify because the Industrial Growth Society is, in systems' terms, on exponential "runaway"—accelerating toward its own collapse.

A HEALTHIER RELATIONSHIP TO TIME

Even as we see its consequences, we must remember that this relation to time is not innate in us. As humans we have the capacity and the birthright to experience time in a saner fashion. Throughout history, men and women have labored at great personal cost to bequeath to future generations monuments of art and learning, to endure far beyond their individual lives. And they have honored through ritual and story those who came before.

To make the transition to a life-sustaining society, we must retrieve that ancestral capacity—in other words, act like ancestors. We need to attune to longer, ecological rhythms and nourish a strong, felt connection with past and future generations. For us as agents of change, this isn't easy, because to intervene in the political and legislative decisions of the Industrial Growth Society, we fall by necessity into its tempo. We race to find and pull the levers before it is too late to save this forest, or stop that weapons program. Nonetheless, we can learn again to drink at deeper wells.

"Deep Time" work has arisen over the last fifteen years for that express purpose: to refresh our spirits and inform our minds by experiencing our present lives within larger, temporal contexts. This work has brought tremendous rewards in both immediate gladness and lasting resilience.

Some of the Deep Time exercises, such as the "Evolutionary Remembering" and "Our Life as Gaia," extend our mental reach beyond human history; these are offered in Chapter 10. In this chapter you will find exercises focusing on our human ancestors and descendants.

EXERCISES

Invoking the Beings of the Three Times
(5 to 10 minutes)

Purpose
This invocation, to which the group adds its voices, reminds us of our place in time and our connectedness with those who have gone before and those who come after us, as well as those living now. It evokes our solidarity with them and the inspiration they can offer us in our work for the world. It heightens our sense of gratitude and responsibility, and strengthens the will.

Description

The invocation, which has also been used in a public talk and at conferences, can be used to open a workshop, or that portion given to Deep Time work. It could precede any of the exercises that follow.

Bring the group into a standing circle. Speaking with respect and conviction, invoke first the beings of the past, pausing at the end for people to murmur names of specific ancestors and teachers. Here are words that we use, that may inspire your own.

> *Be with us now all you who have gone before, you our ancestors and teachers. You who walked and loved and faithfully tended this Earth, be present to us now that we may carry on the legacy you bequeathed us. Aloud and silently in our hearts we say your names and see your faces....*

Then call on the beings of the present: *All you with whom we live and work on this endangered planet, all you with whom we share this brink of time, be with us now. Fellow humans and brothers and sisters of other species, help us open to our collective will and wisdom. Aloud and silently we say your names and picture your faces.* Again, pause to allow people to murmur names.

Lastly, invoke the beings of the future: *All you who will come after us on this Earth, be with us now. All you who are waiting to be born in the ages to come, it is for your sakes, too, that we work to heal our world. We cannot picture your faces or say your names—you have none yet—but we would feel the reality of your claim on life. It helps us to be faithful in the work that must be done, so that there will be for you, as there was for our ancestors, blue sky, fruitful land, clear waters.* Here again a pause, this final one in silence.

Variations

Before starting the invocation, teach the group this simple chant, using two notes of your choosing: *Gather with us now in this hour. Join with us now in this place.* The group repeats the chant three times after each part of the invocation.

If there is sufficient time for preparation, invite three people to speak in turn one part of the invocation. The group can then respond with the chant.

Harvesting the Gifts of the Ancestors
(60 minutes)

Purpose

This extended exercise connects us vividly with our human past on Earth, and deepens awareness of the strengths it offers us. The expanses of time which we enter remind us that the Industrial Growth Society is a momentary episode—and that to move beyond it, we can draw on a far larger and more deeply rooted legacy. As we progress through countless generations, respect and gratitude arise for our forebears' capacity to weather adversity, and to respond collectively and creatively to enormous challenges. The process helps us to believe that these capacities have not forsaken us and to want to use them now, at this crisis point for life on Earth.

Description

The process consists of a slow walk through time, first backwards to the start of the human story, then forwards to return to the present. Allow forty minutes or so for the walk and then another twenty for people to reflect in small groups.

Deep-toned, flowing music widens access to deeper levels of consciousness, stirring images and "memories" of our long human journey. Joanna likes to use portions of *Ignacio* by Vangelis, rerecording them on the same tape to make an hour of background music.

In order to keep walking for an extended length of time, people move in a revolving fashion around a center point in the room. Let them space themselves around the room with their right shoulder to the center, and stand still as you explain the process. They are to move very slowly backwards, after the music has begun and your words give the cue. Their eyes will be half-closed to invite feelings and images from within, while permitting enough vision to maneuver. They will feel the others moving alongside them, occasionally bumping and even stepping into each other, for paces vary. That is to be expected and is appropriate enough, because this is not about a solo journey; we made it together. When people get into a clump and feel impeded, they are just to raise their eyes, look around for a more open area, and relocate themselves.

Halfway through, they will have reached the start of the human journey. Your words will make this clear and cue them to stop still. Then they will move forward, still very slowly, in a clockwise direction. They will be harvesting the gifts of the ancestors. It will help to make bodily gestures of gleaning, scooping, picking from below and above, as they take to themselves the gifts.

After the explanations, the guide dedicates this piece of work to the healing of our world. The walk now begins, with music in the background and voice-over from the guide. The guide's job is to offer a running series of verbal cues. These provide both sequential structure, to assist people's passage through time, and also phrases to evoke personal and collective memories. The tone is steady, assured, and slightly impersonal. *What* is said varies with the history and culture of the group. *How much* is said varies with the guide. Better to say too little than too much. You're not giving a history lesson; you're simply allowing vistas to open and collective experiences to surface. The knowledge most needed is already there.

In other extended verbal reflections like the Cradling, reading a script makes for distance. Here, however, feel free to use extensive notes, because there is so much to remember to say. Here is a rendering of the cues we have offered. (You may not want to talk so much.)

From this present moment on (date) in (place), you begin to walk slowly backwards in time. Move back through the events of this day...to your waking up.... Keep walking back through this last week, the last month...the times at home, and at work, and in your wider community.... Move back through the months to the turn of the year. Now you are walking back through last year through its seasons and encounters....

Keep walking backwards through the decades of your life. See perhaps the loss of someone close, perhaps the birth of a child, or children.... Encounter again the relationships, passions, adventures....

You are moving back through your young adulthood, to your teenage years, their hopes and heartache.... You're entering your childhood, seeing the places and faces you knew, sensing the radiance of the child you were. You are growing smaller; you are carried in arms. You are back in your mother's womb...approaching the point of your conception in this life.

What is alive in you did not begin at that conception.... So step back into your parents' lives, that man and that woman who turned and saw each other, and in their coming together gave you life... Move back through the work they did, the struggles they faced, the mistakes they made, the joys they knew. You are moving through their teenage years,... their childhood, their infancy, their birth, back into the wombs that bore them....

Continue walking back, back into the lives or your grandparents, and your great-grandparents, back through this century of wars and explosions of technology, back before the automobile, the telephone, before electricity. See the shadows of gas lamps, into the lives of ancestors whose names you no longer know, but of whom a gesture, a smile, or turn of the head lives on in you.

Moving back along this river of life, back through the Industrial Revolution, through the dark factories and teeming city streets, into lives of your people, some uprooted from the land into sweatshops and mines and armies...

You're moving back through the centuries now... through wars and revolutions, through the excitement of new discoveries and the steady sameness of tilling the earth.... Generations of ancestors, some settled for centuries in a place, others roaming or carried off, starting new in far-off places...

Moving back into harsher, simpler times marked by the seasons. Walking back through the lives of men and women—peasants and magistrates, scholars, artisans, thieves, beggars, slaves and slaveholders, generals and foot soldiers forced into battle... Even then they carried you within them like a seed. These are your ancestors....

Back through times of torment, plagues and burnings, millions of women and men tied to stakes, your ancestors perhaps both victims and executioners...

Enter as well the lives of ancestors versed in the ancient arts of healing... with eyes like yours, hands like yours, baking bread, gathering herbs, ministering to others.

You are passing back through the rise and fall of entire civilizations, thousands of years passing, the first cities rising from the red clay.... You move back before the days of empire, before the land was tilled in parcels that were owned....

Back to our earlier, nomadic times, tribes in forest settlements and in long migrations... You are walking back through the thousands of years when the earth provided deer and wild boar, berries and roots, through a time unmarked by wars....

Entering the long treks of your ancestors across the continents, their voyages in rafts, the long marches in the ages of ice... Back through the millennia you walk with them, to your beginnings, twenty or thirty thousand generations ago. Can you remember, was it in the heartland of Africa, or another primordial land?...

And now you stop. Now with the very first ones, you stand at the edge of the forest. Pause now, looking out over the savanna. The journey of your people lies ahead. You cannot imagine what it will bring or the challenges you will face....

Walk forward on that journey now, retracing your steps, returning through time. You come from an unbroken line of survivors and each has gifts to bestow. Open your arms and hands to receive these gifts; gather them in.

These people are giving to you the texture of your skin, the shape of your back, the marrow of your bones. They give to you courage and strength and perseverance as they travel through the land: hunting, playing, making babies, dying.

Take these gifts. Take the joy of two young girls splashing in a stream 30,000 years ago.... Coming forward through the years, harvesting the gifts of your ancestors, receiving what they offer—receiving all that you need.

Walking up through the centuries, see the trust in the eyes of the children, the passion in the eyes of the young. See the wisdom in the eyes of the aged. Receive these as gifts.

Receive the creativity of your ancestors, making tools, weaving cloth, building homes.

The compassion of your ancestors, caring for the injured or praying with the dying: that, too, is for you.

Know their love of beauty, music of a flute coming from the hills, hands carving jewelry, feet dancing to the rhythms of drums. Receive that celebration as their gift to you.

Know the intelligence of your ancestors as they track the movements of stars, learn the ways of the plants and animals, hold councils to choose the wisest action. Receive that intelligence as their gift.

Can you sense the love that burns in your ancestors, their devotion to their families, their land? Receive that love as their gift to you.

Relish their wit and humor, too. Your ancestors' jokes and jibes as they work together, the banter of young couples, the merriment of festivals. Receive the laughter of your ancestors as their gift to you.

Your ancestors have gifts from their suffering, too: courage, endurance, resilience, stubborn perseverance. Receive these as their gifts to you.

Moving forward through the centuries, receive the gifts your ancestors offer you....

You're entering now the twentieth century and the lives of your grand-parents, and your parents. Receive the gifts they offer.... Take the strength of your parents and especially that greatest gift they gave you: your own life to live.

Move forward through the years of your own life. Accept the gifts of your own experience, your appetites and your sorrows, your fierce caring for the world....

Coming now to this present moment, you stop. You are once again on a brink of time. You cannot see clearly the way ahead or imagine what will be asked of you. But you do not go forward empty-handed. The ancestors who loved and tended this Earth, and cared for each other, offer you the strength you need now, to do what needs to be done—so that their journey and yours may continue.

Variation

The entire process can be done as a guided meditation with participants seated—in an auditorium, for example. You miss the bodily dimension which walking backwards and forwards provides, but participants can still use their arms to gather in the gifts.

Thirty Years Hence
(20 to 30 minutes)

Purpose

This exercise enlarges our usual time frame by helping us imagine a personal conversation with a child of the future. The child's queries elicit responses that bring fresh respect for the challenges we now face, and fresh inspiration and insight into the strengths and purposes of our present lives. The exercise also uncovers the participants' intuitive grasp of mutual belonging and synergy.

Description

Participants relax by stretching, yawning, and then focusing on the breath for a few minutes. Closing the eyes, they imagine moving forward thirty years in time; from that vantage point and in response to three questions from a child, they look back at the present. Participants, whose age might make another thirty years of life unlikely, are simply asked, for the sake of the exercise, to imagine they're still around. Brief silence of about a minute follows each of the child's queries, which focus on: 1) the reality of the dangers we faced "back then" in that time of crisis; 2) how we felt about them; and 3) how we found the strength to respond to them creatively. After returning to the present, participants gather in threes to reflect on their responses to the child, and, when time permits, bring these reflections to the larger group.

Here is a version of how we lead this exercise:

> *By the power of our imagination, let's move forward through time—30 years. We can make the sound of time passing swiftly.* (This suggestion enlists participation from the start, and the playfulness of the ensuing sound effects relaxes the mind.) *Now we've arrived at* (name the date and hour 30 years from the present moment). *You find yourself in one of your favorite spots. It hasn't changed much, nor have you essentially. Some of us are pretty long in the tooth by now, but we're still alive, same gestures, same action of heart and lungs. Don't worry about figuring out how the world has changed. Just know that the major crises that threatened life on Earth have been averted, the weapons have been dismantled, as have the technologies and institutions that polluted and decimated life. Those destructive patterns were so interlocked that the Great Turning to a sustainable society in the early years of the century happened faster than anyone expected. By now, that transition seems so logical and inevitable that you take it for granted.*

> *As you sit relaxing in this familiar spot, you see approaching you a child of about eight or nine. She's eager and timid, for she has heard in songs and stories what you and your friends did back then to save the world from disaster. You listen to the questions she wants to ask you. The first is this: "Is it true what they say about life back then? Were there really millions and millions of sick and hungry people? And bombs that could blow up whole cities? Could that be so?" She clearly finds it hard to believe. Listen now, as you answer her...*

> *Now she asks you a second question. "What was it like for you to live in a world like that? Weren't you sad and scared all the time?" Hear your own reply...*

> *The child listens carefully; there is one more thing she wants to ask. "Where did you and your friends find the strength to do what you did? How did you keep on going?" Hear within yourself how you answer her now...*

The child is ready now to go back to her friends. As she starts to run off, she turns back, looks up at you, and says, "Thank you."

You watch her go. Now it is time to return to (present year). We go back now to that period when there was still so much to be done, though the Great Turning had already begun and may have been further along than we thought. So let's make sounds of time flowing backwards... until... here we are again, back in (place and time).

Comments

Note that the child's first two questions provide a brief, internal form of despair work—an acknowledgment of the pain we carry in this historical moment, made more natural by virtue of seeing it within a larger time frame. Note also that her third and most important question does not ask us *what* we did to save her world, but *how* we found the strength and perseverance to do it. The exercise is a good precursor to strategy-making exercises in Chapter 1. It is, by the same token, a good complement to the conceptual work of Chapter 8, especially in relation to the revolutionary shift in our understanding of power. On those occasions, at the conclusion of this exercise, the guide may give participants a chance to share their answers to the third question with the larger group, noting them on a sheet of newsprint. These make good talking points for the conceptual discussion to follow, for to a striking extent the sources of strength which were named converge with systems-based understandings of power and synergy. It is gratifying to people to realize that these new understandings are already within them.

Tape Recording to the Future
(15 to 30 minutes)

Purpose

In facing a particular situation or issue, the act of describing it aloud to future generations heightens appreciation of what is at stake in the long term. The larger timeframe deepens the sense of responsibility, stimulates creativity, and increases readiness to "hang in there for the long haul."

Description

People pass around a small recorder, speaking into it one at a time. They imagine they are making a tape to be found and heard in that place by people of a coming generation or century. Alluding to choices presently confronting them, they tape personal messages to the future. This exercise has been used predominantly in gatherings around specific issues, such as clearcutting, toxic dumping, and legislative lobbying for ecosystem and species' preservation.

Background

This process originated in New Mexico at an ad hoc "People's Council" about government plans to deal with radioactive waste by burying it. The activists were concerned about the likelihood of leakage and eventual human intrusion at the site. Up to that point their opposition to these plans for disposing of nuclear waste was limited to the "NIMBY (not in my back yard) syndrome"; they didn't consider the waste to be their responsibility. *"Let's imagine,"* Joanna said, pulling out a small recorder, *"that if we don't manage to stop the waste from being dumped under Carlsbad, we can at least place this cassette there on the surface for future generations to find and listen to. What do we want to say to them?"*

Passing the recorder around the Council circle, the men and women spoke into it with increasing urgency. *"My name is George. I'm back in 1988 and trying to stop people from burying radioactive waste here. If they do and if you hear this, listen. Don't dig here, don't use the water, stay away! This stuff is deadly and contaminates all it touches. Take care!"* As the words poured out, the unborn generations became more real, as if they too were entering the Council, and the activists began to feel some responsibility for the wastes their own generation had produced. The NIMBY response began to evaporate, replaced by a determination to protect the beings of the future by developing less dangerous alternatives than burial—such as monitored surface storage. This is now, among citizen activists, the preferred strategy.

Letter from the Future
(40 minutes)

Purpose

This writing exercise helps us to identify with a human living on Earth one or two centuries from now, to see our current efforts from that perspective, and to receive counsel and courage.

Description

Closing their eyes, participants are invited to journey forward through coming generations and identify with a human living one or two hundred years from now. They need not determine this person's circumstances, but only imagine that he or she is looking back at *them* in their present lives. Nonprogrammatic music helps free the mind. "Now imagine what this being would want to say to you. Open your mind and listen. Now begin putting it on paper, as if this future one were writing a letter just to you."

Allow ample time for the writing, because messages can come from deep within and tap into the collective wisdom of our planet's people. After twenty minutes or so, those who choose, share their letters aloud in small groups. According to many reports, these letters can bring people their "marching orders," and they are often very meaningful to the hearers as well.

The Double Circle*
(60 minutes)

Note: This exercise can serve as the sole experiential component of a short workshop or evening gathering.

Purpose
Including elements of preceding exercises, the Double Circle serves the same goals. By virtue of its content, interactive format, and greater length, it embraces more of people's experience and allows for more unexpected insights.

Description
People sit in two concentric circles that face each other. The numbers in each are equal. (If the total numbers are uneven, the guide joins the inner circle, returning to his place in it after completing each stage of instructions.) Thus a double circle is formed of pairs sitting knee to knee, close enough to attend to each other without distraction, and on the same level. (If a mixture of chairs and floor cushions are used, the seat on the inner circle should be at the same height as the facing one in the outer circle.) Considerable concentration is required, so it is appropriate to treat the exercise as a kind of ritual and ask for silence as the double circle forms.

Those in the outer circle (facing in) speak for themselves, out of their own experience; they stay seated in the same place. Those in the inner circle (facing out) are people of a future generation (specify a date in fifty to two hundred years, not more). These future ones do *not* speak (until the

---

* Evolved from an exercise created by John Seed on a workshop tour in Japan.

end) and *do* move. After each encounter, they rise, step back to move one place to the right, and sit again. In this way, the inner circle moves slowly clockwise while the outer circle is stationary. Since the encounters it allows span many generations, we imagine that the double circle is occurring "at a point outside of time." Once the instructions are completed, the group enters this point outside of time by chanting a group sound—perhaps "ah," as in "The Truth Mandala."

Each of the four encounters is initiated by a query *to* the present-day person *from* the future being. It is imagined that this query is made telepathically, or heart to heart, although it is *heard* in the voice of the guide. The present-day people respond by speaking to the future ones directly in front of them, continuing for several minutes. The guide signals when it is time to conclude, provides a brief silence (the pairs often bow to each other), then asks the future beings to move to the right. After the inner group is seated again, the new partners exchange silent greetings (again, usually a bow or "namaste" with hands in gesture of prayer). Then the guide asks the next question (if necessary, after reminding the future beings to remain silent).

The four questions, which the guide speaks on behalf of the future ones (and repeats for clarity), are given here in words *we* tend to use.

1. Ancestor, I have been told about the terrible times in which you lived, wars and preparations for war, hunger and homelessness, the rich getting richer, the poor getting poorer, poisons in the seas and soil and air, the dying of many species.... It is hard to believe. Was that really true? Tell me.

2. Ancestor, what was it like for you in the midst of that? How did you feel?

3. Ancestor, we have songs and stories that still tell of what you and your friends did back then for the Great Turning. Now what I want to know is this: how did you start? You must have felt lonely and confused sometimes, especially at the beginning. What first steps did you take?

4. Ancestor, I know you didn't stop with those first actions on behalf of Earth. Tell me, where did you find the strength and joy to continue working so hard, despite all the obstacles and discouragements?

When the fourth question has been answered, the future ones do not move on, but stay where they are. Now it is their turn to talk, while the other listens. They speak what is in their hearts after all they have just heard from their ancestors. What comes is often deep and surprising, so they take a good four to five minutes, and the pairs then exchange silent expressions of respect.

Now the body of the exercise, which took place "at a point outside of time," is over. To reenter ordinary time, where the future ones' roles are released, the group sounds again, as at the beginning; this provides a firm ritual closing. But the Double Circle does not disband yet. The last pairs stay together for another four or five minutes to reflect informally on the experience as a whole, the roles they played, the new perspectives that arose. This final conversation ends the exercise, but if time permits, it is rewarding to invite the whole group to share observations and insights.

Chapter 10

THE COUNCIL OF ALL BEINGS: REJOINING THE NATURAL WORLD

Our own pulse beats in every stranger's throat,
And also there within the flowered ground beneath our feet;
And—teach us to listen!—
We can hear it in water, in wood, and even in stone.
We are earth of this earth, and we are bone of its bone.
This is a prayer I sing, for we have forgotten this and so
The earth is perishing.
—Barbara Deming [30]

IN THE GREAT TURNING TO A SUSTAINABLE CIVILIZATION, we become aware of how thoroughly we of the Industrial Growth Society have set ourselves apart from the natural world. With our snowballing technologies, with our race for money and global markets and the goods we've learned to crave, we have forgotten what the ancients knew. We forgot that "we are earth of this earth, bone of its bone," and so, as the poet says, "the earth is perishing." That amnesia is fundamental to our willingness to wreak havoc on our planet's living systems for our own ephemeral gain. We seem to think we could survive without the soil, the trees and waters, the intricate web of life. That delusion is reflected in the very term "environment": the word suggests some periphery or backdrop to our lives—rather than the stuff of our very bodies, igniting every sensation and perception, renewing us with every breath.

THE GENESIS AND PURPOSE OF DEEP ECOLOGY WORK

It is our good fortune to be living now, when countless thinkers and poets call attention to this split in the depths of the modern psyche. And it is a privilege to take part in work that seeks to heal our illusory but fateful separation from the living body of Earth, and the loneliness, the viciousness, this alienation engenders. As described in Chapter 3, an arising of new scientific thought and a resurgence of ancient teachings are helping us now to come back to life. In addition, over the last twenty years, a body of experiential group work has developed to help us awaken to our mutual belonging in the web of life. Often called "deep ecology work," it is described throughout this book. In this particular chapter, we offer those methods which most specifically serve to reconnect us with our brother-sister species and with our wider biological nature.

In offering these practices, we do not need to be naturalists or ecologists or charismatic group leaders. The essential is already present in our desire that life continue, a desire which led you to pick up this book. Nothing more is required than a place large and protected enough for people to feel at ease, the guiding skills described in Chapter 5, and clear intention.

The intention we start with, and make explicit to the group, is all important. We can phrase it in many ways—to heal our separation from the natural world, or to know our interexistence with all beings, or to find in the web of life the power that will help us act in its self-defense... Having owned that intention, we are then in service to it—not to our own success as guides, and not to the whims of the group, but to our life as Earth. That bottom-line motivation will carry us through any difficulties or challenges that may arise.

One of the most widely known of these "deep ecology" methods is the Council of All Beings, in which participants speak on behalf of other life-forms. Arising first in Australia in 1985, with Joanna, John Seed, and their colleagues Down Under, this communal ritual has spread through many countries of the world, maintaining its essential form and purpose, while accruing colorful cultural variations. In the process, the name "Council of All Beings" has come to be used in two ways: to refer to the ritual itself, and also to refer to the workshop or gathering in which it is held, along with the body of practices surrounding it. That dual usage is reflected in this chapter and its title. Here we describe both the Council *per se* and a number of related exercises; these can be used in tandem with the Council or in lieu of it. They combine well with other methods in this book.

Reporting to Chief Seattle
(30 to 60 minutes)

Purpose and background

This process helps people confront, in their own words, the contrast between attitudes and behaviors endemic to the Industrial Growth Society and the reverence with which our indigenous ancestors cared for the natural world. Reminding us that respect for the web of life is our birthright, it evokes both sorrow for its loss and a yearning for its return. In systems terms, this exercise allows "self-referencing"—that is, seeing ourselves and our actions from the perspective of the larger context.

The exercise is based on the speech which Chief Sealth, or Seattle as he is now known, delivered to his tribal assembly in 1854. Its words and images are familiar to many. The version best known to us was adapted in 1970 by film scriptwriter Ted Perry, from the notes of a settler who heard the original speech. Here we use it not as an historical document, but for its powerful evocation of Native American reverence for Earth, and its foreboding of what the white man's lack of reverence would bring.

Description

Sitting in a circle, members of the group read aloud significant portions of Seattle's speech (see Appendix A). A lit candle in the center of the circle, or better yet a natural object—a plant or rock or driftwood sculpted by wind and water—helps to ground the process and lift the mind beyond the pace and pressures of our daily lives. Quietly, reflectively, people listen to the message which the great chief uttered a century and a half ago in response to the U.S. government's decision to buy—or take—his people's land. Among the now familiar words are these:

> How can you buy or sell the sky, the warmth of the land? This idea is strange to us. If we do not own the freshness of the air and the sparkle of the water, how can you buy them? Every part of this earth is sacred to my people. Every shining pine needle, every sandy shore, every mist in the dark woods, every clearing, and humming insect is holy in the memory and experience of my people.... All things share the same breath.

> We will consider your offer to buy the land. I will make one condition: the white man must treat the beasts of this land as his brothers.... What is man without the beasts? If all the beasts are gone, men would die from a

great loneliness of spirit. For whatever happens to the beasts soon happens to man. All things are connected.

This we know. The earth does not belong to man; man belongs to the earth. This we know. All things are connected like the blood which unites one family. All things are connected. Whatever befalls the earth befalls the sons of the earth. Man does not weave the web of life; he is merely a strand of it. Whatever he does to the web, he does to himself.

After a pause, upon completion of the reading, the guide invites people to speak to Chief Seattle. They are to imagine that his spirit is present in the center of the circle. Speaking spontaneously at random, they can tell him now what has happened to his land: how we are treating it and each other, and what life is like for us now. To give weight to each person's words, the others can say simply, "Yes, it is so."

No further guidance is necessary. Whether people choose to tell Seattle about deforestation or factory farms, toxic dumping, poisoned air, or homelessness, they will be glad for the chance to speak of these current facts of life within a larger, encompassing context. The web of life so revered by Seattle lets this truth-telling become redemptive, because it both owns the grief and opens us to possibilities of change and healing. The guide, after allowing ample time for people's words, and for reflective pauses between them, will know when it is time to close. To conclude the process, say something like, *"May our words to Chief Seattle, like his to us, remain with us for the healing of our world."*

The Evolutionary Gifts of the Animals*
(or The Eco-Milling)
(15 to 20 minutes)

Purpose
Using our own bodies, we learn about our kinship with other life-forms, and the debt of gratitude we owe to those who first invented key features of our anatomy.

Description
This process is usually conducted as a "milling" (see page 95) which allows it to be lively, as well as instructive. At each encounter in the milling, when people stop to connect without words, their attention is

---

* Inspired by Tyrone Cashman, philosopher of biological science. A wealth of information on the creativity of our evolutionary ancestors is in *Buddha's Nature*, by Wes Nisker, Bantam, 1998

directed to a particular biological feature which they all share. They are asked to note it in the person before them, to sense the wonder of this gift, and to honor the animal ancestor who bequeathed it. It is not necessary, however, to do a milling, or for people to move about and encounter others. For this kind of reflection, people can always use their own bodies—even sitting in a lecture hall. Here, as we present them in a milling, are features we use to show that endowments, which we tend to take for granted as "our own," are really gifts from other and ancient beings.

The bloodstream. *Can you feel the pulse in your partner's wrist? Blood is circulating. That capacity common to all life-forms arose with the first multicelled creatures who devised ways to transfer nutrients to their inside cells. As they developed some of them invented a muscular pump, a heart. That pulsing you feel is the gift of ancient Great-Grandmother Worm.*

The spinal column. *Feel the bones in the neck, the back. Those vertebrae of the long spine are separate, but ingeniously linked. They cover the central neural cord and, at the same time, allow flexibility of movement. Grandfather fish did the design work, because he couldn't swim if his backbone were one solid piece. We can thank him for this marvel, that now permits us to stand and walk.*

The ear. *Hum in your partner's ear; ah, you can hear one another! That's because tiny bones vibrate in the inner ear, and that's a gift from ancestor fish as well. They were once his jawbones and they migrated into the mammalian ear to carry sound.*

The limbic brain. *Inside the base of the skull lives the limbic region of the brain, gift from our reptilian grandmothers and grandfathers. It allows deep pleasure. It also allows us to protect ourselves by fighting or running away.*

Binocular vision. *See the eyes are no longer on the sides of the head, as with our fish and reptile cousins and many mammals, too. Our tree-climbing primate ancestors moved their eyes around to the front, to function together, so they could know the exact location and distance of branches to leap for. We thank them for our binocular vision.*

Hand. *And see how the hand curls over; see the size of the space it encloses between fingers and thumb. That's just the right size for a branch able to hold a swinging body. Grandmother Monkey designed that hand. And the branch was designed by sun and wind and gravity, as well as Grandfather Tree himself as he grew high to reach the light, and limber to allow the wind. So we, with these hands, are grandchildren of tree and sun and wind, as well.*

The Remembering [31]
(45 minutes or more)

Purpose
With this guided visualization, our evolutionary journey becomes more real to us than before. We reawaken to our long panoramic history as integral parts of the evolving universe, and feel within us the presence and summons of this history. Setting our recent chapter as humans within the context of our far larger story, the Remembering evokes the ecological self and loosens the grip of the anthropocentrism of today's culture. At the same time it fosters a sense of authority, which we can claim when we act on behalf of Earth; that is, it encourages us to "act our age"—our true age of fifteen billion years—and take part in the Great Turning to a sustainable society.

Description
The Remembering can be offered as a guided meditation with people sitting or lying, or as spontaneous enactment, in which people use bodily movements and sensations to imagine or recapture evolutionary memories. Rocking, nosing, wriggling, crawling, pushing up all help us imagine the inner body sense of amphibian and reptile and early mammal. Even if we only imagine them now, these memories are embedded in our neurological system; each one of our bodies recapitulated our evolutionary journey in the womb. In offering this process, we often use a drum to sound a heartbeat; it enhances the sense of connection with the pulse of life in all beings through time.

Come with me on a journey to the past, a journey to help us remember who we are. We begin with the heartbeat; place your hand over your heart and feel this beat, listen to this beat. Follow this pulse all the way back, back through the long eons... follow it back to the first fire at the beginning of time, the immense hot birth of the universe some fifteen billion years ago. You were there. I was there, for the cells in our body burn with that same energy today.

We began, long ago, as great hot swirls of gas and dancing particles. Our galaxy formed, and then our sun, and then, four and a half billion years ago, our Earth. The Earth was rock and crystal, beneath which burned tremendous fires. Through eons it cooled to below boiling, and began to rain, and the oceans were born.

In these warm seas, under a brown sky, from this dance of rock and air, water and fire, organic life arose. Can you remember your life as a single-celled creature, a simple being floating in the Mother Ocean? Only bounded by a thin membrane, you are a bacterium feeding on the minerals in this salty soup. In the warm sea, you are pulled by the currents, stirred by the wind. How does it feel to reproduce by simply becoming two identical beings, and then four.... Every cell in our bodies is descended from those first ones.

Some of us learn to utilize the energy of the sun directly and become plants. But you and I from early on take our energy by eating others and we become one-celled animals. In our constant search for food, we actually invade other cells and combine our nuclei. In time this leads to a new way of creating life. Through sexual reproduction, unique individual creatures come into being, to live, to reproduce in turn, and to die.

Float on and remember linking up with other single-celled beings. Joining together, we become a sponge, or perhaps a jellyfish. What are our sensations now?

Can you remember our childhood drifting in the warm seas? Even today, some of our relatives continue to live in the ancient ways: the corals and snails, worms and plankton.... They have never forgotten what we once knew and now try to remember.

Can you remember being a slim silvery creature, a few inches long? Feel the muscles from your head all the way down your body. Feel the strength and support that slowly solidifies, and becomes over eons a string of vertebrae, extending the length of your body. We have evolved the first backbone. Now we can swim expertly with our fins, the water streaming past and through our gills.

Immensities of time are passing. Our gills slowly change to lungs. We begin to breathe the rich, harsh air, as our fins become strong lobes we use to drag ourselves through the mud of the receding lakes. We return to the waters to spawn, and our young still begin their lives there. Can you remember raising your eyes from the water into the sunlight, as our amphibian cousins, the frogs and toads and salamanders, do today? Blink your eyes in this brightness, and venture further and further into this strange new world.

Millions of years pass as we dream amphibian dreams, and the world around us changes. The swamps are drying up and we learn to carry the water necessary for our young ones in the shells of our reptilian eggs. We can live now completely on dry land. We have evolved limbs which straddle out from our body and move together, alternating from side to side. How does it feel to move in this new way, crawling over the land, eating insects and other small creatures? We store the sun's warmth in our body by day, let our hearts slow down and rest at night. Some of our cousins grow huge and toothy, and send bellows echoing over the once silent earth. Some of our cousins let their legs become wings, their scales become feathers, their bones hollow, their hearts fast and hot. Their children live today as birds. And some of our cousins are content as lizards, as turtles and alligators and snakes; crawling on bellies, they keep today the old wisdom, adhere to the old ways.

But we and other cousins take another path. We grow fur and keep the sun's warmth in our bodies by using the heat stored in our food. We let our young ones grow within us, to keep them safe and warm. More of our children survive, although they require more care. Our legs grow longer and swifter. As early mammals, we are nocturnal, hiding from dinosaurs during the day, and hunting at night. How alert we are as we dart among the roots of the huge trees, searching for food, ready to flee the great jaws. Remember returning to our underground den and curling up to sleep all warm together.

As we sleep, the rule of the dinosaurs fades away, and we mammals can spread now across the land. Some of our cousins return to the water and become dolphins and great whales. Others, like us, remain on land and become gazelles and lemurs, kangaroos and mice, and great cats. Except for resting, our belly seldom touches the ground. We take on thousands of shapes, try thousands of ways of life, and the ones that succeed are passed down. All around us now in the descendants of these cousins are unimaginable storehouses of wisdom and diversity of ways.

We go our own way. We move on hands and feet with greater lightness, leaping and climbing. In the big trees, we run along branches and swing on them. Our acute binocular vision lets us judge accurately the distance between branches. Our strong opposable thumbs help us grip and release. Our fingers are sensitive, able to test the ripeness of fruit, to groom a friend. Life is easy and full. The food we need is all around us. We are curious, playful, adventurous. Some of our close cousins live this way still.

Night falls; we nest in the trees. As we sleep and dream the dreams of monkeys, another transformation takes place. We awake with a body that is stronger and heavier. We balance easily on two legs and look to the far hori-

zon. *We call to each other with strong voices.*

As we sleep in our family groups, dreaming the dreams of great apes, our forests slowly give way to grasslands. We awaken to the next chapter of our story, where on the open savanna we learn to walk upright. Without trees to escape into, we are more vulnerable to the big cats and other large hunters that roam our world. But we are inventive, adaptable. We make intricate sounds that let us plan together in our groups. We send some members out to hunt while others gather plants for food and medicine, maintain the camp, and nourish the young. We learn in great leaps now, one discovery leading to another: tools, language, making fire, music, art, telling stories. It all happens so quickly.

We bury our dead with flowers, laying their heads to the east, to await rebirth in the womb of Mother Earth. We know we are related to all the cousins and that we are connected to all life, and we live in grateful harmony with cycles and seasons. We take the shape we now have; from now on we evolve through our minds and hearts as we live as gatherers and hunters for thousands of generations. Can you remember? Can you see the faces of the grandmothers and grandfathers lit by the evening fire, hear their songs and stories, lean against their solid bodies, feel their arms around you, see in them features you wear today? Much has been forgotten, much passed on.

Only four hundred generations ago, we begin to cultivate food on land we have wrested from our cousin species. It all happens so quickly. Farming, property, domesticated animals, towns, markets, temples, governments, writing... We build fences and fortifications; we have houses in which to keep our goods and sleep safe from one another. Some of us begin to believe that we are separate from our world, and special.

Night falls, we sleep again, and now we open our eyes as modern humans. We awaken enclosed by the walls of a city apartment or suburban house, in a world constructed by machines. What do we smell and touch, see and hear? How did it happen so fast?—automobiles, freeways, skyscrapers, airplanes, television screens, endless aisles in supermarkets filled with cans and boxes of processed food. We push our way along crowded city streets. We have not touched the earth or a wild cousin for weeks. Forces we've unleashed are darkening the air, cutting down and burning the trees, suffocating us and all our relatives. It all happens so quickly.

Yet we are the ones who can remember. We can remember who we have been. We can know once again that we are related to all things, that we are a dance of earth and air, fire and water. And we know we are more than this, too: we are the laughter of a child, the strength of compassion, the gathering under the full moon, the shiver of poetry, the melody of a song not yet sung. We are the part of the world that can gasp with wonder, be moved to tears, and imagine what can come. We are the witnesses and worshipers, the warm brainy ones with clever hands, ones who can love and who can destroy.

Let us enter once more into sleep and dreaming. Can you imagine the capacities that wait to take form in us, through us? This time as we awaken, let us bring forth the powers and abundance of our evolutionary journey, and imagine we can help to recreate a life-affirming world. Let us once again take joy in our bodies and each other, and all our relatives in the more than human world. You and I have lived in harmony with the Earth for millions of years, and this knowledge has not been lost. It is time now to draw on these memories and these strengths, and to let new ways emerge, so that the fire can still burn, so that the heartbeat will not be lost, so that the dance will go on.

The Bestiary
(30 minutes)

Purpose and background

This process elicits and provides a structure for despair work about what we are doing to our brother-sister species. As a ritual it also serves to honor, and hold in memory, the unique and irreplaceable forms that are passing from us. It often precedes the Council of All Beings. It first arose in 1981, at a midnight gathering of several hundred people in Minnesota, in the form of a simple, solemn reading of the list of threatened and endangered species. At its close, people were invited to call out and name other threatened aspects of our common life on Earth; then they expressed their sorrow by the ancient act of keening. Joanna's poem, The Bestiary, grew out of that experience, although she named only other animals, and did not include trees or plants. In subsequent years, more often than not, the reading of this poem has been used in lieu of the unadorned list of threatened and endangered species.

Description

The group sits in a circle and listens as the Bestiary (see Appendix B), or selections of a governmental list of threatened and endangered species, is read aloud. Use several voices (four is a good number) spaced around the circle; the pace should be unhurried, as befits a funeral. After the naming of each species, a clacker is struck or a drum is sounded in one strong beat. Take your pick: the drum has a funereal connotation, the clacker (two pieces of wood struck sharply together as in a zen meditation hall) has the finality of a guillotine. In using the Bestiary, the reader who names the species immediately before a paragraph proceeds to read that reflective paragraph as well.

As the names are read, it is easy to feel guilty as a human. So, before the reading, the guide makes clear that this is not the point of the exercise. Guilt tends to close us down. Instead, as each name is read, people should take the opportunity silently to honor the beauty and wisdom of that unique, irreplaceable species. This suggestion helps people to open to the grief that is in them.

At the conclusion of the poem or selected list, the guide invites people to name things that are disappearing from their world. The intent remains the same as with the endangered species: to take consciousness of the loss by publicly naming it, and to keep the memory of what once had been here. After each naming—"clean beaches," "birdsong," "safe food," "stars over cities," "hope"—the clacker or drum continues to sound. Again the pace is slow, for each utterance comes from below the busy mind. The guide concludes with words that honor the losses that have been spoken and the honesty and solidarity that their naming brings us now for our work in the world.

Variations

Hand out copies to all the participants, and have each person in succession read a name around the circle. The leader, or a volunteer, reads the reflective sections when they appear. People can also walk slowly around in a circle to a drumbeat while they read the names, or listen to the names being read.

> *Short-tailed albatross*
> *whooping crane*
> *gray wolf...*

The Cairn Of Mourning
(30 to 60 minutes)

Purpose
Similar in function to the Bestiary, this ritual-like exercise allows people to express more personally—and often more poignantly—their grief for what is happening to the natural world. In knowing the depth of this sorrow, they can know the depth of their belonging, from which comes the power to endure hardship and to act for the well-being of all.

Description
The Cairn of Mourning, constructed of natural objects, is usually made out-of-doors, though the process can be held inside, as well. Invite people to wander outside alone, reflecting on their love for the natural world, and calling to mind a particular part of that world—a place or being—which was precious to them and which is lost now or disappearing from their life. They are to find an object—say, a rock, a fallen branch, a leaf or stick—to represent that which they mourn and, after an allotted time, bring it back to the circle.

When all are seated in a circle, the simple ritual begins. One by one, at random, people arise, walk to the center and place their object. As they do, they speak. They identify what the object symbolizes for them, describe it along with their connection to it and their feelings for it; then they honor that connection by formally saying good-bye to it. All those in the circle serve as supportive witnesses, as each offering is made and the objects pile up, to form a heap or low "cairn." They acknowledge the speaker by saying, "We grieve with you," or "We share your loss," or similar response. The ritual often ends with the group holding hands, and chanting or singing together.

Note for the guide
Remind people initially, and a couple of times during the ritual, to keep breathing. We have a tendency when feeling strong emotions, especially sadness, to hold our breaths, as if that will keep the feelings at bay. Actually, breathing deeply enlarges our capacity for feeling and compassion. The suggestions for the guide in the Truth Mandala exercise in Chapter 7 apply here as well.

The Council of All Beings*
(2 to 3 hours)

Purpose

This colorful, sometimes solemn, and often lusty communal ritual allows us to step aside from our human identity and speak on behalf of other life-forms. It is excellent for growing the ecological self, for it brings a sense of our solidarity with all life, and fresh appreciation for the damage wrought by one upstart species.

Description

Following a ritual opening, participants allow themselves to be chosen by another life-form, for whom they will speak in Council. They prepare themselves to do this by reflecting on their life-form, often by making a mask to represent it, sometimes practicing moving and speaking as that life-form, and finally gathering in a formal, structured Council to speak of the grave threats faced by nearly all life-forms today.

Each Council, being the extemporaneous expression of those present, is different from all others. Each has its own character and flow. Some release torrents of intense feelings; others appear lighthearted or relatively staid. Remember that appearances can be misleading: participants who seem awkward in their roles, or relatively silent and uninvolved, can be deeply affected by the Council.

Invocation

To begin the process, the guide can call upon the Beings of Three Times (see invocation in Chapter 9) and the Four Directions. The blessing of the Four Directions is found in many indigenous traditions; use a form familiar and comfortable to you. Other ritual openings include smudging everyone with sage or sweetgrass smoke, and chanting.

Being chosen

In this process, we imagine that other beings, other life-forms apart from humans, seek to be heard at our Council. The participants take time alone to let themselves be chosen. If time and setting permit, they walk outside for fifteen or twenty minutes. Indoors, allow five to ten minutes. Play a tape of wilderness sounds or a meditative drone; avoid music which might distract or direct attention. Ask people to relax deeply, opening their mind wide like a radar dish.

Encourage people to stay with the first impulse that arises. It is not a question of choosing a species one knows a lot about, but rather allowing oneself to be surprised by the life-form that comes, be it plant, animal, or

---

* For a fuller treatment, with a narrative, see Seed, Macy, Fleming, and Naess. *Thinking Like A Mountain*. Gabriola Island, BC: New Society Publishers, 1988.

ecological feature, such as swamp or mountain—any nonhuman being. Suggest that they visualize this being fully and from every angle, its size and shape and ways of moving. Then they request this being's permission to enter it, so they can imaginatively sense its body from within. Finally, they ask the being how it wishes to be represented and, if masks are to be used in the Council, what symbolic form the mask can take.

Mask-making

Lay out materials (cardboard, color markers, paste, tape, scissors, string, fabric scraps, etc.) on tables or groundcloths. Let people also gather their own materials from nature. A half-hour should suffice; give a five-minute warning before the end of the allotted time. Everyone works without speaking. People can attach their masks with string, elastic, or by taping the mask to a stick to be held in front of the face. Be sure everyone cuts holes to see and speak through; a mask which blocks the mouth makes it hard to be heard.

Practice moving and speaking as the life-form

If time allows, this practice session helps people identify more fully with their life-form. Either or both of the following activities can help alleviate self-consciousness, which activates our human egos.

1. The guide invites participants to start moving as their life-form, beginning with eyes closed.

Breathing easily, begin to let yourself feel how it is to take body in this new life-form... what shape are you? How much space do you take up now?... What is your skin or outer surface like?... How do you take notice of what is around you?... How do you move, or how are you moved by other forces?... Do you make any sounds? Play with those sounds.

2. In groups of three or four, participants don their masks and practice using their human voice to speak for their adopted life-form. Each being speaks in turn for three to five minutes to their small group, introducing themselves, describing how it feels to be who they are, and naming their special strengths and qualities. Here they stay focused on their physical nature and way of life as it has been from the beginning of time (saving comments about present conditions for the Council itself).

Gathering in Council

The masked beings, dispersed around the area, move to the Council ground "in character" when summoned by drumbeat or animal call. When they are all in the circle, the guide, as her adopted life-form, welcomes them to this council on what is befalling their Earth and their lives.

She invites them to identify themselves. One by one around the circle, each being introduces itself in a ceremonial fashion: *"I am Wolf and I speak for the wolf people." "I am Wild Goose and I speak for the migratory birds." "I am River and I speak for the waters of the world."* It is important that this initial roll-call precede any lengthier statements.

Three stages of the Council

1) Now, speaking at random, the beings express the particular concerns they bring to the Council. For example: *"As Wild Goose, I want to tell the Council that my long migrations are hard now because the wetlands are disappearing. And the shells of my eggs are so thin and brittle, now they break before my young are ready to hatch. I fear there is poison in my bones."* The Beings in the Council respond with *"We hear you, Wild Goose."*

"As Mountain I am ancient, strong, solid, enduring. But now my forest skin is being torn off me, and my topsoil washes away, my streams and rivers choke. Blasts of dynamite shake me and mines carve into my depths. I cannot care for the beings to whom I have always given refuge." "We hear you, Mountain." One by one they speak, and are heard. Rainforest, river, soil, wheat, badger, mouse.

2) After a while, say, a dozen testimonies, the guide reflects that all the suffering that the beings describe seem to derive from the activities of one single upstart species. *"It would be good for humans to hear what we have to say. Let us summon them to our Council, to listen only. Would five or six of you put down your masks and move to the center to be humans?"* The guide beats the drum and humans come to sit back to back in the middle, facing outwards. From now on, they are addressed directly: *"Hear us, humans. This is our world, too. And we've been here a lot longer than you. Yet now our days are numbered because of what you are doing. Be still for once, and listen to us."*

The humans silently listen as the Council continues. *"Oh, humans, as River I was a bearer of life. Look at what I bear now that you've poured your wastes and poisons into me. I am ashamed and want to stop flowing because I have become a carrier of sickness and death." "We hear you, River,"* say the other beings. After a time, when more beings have spoken, the drum beats again and other humans replace the ones in the center, who return to the periphery and pick up their masks. In this fashion, everyone takes a turn to listen as a human.

3) When all the beings have had a chance to address the humans and call them to account, a major shift occurs. The guide may reflect, *"For all their machines and apparent power, the humans now are frightened. They feel overwhelmed by the momentum of the forces they have unleashed. It does not*

serve our survival for them to panic or give up, for truly our life is in their hands. If they can awaken to their place in the web of life, they will change their ways. What strengths and gifts can each of us give them to help them now?"

Now each being has the chance to offer to the humans, and receive as a human when they come to the center, the powers that are needed to stop the destruction of the world, the strengths and gifts inherent in each life-form. Sometimes the humans break their silent listening to say simply *"Thank you."*

"As Mountain, I offer you my deep peace. Come to me at any time to rest, to dream. Without dreams, you may lose your vision and your hope. Come, too, for my strength and steadfastness whenever you need."

"I, Condor, give you my keen far-seeing eye. Use that power to look ahead —beyond your day's busyness, your short-term concerns—to heed what you see, and plan."

"I, Wildflower, offer my fragrance and sweet face, to call you back to beauty. Take time to notice me, and I'll let you fall in love again with life. This is my gift."

Ending

Each Council ends a little differently, given its dynamics. Some wind up reflectively in silence. Some end intimately when everyone has joined the humans in the center to receive the gifts, and find themselves embracing and sounding together. Other Councils burst into vigorous drumming and dancing, with hoots and howls and other wild calls.

In whatever way the Council ends, a formal releasing and thanksgiving should take place. People are asked to speak to the life-forms they adopted, thanking them for the privilege of speaking for them, and then letting that identity go. Then, placing their hands and foreheads on the ground, they return the energy that has moved through them to the earth, for the healing of all beings.

Now what to do with the masks? The group may burn them in a reverent way, or compost them, or take them home to keep for a while.

John Seed and Joanna sometimes end with another suggestion. Participants can retain as their true identity the life-form for whom they have spoken—and put on a human "mask" (their own face) to reenter the world.

Variations

1. When time is short, or the materials are not at hand, drop the mask-making. If desired, use stick-on labels instead, on which people can draw a figure or symbol. Drop the practice sessions of movement and/or speaking in small groups.

2. When time is very short, say, you have just an hour, you can still offer a key feature of the Council: the chance to step aside from one's human identity and speak on behalf of another species.

In this abbreviated form, people cluster in foursomes. Closing their eyes, they follow the guide's suggestions on how to let themselves be chosen by another life-form. Then one by one, in their small group, they begin to speak as that being. It helps to lean forward, heads together, eyes half-closed.

Each person's turn takes about ten minutes and covers three parts, which the guide delineates beforehand, perhaps noting them on a sheet of newsprint:

a) Describe what it's like to *be* this life-form, the powers and per- spectives you are given, the relationships that nourish you and that you nourish in turn.

b) Describe the alterations and difficulties you may be experiencing now, due to loss of habitat, pollution, toxic dumping, drift nets, clearcut- ting, factory farming, etc.

c) Since humans are causing these difficulties and abuses, and only they can correct them, consider what strengths of yours you can offer to the humans to help them make the changes necessary to your survival— and the survival of life on Earth.

The guide, who has given a time signal for each ten-minute turn, may conclude the exercise by reflecting that the gifts each life-form has given are already present within us by virtue of the web of life. Otherwise they would not have occurred to us. When the whole group has drawn together, people may share what life-forms spoke through them, what gifts they offered, and what they discovered in the process.

Chapter 11

GOING FORTH

Go forth on your journey,
for the benefit of the many,
for the joy of the many,
out of compassion for the welfare,
the benefit and joy of all beings.
—The Buddha

THE CULMINATION OF THE WORKSHOP serves as a bridge between the experiences and learnings of our work together (described in the last five chapters) and the actual daily lives we are about to resume. We have come to see with new eyes our ineluctable place in the web of life, our connections with all beings through space and time, and the kind of power that is ours for creating a sustainable civilization. Now we use this new vision to discern the distinctive role we each can play in the Great Turning, and prepare ourselves for it.

This chapter offers exercises for doing this. Before describing them, let us look at the Work That Reconnects to be clear about what it does not provide us, and what it does. It gives us no dogma or ideology, no panacea for society's ills, no blueprint for resolving the global crisis—not even a certainty that we can act in time to save life on Earth. Such a guarantee, were it possible, would not be likely to summon forth our best efforts—the leap of courage and creativity that is required of us now.

LEARNINGS WE BRING BACK INTO OUR LIVES AND COMMUNITIES

What then can we expect to take with us, as we go forth into the world and our individual lives? From the learnings we gained as we experienced at least parts of the preceding three stages—gratitude (Chapter 6), despair work (Chapter 7), the shift (Chapters 8 to 10)—we have harvested priceless gifts to carry with us. Because they are invisible, it is good to name them:

- a heightened awareness of the suffering and dangers besetting our world; and a heightened self-respect, for our capacity to face them and know them, without dodging, denying or numbing out;

- an upsurge of personal vitality for having acknowledged and integrated our pain for the world, reframing it as compassion, and necessary feedback;

- a wider sense of identity and self-interest as an integral part of the living body of Earth—i.e. the ecological self;

- a powerful, nourishing sense of community—with each other, with our brother-sister species, with our ancestors and future generations. We feel not only accountable to them, but also inspired and supported by them;

- a sturdier motivation to join with others in healing our world; and confidence in the power that can sustain us, because it derives not from our separate selves, but from each other and our interactions in service to life;

- an appreciation of our diversities of gifts, and of the many different and interdependent roles we can play in the Great Turning;

- hence also a gratitude for our own unique self, with all its strengths and limitations, and a respectful cherishing of our own intention to be of use in this planet-time;

- (especially if we have been able to do some Deep Time work, as in Chapters 9 and 10) a liberation from dependence on immediate measurable results, and a commitment to long-term goals that extend beyond our individual lifetime; and

- a gladness in being alive now, in this epochal moment on Earth, and a sense of the privilege that is ours, to take part in the Great Turning.

Now, as we approach the end of the workshop, we both digest these gifts of learning and see quite specifically how they can shape our lives and our actions.

EXERCISES

Tales of Power*
(30 minutes)

Purpose
Recounting incidents from our own lives, we recognize our capacity to create positive change, and understand it as power. This is all the more valuable since we are not accustomed to sharing this kind of experience.

Description

Think of some times in your life when something important and good happened because of a choice you made, because of something you said or did, because of the way you were. Choose one of these times...recapture the scene...play it back for yourself.... Now in groups of four, tell that story, taking turns and listening to each other without comment until you all have finished.

Note that the guide does not use the word *power* until later, in the general discussion that follows. When the foursomes are finished, ask that a few of the stories be shared with the whole group, either by the one who told it or by one who heard it. In most cases, people have not seen their particular experience as an exercise of

> To find our calling is to find the intersection between our own deep gladness and the world's deep hunger.
> —Frederick Buechner

power, but now the guide can name it as such. She reminds the group of the new understandings of power arising in the Great Turning (see Chapter 3 and the work described in Chapter 8).

"I got the principal's permission to start a recycling program at our school." "Instead of backing off, I just stood there and talked to the guard at the nuclear power plant." "I was presiding at the board meeting and felt stuck; I decided to relinquish my role as leader, and then everyone was able to decide what to do." Many say that it had not occurred to them before that their flexibility and courage, and their ability to help others be effective, could be forms of power.

At one workshop, one man still insisted that he experienced no power in his life. "What gives you pleasure?" the guide asked. "Well, I don't know. I feel good when I ride my bicycle." "What is that like?" "Well, I tell you now, it feels good when I'm riding home from work and the traffic is jammed. I just speed by all those stuck cars and trucks; they

* Thanks to Kevin McVeigh for creating this exercise.

can hardly move and I'm going where I want to go." "That sounds like a powerful feeling," said the guide. "You bet!" said Jim beaming. "I guess that is a kind of power, isn't it?" And he recognized with pride the guerrilla-power of ingenuity and flexibility.

Imaging Our Power
(40 minutes)

Purpose

Imaging on paper with colors can give us access to intuitive wisdom. Here we allow a subliminal sense of potential to emerge in graphic form. This is especially useful following the previous exercise.

Description

This process is similar to "Imaging with Colors" in Chapter 7, and it may help the guide to review the description of that exercise. After people have arranged themselves and their paper and colors, suggest something like this:

> *Our sense of the power that is in us can be hard to convey in words. Close your eyes and breathe deeply for a moment or two...then try to sense what your power is like.... Let images and sensations emerge.... Then take your paper and colors and begin to draw how that power feels to you or appears to you at this moment. Do this quickly, without too much thought.*

After five minutes or so, the drawings are shared in small groups. Some are nonfigurative swirls and shadings of color; some are symbolic (a heart with a sun, a tree with deep roots and many creatures in its branches). One woman drew a river winding through the landscape and in its curly rushing waters were many objects: first nuclear missiles and cooling towers, stick figures of soldiers and hungry children, and then as the river progressed, trees, flowers, birds, musical notes. "My power is not to close myself off any more, but to be open to the horror and awfulness, to let it all flow through me, and to let it change into what I choose to make happen. These tributaries flowing in are all the people who are doing the same thing. So I guess it isn't my river or my power anymore, but everybody's."

The drawing of one man, an engineer, appeared to be a huge fish net. "I started to draw my anger, see this part here is a gun, but then it started connecting with the anger of others, and then with their needs, and then with their hopes. And now I'm not sure which part of the net I am. I am part of it all. I guess that is my power."

Goals and Resources*
(1 to 1-1/2 hours)

Purpose

This practice helps people to clarify their vision of their part in building a sustainable world, and to bring into focus a specific path or project to pursue (or continue pursuing). It helps them recognize the many, and often unsuspected, resources available to them, and identify immediate steps to take. Because it is done in pairs, it also creates a strong sense of mutual support. Without fail, over the years, we have found this exercise to invigorate people and strengthen their confidence; we make room for it in almost all our workshops.

Description

People work in pairs, taking turns. In response to questions from the guide, one speaks while the other serves as "scribe," recording the speaker's answers on paper. Encourage the speaker to take full advantage of having a scribe, and relax—maybe stretch out to give freer rein to the mind. At the end of each series of questions, the speaker gives the scribe a hand massage, before they reverse roles.

A series of questions we frequently use are:

1. *If you knew you could not fail, what would you be doing for the healing of our world? Here is our chance to pull out the stops and think big, with no "ifs" or "buts" getting in the way.*

   An alternative first question is: *If you were liberated from all fear and open to all the power available to you in the web of life, what would you do for the healing of our world?*

2. *In pursuing this vision, what particular project do you want to undertake? It can be a new direction in work you're already doing, or something entirely new. Here's our chance to get specific. Think in terms of what could be accomplished, or at least well underway, in a year's time.*

3. *What resources, inner and outer, do you now have that will help you do that? Inner resources include specific strengths of character, and relevant experience, knowledge, skills you've acquired. External resources include relationships,*

---

* Thanks to Barbara Hazard and Kevin McVeigh for creating the initial form of this exercise.

contacts, and networks you can draw on—not to forget babysitters, rich uncles, computer-savvy friends—as well as your location, employment, real goods, and money in the bank.

4. *Now what resources, inner and outer, will you need to acquire? To do what you want to do, what will you need to learn and to obtain? These can run from assertiveness training to grants to contacts among organizations, churches, local merchants, and the support they can give you.*

5. *How might you stop yourself? What obstacles might you throw in the way of fulfilling your goals? We all have familiar patterns of self-doubt and sabotage.*

6. *How will you overcome these obstacles? Draw upon your past experience in dealing with these self-imposed obstacles, and perhaps some new ways of moving around them will occur to you.*

7. *What can you do in the next 24 hours, no matter how small the step—if only a phone call—that will move toward this goal?*

When both partners have scribed the other's responses (and exchanged hand massages), the two take turns reporting back to each other from the notes they have taken. Instruct each scribe to use the second-person pronoun: you want to, you have, one way you might stop yourself, etc. And the other is to listen as if hearing, at long last, their orders from the universe. The papers of notes are then exchanged, so that each can take with them their answers, their plans.

Variation
If time is too short for the whole process, skip the scribing. Have people work alone, noting on paper their own responses to each question, then to share their answers with another person.

Consultation Groups*
(60 minutes)

Purpose
As a follow-on to the above exercise, these four-person consultations allow participants to "get real" with their hopes and plans. They provide feedback and counsel, including specific leads to pursue. They can offer breakthrough suggestions about contacts and resources, and often eventuate in continuing support and even collaboration.

---

* Thanks to Fran Macy for this process.

Description
Each pair from the "Goals and Resources" practice now joins with another
pair to make a group of four, bringing the notes of their plans.

> *You are now provided an unparalleled opportunity. You are offered what
> money cannot buy: topflight consultants, who are allied with your vision. Take
> a moment to reflect on the plans you've been hatching. Where can you use some
> excellent advice? Is it to get clearer on your project and what you can achieve?
> Is it how to find the resources you need, or how to deal with particular obsta-
> cles? You each have ten minutes (or fifteen). Refine your questions in your
> mind, so that you can speak briefly and allow time for the others to respond.*

It is hard to bring these groups to a close, so allow some elasticity at
the end of the process, and remind people that they'll have time, when
the workshop finishes, to confer further and take additional notes on
leads and ideas.

Planning Actions
(2 hours)

Purpose
This rewarding three-part exercise reveals how a group can work together
and empower its members, as it moves from a general or abstract goal to
steps for immediate and concrete actions. Adapted from processes developed by the Movement for a New Society, it has been equally effective in
south Asian villages and American campuses.

Description
The process unfolds in three stages.

1. Envisioning goals. (45 minutes)
From the categories listed on newsprint, people select which aspect of a
desired future they wish to envision: education, health, food production
and processing, communications, transportation, community life, habitat restoration/preservation, etc. They should feel free to choose an area
in which they lack expertise, for it is the amateurs who often bring the
most novel and ingenious ideas. They then convene in simultaneous
topic-specific groups.

First, in silence, each person dreams a bit and then jots on paper
notions of an optimal way this particular aspect of society might func-

tion (5 minutes). Then they take turns sharing their ideas with their group (a scribe in each may record them on newsprint). The group then chooses the four or five ideas it finds most appealing (15 minutes). The different groups then report these ideas to the whole gathering (15 minutes).

If time is short, this part of the exercise can be omitted.

2. Progressive brainstorm. (20 to 30 minutes)

Having heard these ideas, the whole group chooses one it wishes to focus on. Note: the specific issue *per se* is less important than the experience of bringing our collective creativity to bear on something. (If the first stage is skipped, pick a goal at random: clean air or free public transportation.) With the goal written at the top of a large sheet of newsprint, the group begins to brainstorm: what conditions would this goal necessitate? (See rules for brainstorming in Chapter 6.) After four or five minutes, the group chooses one of the ideas which has arisen, and brainstorms the conditions this more specific goal would necessitate. This process continues in four to five minute rounds until the goals are quite specific, so that each person could conceivably do something about one of them in the next 24 hours. From the distant goal, the group has moved to specific and immediate steps.

Take the goal of clean air. What conditions would free us from air pollution? These are listed in Round One of the brainstorm. The group then chooses one of the ideas, say, "reduce the use of automobiles." This is written at the top of another piece of newsprint and the group moves quickly into a second brainstorm on what we would need to do to reduce the use of automobiles. Many ideas surface here, too: mandatory carpools, blocked streets, public bicycles, new forms of mass transit. Again, one of these is chosen and brainstormed further as to how it might be implemented. The process continues until concrete actions are suggested that can be immediately implemented, e.g.. a door-to-door canvass to enlist support for a cooperative bicycle delivery system. At this point, the group moves into the third stage of the exercise.

3. Role-play.

Now that the group has an immediate (though still hypothetical) action to undertake, how will we obtain the resources and cooperation needed? How will we enlist people? What types of persons or situations present a particular challenge? Role-playing such encounters helps us move beyond the blocks we often feel at this juncture, which keep some of our finest ideas trapped in the world of dreams.

In the example above, the group has decided to organize a cooperative delivery system by bicycle, and for that purpose teams will call on everyone in the community to elicit their support and involvement. We role-play conversations between team members and senior citizens, or high school students, or the owner of a bicycle store, or an official in the Highway Department. After a while, in mid-conversation, we reverse roles, "team members" becoming the people addressed, and vice versa.

The exercise is as instructive as it is entertaining. It forces us to discover how well we can think on our feet, what we need to know and say in order to be convincing. Moreover, reversing roles in mid-conversation gives us insight into the thoughts and feelings of the people we are trying to enlist. It breaks us out of polarized we/they thinking, helps us to identify with others, and enhances our confidence and effectiveness.

Communicating Our Concerns and Hopes—Exercise

(30 - 45 minutes)

Purpose

At each step in our work for the healing of our world, we engage with other people. Many give little evidence of sharing our concerns, but because of their relationship to us or their position or responsibilities, we want to enlist their support, or at least their understanding. Assuming that they are opposed to our views, we often feel intimidated and reluctant to argue. This role-playing exercise, along with the guidelines which follow, helps us to be more skillful and confident.

Description

Think of someone with whom you find it hard to talk about your concerns for the world and about the actions you want to take. It could be your father or sister, your employer or lover, or even the President or the Secretary of Defense. Assign that identity to your partner along with some clues as to how to play the role, what responses this person might give. Partners, feel free to ask for clarification, and let your intuition guide you, too.

Then begin the role-play. Speakers, tell this person what you see and how you feel, and what you feel impelled to do about it. Note the sense of awkwardness, shame, or powerlessness that may arise, and continue nonetheless. Partners, respond in your role, keeping your replies fairly brief, so the burden of communication is on the speaker.

After a few minutes, the guide asks the pairs to reverse roles, the speakers taking on the identities of the persons they have chosen to address, and their partners taking up the role of speaker. This reversal of roles is revealing and productive, breaking through our old, automatic assumptions about the person we are addressing. We may experience his confusion and fear; we may see our own self in a new light. We discover how we tend to lock people into adversarial positions by our presuppositions and projections, and our previous history with them. Reversing roles again, the conversation continues, but now the speaker is more aware of the inner person being addressed, and is often more compassionate.

Generally, two rounds of role-playing take place, so that everyone has a chance to practice speaking to a person of their choice. In the general discussion following the role-plays, the guide helps the group create a list of guidelines and principles, drawing on the participants' experience and insights, and the ideas offered below.

Communicating Our Concerns and Hopes—Guidelines

Many of us are reluctant to reveal our concerns about world issues because we don't want to get into an argument, especially with people who are important in our lives, be they coworkers or employers, relatives or neighbors. We can be afraid of triggering their angers or suspicions. We can be afraid of not knowing enough facts to sustain our views, thereby losing their respect, or we can be afraid of appearing judgmental or self-righteous. Society discourages talking about things which evoke strong feelings and opinions; religion and politics are considered off-limits for many social occasions. Not wanting to make anyone else uncomfortable, we often remain silent about our concerns, especially if they seem to conflict with others' points of view. On the other hand, if we do speak up, we may get embroiled in debates that become heated and fruitless, and that leave each party more entrenched in their opinions. At a time when our collective choices are so critical, how can we discuss our concerns without polarizing them?

Here are some guidelines for communicating our concerns, especially with those who hold a different opinion.

1. **Beware of labeling or pigeonholing the other person**, assuming they are automatically going to agree or disagree with you because they are a certain age, dressed in a certain way, come from a particular region or class, or hold a particular job.

2. **Acknowledge the limits of your knowledge.** People will see you as more trustworthy if you admit you don't know everything, and will feel more willing to share their perspectives, which are also based on partial information. We all must make decisions in political life without knowing the whole story; if we put our knowledge and ideas together, we create a more complete picture.

3. **Find common ground before examining differences.** If you begin by ascertaining areas of agreement (e.g. "Nuclear war is possible" or "We need clean air and water for our children"), both parties can trust each other more and proceed to see where their views diverge. Then offering the information that has led to your view can fill a gap in the other's knowledge, and lead to reappraisal of old assumptions. A person may simply not know, for example, about the extent of clearcutting in the Pacific Northwest, or the current level of expenditures on nuclear weapons.

4. **Share feelings as well as facts.** Facts are debatable; feelings are not. Feelings are "givens"; we can report them with varying degrees of accuracy and honesty, but they are not debatable. Sharing your feelings invites other people to share theirs as well, moving the conversation away from argument and towards mutual listening.

5. **Share your personal experience.** The facts and figures we cite take on more reality for people when we describe what led us to the views we hold. Personal experience, like feelings, is not open to debate.

6. **Trust the other person's ability to learn and change over time**. Even if the person seems entrenched in a contrary position, change may be stirring within. And you may never know if change has occurred as a result of your discussion, or what other input the person may receive from others to add to yours. Consider what books, films, speakers, encounters have changed your life; how often was the change agent aware of his or her effect on you?

7. **See yourself and the other within the larger context:** your shared humanity, the stresses of the Industrial Growth Society, the long, uneven journey to a sustainable civilization. This breeds patience and goodwill.

8. **Remember to hold the other person with compassion**, even when you seem to find no common ground. You can "agree to disagree" with goodwill and mutual respect. We can never know what suffering and hardship might underlie another's seemingly intractable position.

Networking

(20 to 60 minutes)

Purpose

Here workshop participants have the opportunity to inform each other of their plans and projects, and as they do so, to offer contacts, leads, and resources. They link up, and help each other link up, in networks of ongoing support.

Description

This is a free-wheeling process within a limited time period. Begin it by inviting people to stand at random ("popcorn" style) to announce the plans they have hatched or clarified in the Goals and Resources exercise. Then everyone mingles, gathering together around particular concerns and themes.

As an alternative, uses sheets of newsprint on the wall. Ask people, after the Goals and Resources exercise, or the Consultation Groups that follow, to post their projects or areas of concern—say, Education, Recycling, Factory Farms, Global Warming, Multinational Corporations, Nuclear Waste, Forests, Transportation, Homelessness, etc. The posting process itself may result in some groupings. Then as people read and move around, they can gather together around common concerns, and share plans and information.

Overcoming Obstacles

(15 minutes, plus 1 or 2 minutes per person)

Purpose

This simple ritual empowers us to go forth for the healing of our world, by helping us to recognize both the internal obstacles we face and our willingness to move beyond them—to burn them up in the fire of our commitment.

Description

With what obstacles are we likely to hinder ourselves from taking part in the Great Turning? What might hold us back? What old timidities and fears might stop us? Let's ponder this in silence for a little while, and then use the markers and paper in the middle of the room to draw images and symbols of them, or write their names.

When people have done this, they reconvene in a circle. In the center of the circle, the guide has lit a candle and set it in a large pan to hold the ashes. One by one, at random, people come forward with their bits of paper, to offer up their obstacles and, naming them, to burn them. "I, Suzanne Smith, relinquish my timidity about speaking out." "I, George Jones, hereby let go of the fear of my own feelings." One man said, "My obstacle is my attachment to money," and instead of his bit of paper, he held a dollar bill to the flame.

The people in the circle respond to each "burnt offering" as if it were a gift. They may chant something together: "Let go and be free," or the Buddhist *"Gaté gaté, paragaté parasam gaté"* ("Gone, gone, completely gone"), or simply a tone which rises after each offering and then quiets again.

Affirming Our Commitment

(15 minutes)

Purpose
At the close of the workshop, this process lets us reflect on the unique role we each can play in the Great Turning, and strengthens our intention.

Description
Each of us has an important and irreplaceable role to play in the healing of our world. Each has distinctive gifts to bring. Closing your eyes, breathing slowly, visualize the conditions of your life and the strengths that have been given to you.... They will allow you to do something no one else can do.... You may not see that path very clearly yet, but the knowledge of it is within you, and it will unfold now, more and more, with each step you take. Feel in the core of your being the strength of that intention....

It is good to offer some ritual act to give outer form to the inner movement of intention and commitment. It can be as simple as a gesture, a stepping forward into the circle, the lighting of a candle, or joining in a chant or song. Sometimes we just invite people to put their hands over their heart (as they hearken to their intention) and then lower their hands in front of them, palms up (when they are ready to commit themselves to follow it).

Circle of Blessings

(2 to 5 minutes per person)

Purpose

In the closing circle, people tell of a particular action or path they intend to pursue, and receive each other's blessings for it. This is, as they prepare to go forth, a kind of reciprocal "commissioning," which lets them receive and carry with them the group's support for their intentions.

Description

One at a time, each person comes (by choice) to the center of the circle. Sometimes a cushion is placed there for them, sometimes they stand and turn, as they speak, to see all the faces. In a sentence or two, they inform the group of a particular work they envisage undertaking, or a task to which they return. From caring for an ailing parent to starting a wilderness school, many of the myriad ways we will serve our world are held now in the group's collective appreciation and resolve.

The person in the center then asks for the others' blessings, naming specific strengths they will need. "To start this composting program, I need wisdom in making priorities and choosing what to drop from my crowded days." "In running for city council, I want courage, and lots of it." "Before I do anything else, I gotta finish my degree; I'd like your blessings on my tired brain, and perseverance."

The encircling group then responds in spontaneous expressions of support. Sometimes these are voiced as specific wishes or blessings. ("May wisdom be yours; you will choose well".... "We see your courage; it will carry you".... "Hang in there with the books; let those neurons fire.") Sometimes the listeners reply by chanting the speaker's name, over and over, with hands outstretched, palms forward. Sometimes the blessings are accompanied by a laying on of hands. As the custom has arisen in German workshops, the one in the center often chooses to lie down and have the group cluster around; then he or she can receive, from many hands and voices, a sonorous cradling of prayers.

It is good for the guide to go first in this circle of blessings, in order to model the process and encourage participation. At the close of many a recent workshop we have asked for the group's blessings for this book. "Wish me a clear head and good use of my time." "I want to remember this is a privilege, and not a chore, so I can work out of gratitude."

The prayers and blessings then showered upon us have certainly been effective. Our writing of this book has been buoyed by gladness—and thankfulness for the countless men and women who have joined in the Work that Reconnects.

Chapter 12

MEDITATIONS FOR
COMING BACK TO LIFE

I would not like to have the bodhisattva think this kind of work
hard to achieve. If he did, there are beings beyond calculation,
and he will not be able to benefit them.
Let him, on the contrary, consider the work easy and pleasant,
thinking they were all his mother and father and children,
for this is the way to benefit all beings
whose number is beyond calculation.
—The Perfection of Wisdom in Eight Thousand Lines [32]

To heal our society, our psyches must heal, as well. Haunted by the desperate needs of our time and beset by more commitments than we can easily carry, we may wonder how to find the time and energy for spiritual disciplines. Few of us feel free to take to the cloister or meditation cushion to seek personal transformation.

We do not need to withdraw from the world or spend long hours in solitary prayer or meditation to begin to wake up to the spiritual powers within us. The activities and encounters of our daily lives can serve as the occasion for that kind of discovery. Here are seven practices that help, transcribed as Joanna has offered them in workshops. Because they are useful in our ongoing lives as well, we present them here in this concluding chapter.

Some of these meditations—on death, loving kindness, compassion, mutual power, and mutual recognition—happen to be adapted from the Buddhist tradition. As part of our planetary heritage, they belong to us all. No belief system is necessary, only a readiness to attend to the immediacy of your own experience. They are to be read slowly with a quiet mind. If you read them aloud for others or put them on tape, allow several seconds when three or four dots (...) appear, and when more appear (......), leave additional time.

The Web of Life

This spoken meditation arose at the turning point of a workshop offered in Washington, D.C., in the first year of the work. It is most effective if participants can stretch out.

Lie, stretch...relax into the floor....

Feel breath... lungs, abdomen...glide on the breath, in, out.... The oxygen ignites each cell, stirs it awake as it burns in the metabolism of life.... Extend your awareness deep within to feel this energy.... It is all around you, too... sustaining the bodies in this room, sparking in the great cycles of air, water, fire, and earth flowing through us all... weaving us into the web of life.

Imagine you can see these interlacing currents, like threads of light, perhaps.... See how they connect us, and extend beyond this room, this moment.... Experience the great multiplicity of strands...formed by countless relationships, woven of the work and food, the laughter and tears you've shared with others.... They shape what you are... they hold you in place.... Sense those filaments, lie into them.

The web sustains your bones and blood and skin, concocted so intricately out of the food you have eaten...out of grains, vegetables, fruit grown in so many places near and far.... The grass and the munching jaws of the cow as she makes her milk for your butter and cheese... The soil that yields the grain for your bread, the boughs of the tree that bears the oranges for your juice... The hands that plow, sow, reap, process... They all are of your body now....

Back through time this web extends...mothers, fathers, our great-grandmothers and great-grandfathers...giving you your coloring and features...your gestures, your tone of voice.... The web extends back through countless generations, through numberless ancestors we share...all the way back to those with gills and wings.... For it is of star stuff evolving that we all are made in the flowing of time.... We are each a jewel in this vast net, that called us into being.... Each of us an unrepeatable jewel, sparkling with awareness, reflect-

ing the world... Sound of gull crying over the sea, sight of mountain ris-ing...colors of sunrise...scents of pine and loam...the excitement of a new idea...the melody of a favorite song.

There is pain, too, coming in along the strands of the web... a friend with cancer... an oil spill coating the beach... an Iraqi mother weeping for her lost children.... Do not shut them out, they inhere in the web of this planet-time.... Open to these sorrows, breathe them in, so the channels may stay open for the flow of energy and life and change.... If we block the pain, we block the joy out, too.... There is power in the flowing of this fluid net, love that has enriched us, and love that we give.... Feel the caring and love that flow through you and out from you.

Open to the pulsing of the web, its murmurs, whispers, tugs.... Through that vast network all forms arose, intelligence arose.... It shaped you as it shaped the mockingbird and the deep-diving trout.... You are of it... of it, even to the terrors we've unleashed now.... Open to it all, unafraid, relaxed, alert.... We are the universe knowing itself.

To all our brothers and sisters we open now... in this time of hardship. We go now through a dark place, but we do not go alone.... And we do not go with-out our own timeless knowledge of the dark.... We come from it, it is behind our eyes...and we will look into it, together, until the dark itself is clear...and home.... There is nowhere you can go where you're not held in the web that sustains us all.

Still sensing these connections through space and time, we stretch now, open our eyes, slowly move to rise....

Gaia Meditation [33]

This simple spoken meditation, composed by John Seed and Joanna, guides us into precise and close identification with the elements, and with Earth's geohistory and life history. This meditation can also be done in pairs, contemplating one another while listening to the words.

What are you? What am I? Intersecting cycles of water, earth, air and fire, that's what I am, that's what you are.

WATER—Blood, lymph, mucus, sweat, tears, inner oceans tugged by the moon, tides within and tides without. Streaming fluids floating our cells, washing and nourishing through endless riverways of gut and vein and cap-illary. Moisture pouring in and through and out of you, of me, in the vast poem of the hydrological cycle. You are that. I am that.

EARTH—Matter made from rock and soil. It, too, is pulled by the moon as the magma circulates through the planet heart and roots such molecules into biology. Earth pours through us, replacing each cell in the body every seven years. Ashes to ashes, dust to dust, we ingest, incorporate and excrete the earth, are made from earth. I am that. You are that.

AIR—The gaseous realm, the atmosphere, the planet's membrane. The inhale and the exhale. Breathing out carbon dioxide to the trees and breathing in their fresh exudations. Oxygen kissing each cell awake, atoms dancing in orderly metabolism, interpenetrating. That dance of the air cycle, breathing the universe in and out again, is what you are, is what I am.

FIRE—Fire, from our sun that fuels all life, drawing up plants and rais-ing the waters to the sky to fall again replenishing. The inner furnace of your metabolism burns with the fire of the Big Bang that first sent matter-energy spinning through space and time. And the same fire as the lightning that flashed into the primordial soup, catalyzing the birth of organic life.

You were there, I was there, for each cell of our bodies is descended in an unbroken chain from that event. Through the desire of atom for molecule, of mol-ecule for cell, of cell for organism. In that spawning of forms death was born, born simultaneously with sex, before we divided from the plant realm. So in our sexu-ality we can feel ancient stirrings that connect us with plant as well as animal life. We come from them in an unbroken chain—through fish learning to walk the land, feeling scales turning to wings, through migrations in the ages of life.

We have been but recently in human form. If Earth's whole history were compressed into twenty-four hours beginning at midnight, organic life would begin only at 5 p.m....mammals emerge at 11:30 p.m....and from amongst them at only seconds to midnight, our species.

In our long planetary journey we have taken far more ancient forms than these we now wear. Some of these forms we remember in our mother's womb wear vestigial tails and gills, grow fins for hands.

Countless times in that journey we died to old forms, let go of old ways, allowing new ones to emerge. But nothing is ever lost. Though forms pass, all return. Each worn-out cell consumed, recycled...through mosses, leeches, birds of prey...

Think to your next death. Will your flesh and bones back into the cycle. Surrender. Love the plump worms you will become. Launder your weary being through the fountain of life.

Beholding you, I behold as well all the different creatures that compose you—the mitochondria in the cells, the intestinal bacteria, the life teeming on the surface of the skin. The great symbiosis that is you. The incredible coordination and cooperation of countless beings. You are that, too, just as your body is part of a much larger symbiosis, living in wider reciprocities. Be conscious of that give-and-take when you move among trees. Breathe your pure carbon dioxide on a leaf and sense it breathing fresh oxygen back to you.

Remember again and again the old cycles of partnership. Draw on them in this time of trouble. By your very nature and the journey you have made, there is in you deep knowing of belonging. Draw on it now in this time of fear. You have earth-bred wisdom of your interexistence with all that is. Take courage and power in it now, that we may help each other awaken in this time of peril.

Meditation on Death

Most spiritual paths begin by recognizing the transience of human life. Medieval Christians honored this in the mystery play of *Everyman*. Don Juan, the Yaqui sorcerer, taught that the enlightened warrior walks with death at his shoulder. To confront and accept the inevitability of our dying releases us from triviality and frees us to live boldly.

An initial meditation on the Buddhist path involves reflection on the twofold fact that: "death is certain" and "the time of death is uncertain." In our world today, nuclear weaponry, serving in a sense as a spiritual teacher, does that meditation for us, for it tells us that we can die together at any moment, without warning. When we allow the reality of that possibility to become conscious, it is painful, but it also jolts us awake to life's vividness, its miraculous quality, heightening our awareness of the beauty and uniqueness of each object and each being.

Look at the person you encounter (stranger or friend). Let the realization arise in you that this person lives on an endangered planet. He or she may die in a nuclear war, or from the poisons spreading through our world. Observe that face, unique, vulnerable... Those eyes still can see; they are not empty sockets... the skin is still intact... Become aware of your desire that this person be spared such suffering; feel the strength of that desire... Keep breathing... Also let the possibility arise in your consciousness that this may be the person you happen to be with when you die... that face, the last you see... that hand, the last you touch... It might reach out to help you then, to comfort, to give water... Open to the caring and connection that arise in you...

Meditation on Loving Kindness

Loving kindness, or *metta*, is the first of the four "Abodes of the Buddha," also known as the *Brahmaviharas*. Meditation to arouse and sustain loving-kindness is a staple of the Sarvodaya Shramadana Movement for community development in Sri Lanka, and is accorded minutes of silence at the outset of every meeting. Organizers and village workers find it useful in developing motivation for service and overcoming feelings of hostility or inadequacy.

Joanna first received instruction in this meditation from Sister Karma Khechog Palmo, a nun in the Tibetan Buddhist tradition. Here is a version that she has adapted for use in the West.

Close your eyes and begin to relax, exhaling to expel tension. Now center on the normal flow of the breath, letting go of all extraneous thoughts as you passively watch the breathing-in and breathing-out....

Now call to mind someone you love very dearly.... In your mind's eye see the face of that beloved one... silently speak her or his name.... Feel your love for this being, like a current of energy coming through you.... Now let yourself experience how much you want this person to be freed from fear, how intensely you desire that this person be released from greed and ill-will, from confusion and sorrow and the causes of suffering.... That desire, in all its sincerity and strength, is metta, the great loving-kindness....

Continuing to feel that warm flow coming through the heart, see in your mind's eye those with whom you share your daily life, family members, close friends and colleagues, the people you live and work with.... Let them appear now as in a circle around you. Behold them one by one, silently speaking their names... and direct to each in turn that same current of loving-kindness.... Among these beings may be some with whom you are uncomfortable, in conflict, or tension. With those especially, experience your desire that each

*be free from fear, from hatred, free from greed and ignorance and the causes
of suffering....*

*Now allow to appear, in wider concentric circles, your relations, and
your acquaintances.... Let the beam of loving-kindness play on them as well,
pausing on the faces that appear randomly in your mind's eye. With them as
well, experience how much you want their freedom from greed, fear, hatred and
confusion, how much you want all beings to be happy......*

*Beyond them, in concentric circles that are wider yet, appear now all
beings with whom you share this planet-time. Though you have not met, your
lives are interconnected in ways of knowing. To these beings as well, direct the
same powerful current of loving-kindness. Experience your desire and your
intention that each awaken from fear and hatred, from greed and confusion...
that all beings be released from suffering....*

*As in the ancient Buddhist meditation, we direct the loving-kindness
now to all the "hungry ghosts," the restless spirits that roam in suffering, still
prey to fear and confusion. May they find rest...may they rest in the great loving-kindness and in the deep peace it brings......*

*By the power of our imagination let us move out now beyond our plan-
et, out into the universe, into other solar systems, other galaxies, other
Buddha-fields. The current of loving-kindness is not affected by physical distances, and we direct it now, as if aiming a beam of light, to all centers of
conscious life.... To all sentient beings everywhere we direct our heartfelt wish
that they too be free of fear and greed, of hatred and confusion and the causes
of suffering.... May all beings be happy......*

*Now, from out in the interstellar distances, turn and behold your own
planet, your home.... See it suspended there in the blackness of space, like a
jewel turning in the light of its sun.... That living blue-green planet laced with
swirls of white is the source of all you are, all you've ever known and cher-
ished.... Feel how intensely you desire that it surmount the spreading wounds
and dangers of this time; direct toward it the strong current of your compassion and prayerful wishes for its healing....*

*Slowly approach it now, drawing nearer, nearer, returning to this part of
it, this region, this place.... And as you approach this place, let yourself see the
being you know best of all... the person it has been given you to be in this lifetime.... You know its need for love, know how hard it tries.... Let the face of this
being, your own face, appear before you.... Speak the name you are called in
love.... And experience, with that same strong current of loving-kindness, how*

deeply you desire that this being be free from fear, released from greed and hatred, liberated from ignorance and confusion and the causes of suffering.... The great loving-kindness linking you to all beings is now directed to your own self... know now the fullness of it.

Breathing Through

Basic to most spiritual traditions is the recognition that we are not separate, isolated entities, but integral and organic parts of the vast web of life. We can open to the pain of the world in confidence that it can neither shatter nor isolate us, for we are not objects that can break. We are resilient patterns within a vaster web of knowing.

Because we have been conditioned to view ourselves as separate, competitive and thus fragile entities, we need to relearn this kind of resilience. One way is to practice simple openness, as in the exercise of "breathing through," adapted from an ancient Buddhist meditation for developing compassion.

Closing your eyes, focus attention on your breathing. Don't try to breathe any special way, slow or long. Just watch the breathing as it happens, in and out. Note the accompanying sensations at the nostrils or upper lip, in the chest or abdomen. Stay passive and alert, like a cat by a mousehole....

As you watch the breath, note that it happens by itself, without your will, without your deciding each time to inhale or exhale.... It's as though you're being breathed—being breathed by life.... Just as everyone in this room, in this city, on this planet now, is being breathed by life, sustained in a vast living breathing web....

Now visualize your breath as a stream or ribbon of air. See it flow up through your nose, down through your windpipe and into your lungs. Now from your lungs, take it through your heart. Picture it flowing through your heart and out through an opening there to reconnect with the larger web of life. Let the breath-stream, as it passes through you and through your heart, appear as one loop within that vast web, connecting you with it......

Now open your awareness to the suffering that is present in the world. Drop for now all defenses and open to your knowledge of that suffering. Let it come as concretely as you can... images of your fellow beings in pain and need, in fear and isolation, in prisons, hospitals, tenements, refugee camps... no need to strain for these images; they are present to you by virtue of our interexistence. Relax and just let them surface... the vast and countless hardships of our fellow humans, and of our animal brothers and sisters as well, as they swim the seas and fly in the air of this planet.... Now breathe in the pain like dark granules on the stream of air, up through your nose, down through your trachea, lungs, and heart, and out again into the world net.... You are asked to do nothing for now, but let it pass through your heart.... Be sure that stream flows through and out again; don't hang onto the pain.... Surrender it for now to the healing resources of life's vast web....

With Shantideva, the Buddhist saint, we can say, "Let all sorrows ripen in me." We help them ripen by passing them through our hearts...making good rich compost out of all that grief... so we can learn from it, enhancing our larger, collective knowing....

If no images or feelings arise and there is only blankness, gray and numb, breathe that through. The numbness itself is a very real part of our world....

And if what surfaces for you is not the pain of other beings so much as your own personal suffering, breathe that through, too. Your own anguish is an integral part of the grief of our world, and arises with it....

Should you feel an ache in the chest, a pressure in the ribcage, as if the heart would break, that is all right. Your heart is not an object that can break.... But if it were, they say the heart that breaks open can hold the whole universe. Your heart is that large. Trust it. Keep breathing....

This guided meditation serves to introduce the process of breathing through, which, once familiar, becomes useful in daily life in the many situations that confront us with painful information. By breathing through the bad news, rather than bracing ourselves against it, we can let it strengthen our sense of belonging in the larger web of being. It helps us remain alert and open, whether reading the newspaper, receiving criticism, or simply being present to a person who suffers.

For activists and those dealing most directly with the griefs of our time, the practice helps prevent burnout. Reminding us of the collective nature of both our problems and our power, it offers a healing measure of humility. It can save us from self-righteousness. For when we can take in our world's pain, accepting it as the price of our caring, we let it inform our acts, without needing to inflict it as a punishment on others who appear, at the present moment, to be less involved.

The Great Ball of Merit

Compassion, which we generally understand as grief in the grief of others, is but one side of the coin. The other side is joy in the joy of others—which Buddhists call *mudita*. To the extent that we allow ourselves to identify with the sufferings of other beings, we can identify with their strengths, as well. This is very important for a sense of adequacy and resilience, because we face a time of great challenge that demands of us more commitment, endurance and courage than we can dredge up out of our individual supply. We can learn to draw on the other neurons in the neural net. We can see them with gladness as a present resource, like money in the bank.

This practice is adapted from the "Meditation of Jubilation and Transformation" taught in a Buddhist text written two thousand years ago at the outset of the Mahayana tradition. You can find the original version in Chapter Six of *The Perfection of Wisdom in Eight Thousand Lines*. We find it very useful today in two forms. The one closer to the ancient practice is this, which we use in workshops. As you guide the meditation, participate in it yourself as much as possible, especially making the hand gestures.

> *Relax and close your eyes. Open your awareness to the fellow beings who share with you this planet-time... in this town...in this country...and in other lands...... In your mind's eye, behold their multitudes...... Now let your awareness open wider yet, to encompass all beings who ever lived...of all races and creeds and walks of life, rich, poor, kings and beggars, saints and sinners.... See the vast vistas of these fellow beings stretching into the distance, like successive mountain ranges...... Now consider the fact that in each of these innumerable lives some act of merit was performed. No matter how stunted or deprived the life, there was a gesture of generosity, a gift of love, an act of valor or self-sacrifice... on the battlefield, or in the workplace, hospital, or home.... From these beings in their endless multitudes arose actions of courage, kindness, of teaching and healing. Let yourself see these manifold and immeasurable acts of merit......*

> *Now imagine you can sweep together these acts of merit...sweep them into a pile in front of you.... Use your hands.... Pile them up.... Pile them into a heap, viewing it with gladness and gratitude.... Now pat them into a ball.... It is the Great Ball of Merit.... Hold it now and weigh it in your hands.... Rejoice in it, knowing that no act of goodness is ever lost. It remains ever and always a present resource...a means for the transformation of life.... So now, with jubilation and gratitude, you turn that great ball...turn it over...over...into the healing of our world.*

As we can learn from contemporary science and visualize in the holographic model of reality, our lives interpenetrate. In the fluid tapestry of space-time, there is at root no distinction between self and other. The acts and intentions of others are like seeds that can germinate and bear fruit through our own lives, as we take them into awareness and dedicate, or "turn over," that awareness to our own empowerment. Gautama, Jesus, Dorothy Day, Gandhi, Martin Luther King, Mother Teresa, and countless, nameless heroes of our time—all can be part of our Ball of Merit, from which we can draw inspiration and endurance. Other traditions feature notions similar to this, such as the "cloud of witnesses" of which St. Paul spoke, or the Treasury of Merit in the Catholic Church.

The second, more workaday version of the Ball of Merit meditation helps us open to the powers in people around us. It is in direct contrast to the commonly accepted, patriarchal notion of power as something personally owned and exerted over others. The exercise prepares us to bring expectant attention to our encounters with other beings, to view them with fresh openness and curiosity as to how they can enhance our Ball of Merit. We can play this inner game with someone opposite us on the bus or across the bargaining table. It is especially useful when dealing with a person with whom we are in conflict.

What does this person add to my Great Ball of Merit? What gifts of intellect can enrich our common store? What reserves of stubborn endurance can she or he offer? What flights of fancy or powers of love lurk behind those eyes? What kindness or courage hides in those lips, what healing in those hands?

Then, as with the breathing through exercise, we open ourselves to the presence of these strengths, inhaling our awareness of them. As our awareness grows, we experience our gratitude for them and our capacity to partake of them....

Often we let our perceptions of the powers of others make us feel inadequate. Alongside an eloquent colleague, we can feel inarticulate; in the presence of an athlete, we can feel weak and clumsy; and we can come to resent both ourself and the other person. In the light of the Great Ball of Merit, however, the gifts and good fortunes of others appear not as competing challenges, but as resources we can honor and take pleasure in. We can learn to play detective, spying out treasures for the enhancement of life from even the unlikeliest material. Like air and sun and water, they form part of our common good.

In addition to releasing us from the mental cramp of envy, this practice offers two other rewards. One is pleasure in our own acuity, as our merit-detecting ability improves. The second is the response of others who, though ignorant of the game we are playing, sense something in our manner that invites them to disclose more of the person they can be.

Learning to See Each Other

This spiritual exercise is adapted from the Buddhist practice of the Brahmaviharas, also known as the Four Abodes of the Buddha, which are loving-kindness, compassion, joy in the joy of others, and equanimity. It helps us to see each other more truly and experience the depths of our interconnections.

In workshops, it is offered as a guided meditation, with people sitting in pairs facing each other. At its close, we encourage them to use it, or any portion of it they like, as they go about the business of their daily lives. It is an excellent antidote to boredom, when our eye falls on another person, say, on the subway, or waiting in the checkout line. It charges that idle moment with beauty and discovery. It also is useful when dealing with people whom we are tempted to dislike or disregard; it breaks open our accustomed ways of viewing them. When used like this, as a meditation-in-action, one does not, of course, gaze long and deeply upon the other, as in the guided exercise. A seemingly casual glance is enough.

In many cultural settings, it is considered rude to look directly into another's eyes. In high schools and colleges in our culture, sustained eye contact may provoke embarrassment. In such situations, suggest that the partners still sit facing each other, but with their eyes closed, picturing the other's face in the mind's eye. Then from time to time as they wish, they can open their eyes and look at the other's face to refresh their memory, for as long as is comfortable.

The usual guided form in a group goes like this:

Face your partner with eyes closed, remaining silent. Take a couple of slow breaths, centering yourself and exhaling tension. Open your eyes in soft focus and look upon your partner's face.... If you feel discomfort, just note it with patience and gentleness, and come back, when you can, to regard your partner. You may never see this person again; the opportunity to behold the uniqueness of this particular human being is given to you now....

To enter the first abode, open your awareness to the gifts and strengths that are in this being.... Though you can only guess at them, there are behind those eyes unmeasured reserves of courage and intelligence...of patience, endurance, wit and wisdom.... There are gifts there, of which even this person is unaware.... Consider what these powers could do for the healing of our world, if they were to be believed and acted on...... As you consider that, experience your desire that this person be free from fear.... Experience how much you want this being to be released as well from greed, from hatred and confusion and from the causes of suffering.... Know that what you are now experiencing is the great loving-kindness...... Closing your eyes now, rest into your breathing......

Opening them again, we enter the second abode. Now, as you look into those eyes, let yourself become aware of the pain that is there. There are sorrows accumulated in that life, as in all human lives, though you can only guess at them. There are disappointments and failures, losses and loneliness and abuse.... There are hurts beyond the telling.... Let yourself open to that pain, to hurts that this person may never have told to another human being...... You cannot take that pain away, but you can be with it. As you draw upon your capacity to be with your partner's suffering, know that what you are experiencing is the great compassion. It is very good for the healing of our world......

Again we close our eyes, opening them as we enter the third abode. As you behold the person before you, consider how good it would be to work together...on a joint project, toward a common goal.... What it would be like, taking risks together... conspiring together in zest and laughter... celebrating the successes, consoling each other over the setbacks, forgiving each other when you make mistakes... and simply being there for each other...... As you open to that possibility, you open to the great wealth, the pleasure in each other's powers, the joy in each other's joy......

Now entering the fourth and last abode, your eyes open, let your awareness drop deep within you like a stone, sinking below the level of what words can express... to the deep web of relationship that underlies all experience.... It is the web of life in which you have taken being and which interweaves us through all space and time.... See the being before you as if seeing the face of one who, at another time, another place, was your lover or your enemy, your parent or your child...... And now you meet again on this brink of time, almost as if by appointment.... And you know that your lives are as inextricably interwoven as nerve cells in the mind of a great being...... Out of that vast web you cannot fall...no stupidity, or failure, or cowardice, can ever sever you from that living web. For that is what you are...... Rest in that knowing. Rest in the Great Peace.... Out of it we can act, we can risk any-

thing...and let every encounter be a homecoming to our true nature......

This practice helps us realize that we do not have to be particularly noble or saint-like in order to wake up to the power of our connection with other beings. That simple awakening is the gift this planet-time holds for us. For all their horror and stupidity, the very bombs and poisons and wreckage we create are also the manifestation of an awesome spiritual truth—the truth about the hell we create for ourselves when we cease to learn how to love. Saints, mystics and prophets throughout the ages saw that law: now *all* can see it and none can escape its consequences.

For us to regard the bomb, the dying seas, or the poisoned air as monstrous injustices would suggest that we never took seriously the injunction to love. Perhaps we thought all along that Gautama and Jesus were kidding, or their teachings meant only for saints. But now we see, as an awful revelation, that we are all called to be saints—not good necessarily, or pious, or devout—but saints in the sense of just caring for each other.

In that possibility we take heart. Even in confusion and fear, with all our fatigues and faults, we can let that awareness work in and through our lives. Such simple exercises as those offered here can help us do that, help us to see ourselves and each other with fresh eyes.

Let us close with the same suggestion that often closes our workshops. It is a practice that is a corollary to the earlier death meditation, in which we recognize how threatened now is each person we meet. Look at the next person you see. It may be a lover, child, coworker, bus driver, or your own face in the mirror. Regard him or her with the recognition that:

In this person are gifts for the healing of our world. In him or her are powers that can redound to the joy of all beings.

Appendix A

CHIEF SEATTLE'S MESSAGE

CHIEF SEALTH, OR SEATTLE AS HE IS NOW KNOWN, delivered a speech in his native Duwamish to his tribal assembly in the Pacific Northwest in 1854. Dr. Henry Smith jotted down notes on the speech. He later emphasized that his own English, which reflects the usage of his time—including the use of the generic male which may or may not have been found in the original—was inadequate to render the beauty of Sealth's imagery and thought.

The version we now have was in fact recreated from Dr. Smith's jottings by film scriptwriter Ted Perry in 1970. We should note that it contains several historical distortions and anachronisms: Sealth, a Northwest Indian, would never have seen a prairie and unlikely a buffalo, and no railway was built anywhere near his territory until 1869. We recommend his "testimony" not as a historical document, but for its usefulness in eliciting a response from the listener/reader.

The Great Chief in Washington sends word that he wishes to buy our land.

The Great Chief also sends us words of friendship and goodwill. This is kind of him, since we know he has little need of our friendship in return.

But we will consider your offer. For we know that if we do not sell, the white man may come with guns and take our land.

How can you buy or sell the sky, the warmth of the land? This idea is strange to us.

If we do not own the freshness of the air and the sparkle of the water,
how can you buy them?

Every part of this earth is sacred to my people.
Every shining pine needle, every shady shore, every mist in the dark
woods, every clearing, and humming insect is holy in the memory
and experience of my people. The sap which courses through the
trees carries the memories of the red man.

The white man's dead forget the country of their birth when they go to
walk among the stars. Our dead never forget this beautiful earth,
for it is the mother of the red man. We are part of the earth and
it is part of us.

The perfumed flowers
are our sisters;
the deer, the horse, the great eagle,
these are our brothers.
The rocky crests,
the juices of the meadows,
the body heat of the pony, and man—
all belong to the same family.

So, when the Great Chief in Washington sends word that he wishes to
buy our land, he asks much of us.

The Great Chief sends word he will reserve us a place so that we can
live comfortably to ourselves. He will be our father and
we will be his children.

So we will consider your offer to buy our land. But it will not be easy.
For this land is sacred to us.

The shining water that moves in the streams and rivers is not just
water but the blood of our ancestors. If we sell you our land, you must
remember that it is sacred, and you must teach your children that it is
sacred and that each ghostly reflection in the clear water of the lake
tells of events and memories in the life of my people. The water's
murmur is the voice of my father's father.

The rivers are our brothers, they quench our thirst. The rivers carry our
canoes, and feed our children. If we sell you our land, you must
remember, and teach your children, that the rivers are our brothers—

and yours, and you must henceforth give the rivers the kindness you would give any brother.

The red man has always retreated before the advancing white man, as the mist of the mountains runs before the morning sun. But the ashes of our fathers are sacred. Their graves are holy ground, and so these hills, these trees, this portion of the earth is consecrated to us. We know that the white man does not understand our ways. One portion of the land is the same to him as the next, for he is a stranger who comes in the night and takes from the land whatever he needs. The earth is not his brother, but his enemy, and when he has conquered it, he moves on. He leaves his fathers' graves behind, and he does not care. He kidnaps the earth from his children, he does not care. His fathers' graves and his children's birthright are forgotten. He treats his mother, the earth, and his brother, the sky, as things to be bought, plundered, sold like sheep or bright beads. His appetite will devour the earth and leave behind only a desert.

I do not know. Our ways are different from your ways. The sight of your cities pains the eyes of the red man. But perhaps it is because the red man is a savage and does not understand.

There is no quiet place in the white man's cities. No place to hear the unfurling of leaves in the spring or the rustle of insect's wings. But perhaps it is because I am a savage and do not understand. The clatter only seems to insult the ears. And what is there to life if a man cannot hear the lonely cry of the whippoorwill or the arguments of the frogs around a pond at night? I am a red man and do not understand. The Indian prefers the soft sound of the wind darting over the face of a pond, and the smell of the wind itself, cleansed by a midday rain or scented with the piñon pine.

The air is precious to the red man, for all things share the same breath—the beast, the tree, the man, they all share the same breath. The white man does not seem to notice the air he breathes. Like a man dying for many days, he is numb to the stench. But if we sell you our land, you must remember that the air is precious to us, that the air shares its spirit with all the life it supports. The wind that gave our grandfather his first breath also receives his last sigh. And the wind must also give our children the spirit of life. And if we sell you our land, you must keep it apart and sacred, as a place where even the white man can go to taste the wind that is sweetened by the meadow's flowers.

So we will consider your offer to buy the land. If we decide to accept, I will make one condition: The white man must treat the beasts of this land as his brothers.

I am a savage and I do not understand any other way. I have seen a thousand rotting buffaloes on the prairie, left by the white man who shot them from a passing train. I am a savage and I do not understand how the smoking iron horse can be more important than the buffalo that we kill only to stay alive.

What is man without the beasts? If all the beasts were gone, men would die from a great loneliness of spirit. For whatever happens to the beasts, soon happens to the man. All things are connected.

You must teach your children that the ground beneath their feet is the ashes of our grandfathers. So that they will respect the land, tell your children that the earth is rich with the lives of our kin. Teach your children what we have taught our children: that the earth is our mother. Whatever befalls the earth befalls the sons of the earth. If men spit upon the ground, they spit upon themselves.

This we know. The earth does not belong to man; man belongs to the earth. This we know. All things are connected like the blood which unites one family. All things are connected.

Whatever befalls the earth, befalls the sons of the earth. Man does not weave the web of life, he is merely a strand in it. Whatever he does to the web, he does to himself.

But we will consider your offer to go to the reservation you have for my people. We will live apart, and in peace. It matters little where we spend the rest of our days. Our children have seen their fathers humbled in defeat. Our warriors have felt shame, and after defeat they turn their days in idleness and contaminate their bodies with sweet foods and strong drink. It matters little where we spend the rest of our days. They are not many. A few more hours, a few more winters, and none of the children of the great tribes that once lived on this earth or that roam now in small bands in the woods will be left to mourn the graves of a people once as powerful and hopeful as yours. But why should I mourn the passing of my people? Tribes are made of men, nothing more. Men come and go, like the waves of the sea.

Even the white man, whose God walks and talks with him as friend to friend, cannot be exempt from the common destiny. We may be brothers, after all; we shall see. One thing we know, which the white man may one day discover—our God is the same God. You may think now that you own Him as you wish to own our land, but you cannot. He is the God of man and His compassion is equal for the red man and the white. This earth is precious to Him and to harm the earth is to heap contempt on its Creator. The whites, too, shall pass—perhaps sooner than all other tribes.

But in your perishing you will shine brightly, fired by the strength of the God who brought you to this land and for some special purpose gave you dominion over this land and over the red man. That destiny is a mystery for us, for we do not understand when the buffalo are slaughtered, the wild horses tamed, the secret corners of the forest heavy with the scent of many men, and the view of the ripe hills blotted by talking wires.

Where is the thicket? Gone. Where is the eagle? Gone. And what is it to say good-bye to the swift pony and the hunt? The end of living and the beginning of survival.

So we will consider your offer to buy our land. If we agree, it will be to secure the reservation you have promised. There, perhaps, we may live out our brief days as we wish. When the last red man has vanished from this earth, and his memory is only the shadow of a cloud moving across the prairie, those shores and forests will still hold the spirits of my people. For they love this earth as the newborn loves its mother's heartbeat. So if we sell you our land, love it as we've loved it. Care for it as we've cared for it. Hold in your mind the memory of the land as it is when you take it. And with all your strength, with all your mind, with all your heart, preserve it for your children and love it... as God loves us all.

One thing we know. Our God is the same God. This earth is precious to Him. Even the white man cannot be exempt from the common destiny. We may be brothers, after all. We shall see.

Appendix B

THE BESTIARY

by Joanna Macy

short-tailed albatross
     whooping crane
        gray wolf
           peregrine falcon
              hawksbill turtle
                  jaguar
                     rhinoceros

In Geneva, the international tally of endangered species, kept up to date in looseleaf volumes, is becoming too heavy to lift. Where do we now record the passing of life? What funerals or farewells are appropriate?

reed warbler
     swallowtail butterfly
        Manx shearwater
           Indian python
              howler monkey
                  sperm whale
                    blue whale

Dive me deep, brother whale, in this time we have left. Deep in our mother ocean where once I swam, gilled and finned. The salt from those early seas still runs in my tears. Tears are too meager now. Give me a song... a song for a sadness too vast for my heart, for a rage too wild for my throat.

anteater
     antelope

grizzly bear
brown bear
Bactrian camel
Nile crocodile
American alligator

Ooze me, alligator, in the mud whence I came. Belly me slow in the rich primordial soup, cradle of our molecules. Let me wallow again, before we drain your swamp, before we pave it over and blast it to ash.

gray bat
ocelot
marsh mouse
blue pike
red kangaroo
Aleutian goose
Audouin's seagull

Quick, lift off. Sweep me high over the coast and out, farther out. Don't land here. Oilspills coat the beach, rocks, sea. I cannot spread my wings glued with tar. Fly me from what we have done, fly me far.

golden parakeet
African ostrich
Florida panther
Galapagos penguin
Imperial pheasant
leopard
Utah prairie dog

Hide me a hedgerow, badger. Can't you find one? Dig me a tunnel through leaf-mold and roots, under the trees that once defined our fields. My heart is bulldozed and plowed over. Burrow me a labyrinth deeper than longing.

thick-billed parrot
zone-tailed pigeon
desert bandicoot
Southern bald eagle
California condor
lotus blue butterfly

Crawl me out of here, caterpillar. Spin a cocoon. Wind me to sleep in a shroud of silk, where in patience my bones will dissolve. I'll wait as long as all creation if only it will come again—and I take wing.

Atlantic Ridley turtle
pearly mussel

helmuted hornbill
                sea otter
            humpback whale
                    monk seal
                        harp seal
Swim me out beyond the ice floes, mama. Where are you? Boots squeeze
my ribs, clubs drum my fur, the white world goes black with the taste of
my blood.
gorilla
    gibbon
        sand gazelle
            swamp deer
                musk deer
                    cheetah
                        chinchilla
                    Asian elephant
                        African elephant
Sway me slowly through the jungle. There still must be jungle somewhere,
my heart drips with green secrets. Hose me down by the waterhole; there
is buckshot in my hide. Tell me old stories while you can remember.
fan-tailed flycatcher
                flapshell tortoise
                    crested ibis
                    hook-billed kite
                            bobcat
                            frigate bird
In the time when his world, like ours, was ending, Noah had a list of the
animals, too. We picture him standing by the gangplank, calling their
names, checking them off on his scroll. Now we also are checking them off.
ivory-billed woodpecker
                brown pelican
                    Florida manatee
                        Canada goose
We reenact Noah's ancient drama, but in reverse, like a film running backwards, the animals exiting.
    ferret
        curlew
            cougar
                wolf

Your tracks are growing fainter. Wait. Wait. This is a hard time. Don't leave us alone in a world we have wrecked.

Appendix C

A COUNCIL OF ALL BEINGS: THE SITE SPEAKS

Architect Rosa Lane offered us this account of a Council of All Beings she organized in Tilden Regional Park near Berkeley, California, as part of t he planning process for a new park building. We consider it an inspiring example of how the Council can be used as a practical aid in decision-making.

THE SITE SPEAKS:

**Ecological and Emergent Feedback at Tilden Park, Quarry Site
in Response to a Proposed Park Building—Visitors' Center** [34]
with the Ecological Design Seminar
UC Berkeley Department of Architecture
April 21, 1998, 3 p.m. to 6 p.m.
by Rosa Lane, Architect

As an architect, I am interested in systems theory and how this theory provides ecological understanding in architectural practice. As architectural practice moves from a mechanical worldview based on an industrial growth society to an ecological worldview based on a life-sustaining society, the Council of All Beings offers a bridge to designers. Specifically, the Council of All Beings facilitates listening and a process of knowing ecological networks and native biota. These feedback loops of knowledge inform sustainable design, limitations of human settlement, and, where applicable, an architecture that is living, dynamic, and congruent with ecology.

A group of young architects at the University of California, Berkeley, gathered to participate in a three-hour Council of All Beings at the

Quarry Site in Tilden Park, a greenbelt of rolling hills overlooking San Francisco Bay. The nonhuman Council convened to share feedback on the design of the human habitat, and particularly, on the proposed construction of a Visitors' Center at the Quarry Site. The Quarry Site with its acres of open parkland of woodlands and meadows also included several picnic tables which we used for mask-making on.

The event was divided into the following six parts: 1) intention was set within the initial circle gathering; 2) solo journey in nature; 3) mask-making; 4) nonhuman council; 5) nonhuman council with an architect in the center; and 6) a debriefing of learnings. Nonhuman voices brought concerns, questions, gifts, and wisdom to the circle in response to the proposed construction to take place within their home environment. What follows are some of the voices from this Council.

Ant feared that her own home would be displaced and care would not be exercised by the humans. She brought tenacity and "mighty-mite" strength to the Council. Pine Cone thanked Ant for storing and distributing her seeds. Then Pine Cone spoke of herself as a bearer of seeds, seeds that hold visions for the future, of whole forests growing and swaying in the wind, persisting towards greater complexity and life. But she said her dreams, her seeds, and her forests are realized less and less due to the pollution, bad soils, and constant harvesting. Pine Cone offered the new building trees of shade and the sound of water in the slightest breeze in her future branches. But she can only do so much. Unless the architects wake themselves up, they will only contribute more pollution to the site with their closed systems of air-conditioning, heating, and lack of operable windows.

Sun expressed the same frustration at being unseen when she is the one who brings light so that humans can see. Sun yelled, "I am under-appreciated! Why? Why can't they see when I give them light to see! What don't they use me? I can give them warmth. I can give them power. I am here to serve and am free for their taking." She turned to address one of the Council, Stone. "They can store my heat in you, Stone."

Stone said, "Yes, I can also provide them walls so that trees like Young Redwood, Father Tree, and Grandfather Pine wouldn't have to be killed and misused." But Stone feared that the opportunities he brings will remain unrecognized and that he would be thoughtlessly tossed aside as useless waste.

Young Redwood grew sad. She thanked Stone for the thought of substituting himself for her. "I give so much life to other beings. Undoubtedly, they will use me for their picnic tables, fenceposts, and trellises at the new

Park building because I am so durable. Humans will use me as defense against my own friends, my friends the insects and water. Oh, humans have it so mixed up! When they cut me down and use me for such meaningless products, whole beings' families will either die with me or be displaced," Young Redwood said.

Mother Nature provided an overview. "I see us all working together, humans and all of nature." Bringing a ray of hope, Mother Nature assured us, "We must keep up our spirits and keep our relationships in good condition. Humans will eventually learn from their mistakes, and we will move into new relationships with them," she promised.

Grandfather Pine said that in the meantime he worries about his tree cousins in the city. "They're suffocating, missing relationships and rhythms of biological processes, and lacking diversity. It is so hard to see them disconnected, displaced, and growing from concrete."

Father Tree looked around the Council and said he is happy that he provides a home for so many of the rest of us. He went on to say, "I hope I can continue in this. I also give oxygen to the humans so they can breathe, so why do they destroy me?"

Groundhog piped up, "I am also afraid of losing my home. They're sure to put the buildings right where I live—or worse, they'll pave the site and there will be no place for me to go."

Sun/Shadow with her light and dark shaded face, offered the cycles of day and night, of light and dark, as reminders to humans of the non-linear rhythms of life. "Humans light the dark at night and live in the shadows during days. They make no sense."

Wind-in-Grass said he can go anywhere. He can just pick up and leave it all behind if he wants to. Wind, like Sun, has seen it all in deep time. Expanding our frames with quiet dignity, he reminded us of his ancient beginnings: he has swept the shifting tectonic plates, molten action making earth, glaciers. Today, Wind-in-Grass expressed his detachment. "I bring comfort with my breezes. I reveal myself in the swaying grass. I give humans this visual beauty for their building. I also give the humans the comfort of Bay winds to cool themselves from the summer heat."

Midway through the Council, a human architect stepped into the center of the circle and heard our voices. He was receptive because he *needed* to hear us. He said he was sorry for all the times he did not listen to us. He had grown short-sighted and numb. Listening is the key.

The architect's perception of the site/region stepped beyond the usual observer/object split to intersubjectivity. His notion of "client" expanded to include our voices of the site/region. Our nonhuman voices are to be at every collaborative design table as part of the feedback loop. We beings are participants in an emergent process, a bridge between ongoing site ecology and the built space.

The Council thanked the architect for listening. The participants then removed the masks, put them in the center of the circle, thanked the beings for their wisdom, and released them back to their habitats. The young architects experienced the nonhuman community at depths of feelings and perceptions that will enable them to listen to the nonhuman voices of their future site/regions, to map emergent phenomena, and to work in partnership. The Council of All Beings offers a profound tool in designing future human habitats in ecological relationship, as nodes in existing biotic and elemental networks.

Reference Notes

Molly's Preface

1. Cited in Ed Ayers, "The Banality of Evil," *World Watch*, Vol. 11, No. 1, Jan.-Feb. 1998.

2. Ayers, Ibid.

Chapter 1

3. Robinson Jeffers, "The Tower Beyond Tragedy," *The Collected Poetry of Robinson Jeffers*, ed. Tim Hunt (Stanford University Press, 1988), Vol. 1, p. 177. Used with permission.

Chapter 2

4. Wendell Berry, from *A Timbered Choir* (Counterpoint Press, 1998).

5. Dr. Robert Murphy, personal communication.

6. Dr. Leon Balter in his report on the New York Psychiatric Association's study of psychological responses to the nuclear threat, 1982.

7. Anita Barrows, from "Psalm" in *We Are The Hunger* (Unpublished manuscript, 1998).

Chapter 3

8. Gregory Bateson, *Steps to an Ecology of Mind* (Ballantine, 1972), p. 481-2.

9. Norbert Wiener, *The Human Use of Human Beings* (Avon Books, 1967), p. 130.

10. Leon Brillouin, "Life Thermodynamics and Cybernetics," in *Modern Systems Research for the Behavioral Scientist*, ed. Walter Buckley (Aldine, 1968), p. 153.

11. Karl Deutsch, "Toward a Cybernetic Model of Society," in *Modern Systems Research for the Behavioral Scientist*, ed. Walter Buckley (Aldine, 1968), p. 399.

12 . Ervin Laszlo, *Introduction to Systems Philosophy* (Harper Torch, 1973), p. 170.

13. Gregory Bateson, "Toward a Theory of Alcoholism," in *Steps to an Ecology of Mind* (Ballantine, 1972), p. 332.

14. Kazimierz Dabrowski, *Positive Disintegration* (Boston: Little, Brown & Co., 1964).

15. J. Seed, J. Macy, P. Fleming, A. Naess, *Thinking Like a Mountain* (Philadelphia: New Society Publishers, 1988).

16. Ibid, p. 20.

17. Sarah Conn, unpublished article to appear in *Journal of Humanistic Psychology*, 1998.

18. Robert Bly, trans., *The Book of Kabir* (Beacon, 1977).

Chapter 4

19. From *Rilke's Book of Hours*, translated by Joanna Macy and Anita Barrows (NY: Riverhead, 1997).

20 . bid.

Chapter 5

21. Erik Erikson, *Gandhi's Truth* (Norton, 1993).

22. Jack Kornfield, *A Path With Heart* (New York: Bantam, 1993).

Chapter 7

23. We don't know the exact source of this quotation; it was handed to Joanna at a workshop.

24. Roger Harrison, PhD and Margaret Harris at Boise State University, 1996.

25. Jack Belden, *China Shakes the World* (N.Y. Monthly Review Press, 1949), pp. 487-8.

Chapter 8

26. Translated by Jane Hirshfield in *The Enlightened Heart*, ed. Stephen Mitchell (Harper & Row, 1989). Used with permission of translator.

27. Miriam Theresa MacGillis, "The Fate of the Earth," in *The Soul of Nature*, ed. Michael Tobias and Georgianne Cowan (New York: Continuum, 1994).

28. Taigen Daniel Leighton, *Bodhisattva Archetypes: Classic Buddhist Guides to Awakening and Their Modern Expression* (New York: Penguin, 1998).

Chapter 9

29. Denise Levertov, from *Poems 1968-1972* (New Directions Publishing, 1972).

Chapter 10

30. Barbara Deming, "Spirit of Love," from *We Are All Part of One Another: A Barbara Deming Reader*, ed. Jane Meyerding (Philadelphia, PA: New Society Publishers, 1984).

31. This version of the "Evolutionary Remembering," first published in J. Seed, J. Macy, P. Fleming, A. Naess, *Thinking Like a Mountain* (Philadelphia: New Society Publishers, 1988), is adapted from other subsequent adaptations, including one by Gale Warner.

Chapter 12

32. Edward Conze, trans. *The Perfection of Wisdom in Eight Thousand Lines* (Berkeley: Bookpeople, 1973).

33. By John Seed and Joanna Macy, from J. Seed, J. Macy, P. Fleming, and A. Naess, *Thinking Like a Mountain* Gabriola Island: New Society Publishers, 1988).

Appendix C

34. Rosa Lane, *"The Site Speaks"*. Unpublished manuscript used with permission of the author.

Resources

WE LIST HERE SOME OF THE BOOKS which have influenced our thinking, and some of the books we consider to be central texts. This list is by no means exhaustive. Please forgive our omission of many other worthy books.

A number of the older books on this list are out of print, but we include them here because they can still be found with some effort in libraries and used book stores.

World Conditions

Barlow, Maude and Tony Clarke. *MAI: The Multilateral Agreement on Investment and the Threat to American Freedom.* Stoddart Publishing, 1998.

Bowers, C.A. *Education, Cultural Myths and the Ecological Crisis: Toward Deep Changes.* SUNY, 1992.

Brown, Paul. *Global Warming: Can Civilization Survive?* Blandford, UK, 1996.

Carson, Rachel. *Silent Spring.* Cambridge: Riverside Press, 1962.

Chomsky, Noam. *The Chomsky Reader.* Random House, 1996.

Colborn, Theo, Dianne Dumanoski, and John Peterson Myers. *Our Stolen Future.* Penguin, 1996.

Daly, Herman E. *Beyond Growth: The Economics of Sustainable Development.* Beacon Press, 1996.

Devall, Bill, ed. *Clearcut: The Tragedy of Industrial Forestry.* Sierra Club, 1993.

Flavin, Christopher and Nicholas Lenssen. *Power Surge: Guide to the Coming Energy Revolution.* W.W. Norton & Co. and World Watch Institute, 1994.

Helvarg, David. *The War Against the Greens: The "Wise Use" Movement, the New Right, and Anti-environmental Violence.* Sierra Club, 1994.

Hofrichter, Richard, ed. *Toxic Struggles: The Theory and Practice of Environmental Justice.* New Society Publishers, 1993.

Little, Charles E. *The Dying of the Trees: The Pandemic in America's Forests.* Viking Penguin, 1995.

Mander, Jerry. *In the Absence of the Sacred: The Failure of Technology and the Survival of the Indian Nations.* Sierra Club, 1991.

Mander, Jerry and Edward Goldsmith, eds. *The Case Against the Global Economy (and For a Turn Toward the Local).* Sierra Club, 1996.

Meadows, Donella, Dennis Meadows and Randers Jurgen. *Beyond the Limits: Confronting Global Collapse, Envisioning a Sustainable Future.* Chelsea Green, 1992.

Norberg-Hodge, Helena. *Ancient Futures: Learning from Ladakh.* Sierra Club, 1991.

Reich, Charles A. *Opposing the System.* Crown, 1995.

Robbins, John. *Diet for a New America.* Stillpoint, 1987.

Robbins, John. *May All Be Fed: Diet for a New World.* William Morrow & Co., 1992.

Robbins, John. *Reclaiming Our Health: Exploding the Medical Myth and Embracing the Source of True Healing.* H.J. Kramer, 1996.

Shiva, Vandana. *Close to Home: Women Reconnect Ecology, Health, and Development Worldwide.* New Society Publishers, 1994.

Steingraber, Sandra. *Living Downstream: An Ecologist Looks at Cancer and the Environment.* Addison Wesley, 1997.

Taylor, Bron Raymond, ed. *Ecological Resistance Movements: The Global Emergence of Radical and Popular Environmentalism.* SUNY, 1995.

Terry, Roger. *Economic Insanity.* Berrett-Koehler, 1996.

Tirman, John. *Spoils of War: The Human Cost of America's Arms Trade.* New York: Simon & Schuster, 1997.

Wachtel, Paul. *The Poverty of Affluence: A Psychological Portrait of the American Way of Life.* New Society Publishers, 1989.

Weaver, Jace, ed. *Defending Mother Earth: Native American Perspectives on Environmental Justice.* Orbis Books, 1996.

Journals

Earth Island Journal, Earth Island Institute, 3000 Broadway #28, San Francisco, CA 94133.

The New Internationalist, UK: PO Box 79, Hertford, SG14 1AQ. USA: PO Box 1143, Lewiston, NY 14092.

State of the World and *Vital Signs,* published annually by World Watch Institute, 1776 Massachusetts Ave. NW, Washington, DC 20036.

Too Much: A Quarterly Commentary on Capping Excessive Income and Wealth. Council on International and Public Affairs, Suite 3C, 777 United Nations Plaza, New York, NY 10017.

World Press Review. PO Box 228, Shrub Oak, NY 10588.

World Watch: Working for a Sustainable Future. World Watch Institute, 1776 Massachusetts Ave NW, Washington DC 20036.

Deep Ecology

Abrams, David. *The Spell of the Sensuous: Perception and Language in a More Than Human World.* Pantheon, 1996.

Adams, Cass, ed. *The Soul Unearthed: Celebrating Wildness and Personal Renewal Through Nature.* Tarcher, 1996.

Brown, Molly Young. *Growing Whole: Self-realization on an Endangered Planet.* Hazelden, 1993. Now available from Psychosynthesis Press.

Devall, Bill and George Sessions. *Deep Ecology: Living as if Nature Mattered.* Gibbs M. Smith, 1985.

Drengson, Alan and Yuichi Inoue, eds. *The Deep Ecology Movement.* North Atlantic, 1995.

Glendinning, Chellis. *My Name is Chellis and I'm in Recovery from Western Civilization.* San Francisco: Sierra Club, 1994.

Johnson, Chris. *The Lens of Deep Ecology.* Institute for Deep Ecology Education, UK, 1994.

Kaza, Stephanie. *The Attentive Heart: Conversations with Trees.* Shambhala, 1996.

Kwaloy, Sigmund. "Ecophilosophy." In *The Green Fuse.* Ed. J. Button. Quartet Books, 1990.

LaChapelle, Dolores. *Sacred Land, Sacred Sex—Rapture of the Deep: Concerning Deep Ecology and Celebrating Life.* Kivaki, 1988.

Leopold, Aldo. *A Sand County Almanac.* Ballantine, 1970.

Macy, Joanna. *World as Lover, World as Self.* Parallax, 1991.

McLaughlin, Andrew. *Regarding Nature: Industrialism and Deep Ecology.* SUNY, 1993.

Naess, Arne. *Ecology, Community, and Lifestyle.* Ed. And trans. David Rothenberg. Cambridge University Press, 1989.

Orr, David. *Ecological Literacy: Education and the Transition to a Postmodern World.* SUNY, 1992.

Seed, J., J. Macy, P. Fleming and A. Naess. *Thinking Like a Mountain: Toward a Council of All Beings.* New Society Publishers, 1988.

Sessions, George, ed. *Deep Ecology for the 21st Century: Readings on the Philosophy and Practice of the New Environmentalism.* Shambhala, 1995.

Shepard, Paul. *Nature and Madness.* San Francisco: Sierra Club, 1982.

Shepard, Paul. *The Others: How Animals Made Us Human.* Island Press, 1996.

Snyder, Gary. *A Place in Space: Ethics, Aesthetics, and Watersheds.* Counterpoint, 1995.

Snyder, Gary. *The Practice of the Wild.* F S & G, 1990.

Suzuki, David. *The Sacred Balance: Rediscovering Our Place in Nature.* Amherst, NY: Prometheus Books, 1998.

Thomashow, Mitch. *Ecological Identity.* MIT Press, 1995.

Related Ecological, Economic, and Political Thought

Andruss, Van, C. Plant, J. Plant and E. Wright, eds. *Home! A Bioregional Reader.* New Society Publishers, 1990.

Berry, Thomas. *The Dream of the Earth.* Sierra Club, 1988.

Clinebell, Howard. *Ecotherapy: Healing Ourselves/Healing the Earth.* Haworth Press, 1996.

Durning, Alan T. *This Place on Earth: Home and the Practice of Permanence.* Sasquatch, 1996.

Fox, Matthew. *The Reinvention of Work: A New Vision of Livelihood for Our Time.* Harper Collins, 1994.

Goldsmith, Edward. *The Way: An Ecological Worldview.* Shambhala, 1993.

Griffin, Susan. *A Chorus of Stones: A Private Life of War.* Doubleday, 1993.

Hillman, James. *The Thought of the Heart and the Soul of the World.* Spring Pubs., 1996.

Kelly, Petra. *Thinking Green! Essays on Environmentalism, Feminism and Non-violence*. Parallax, 1994.

Kropotkin, Peter. *Mutual Aid: A Factor of Evolution*. Extending Horizons Books, 1988.

Murchie, Guy. *The Seven Mysteries of Life: An Exploration of Science and Philosophy*. Houghton Mifflin, 1978.

Plant, Judith, ed. *Healing the Wounds: The Promise of Ecofeminism*. New Society Publishers, 1989.

Quinn, Daniel. *Ishmael*. Bantam, 1992.

Quinn, Daniel. *The Story of B: An Adventure of the Mind and Spirit*. Bantam, 1996.

Roszak, Theodore. *The Voice of the Earth*. New York: Simon & Schuster, 1992.

Roszak, Theodore, Mary Gomes, and Alan D. Kanner, eds. *Ecopsychology*. Sierra Club, 1995.

Russell, Peter. *The Global Brain: Speculations on the Evolutionary Leap to Planetary Consciousness*. Los Angeles: Tarcher, 1983.

Sale, Kirkpatrick. *Dwellers in the Land: A Bioregional Vision*. New Society Publishers, 1991.

Schumacher, E.F. *Small Is Beautiful: Economics as if People Mattered*. HarperCollins, 1973.

Spretnak, Charlene. *The Resurgence of the Real: Body, Nature, and Place in a Hypermodern World*. Addison-Wesley, 1997.

Starhawk. *The Fifth Sacred Thing*. Bantam, 1993.

Toms, Justine Willis and Michael Toms. *True Work: The Sacred Dimension of Earning a Living*. New York: Bell Tower, 1998.

Williams, Terry Tempest. *Refuge*. Random, 1991.

Winter, Deborah D. *Ecological Psychology*. Harper Collins, 1996.

Zimmerman, Michael, ed. *Environmental Philosophy: From Animal Rights to Radical Ecology*. Prentice Hall, 1992.

Journals

The Ecologist. Ecosystems, Ltd. Cissbury House, Furze View, Five Oaks Rd., Slinfold, W. Sussex PH13 7RH, UK.

Resurgence: An International Forum for Ecological and Spiritual Thinking. Rocksea Farmhouse, St. Mabyn, Bodmin, Cornwall PL30 3BR, UK. USA: Small Changes, 316 Terry Ave. North, PO Box 19046, Seattle, WA 98109.

The Trumpeter: Journal of Ecosophy. Where Philosophy and Culture Meet the Earth. Box 5853, Stn. B, Victoria, BC, Canada V8R 6S8.

Wild Earth. Cenozoic Society, PO Box 455, Richmond, VT 05477.

Group Work and Leadership

Carnes, Robin Deen and Sally Craig. *Sacred Circles: A Guide to Creating Your Own Women's Spirituality Group.* HarperCollins, 1998.

Coover, Virginia, Ellen Deacon, Charles Esser, and Christopher Moore. *Resource Manual for a Living Revolution.* New Society Publishers and Movement for a New Society, 1978.

Gastil, John. *Democracy in Small Groups: Participation, Decision Making and Communication.* New Society Publishers, 1993.

Kaner, Sam. *Facilitator's Guide to Participatory Decisionmaking.* New Society Publishers, 1995.

Poetry and Resources for Ritual

Barks, Colman, trans. with John Moyne. *The Essential Rumi.* HarperCollins, 1995.

Brown, Molly Young. *Lighting a Candle: Quotations on the Spiritual Life.* HarperCollins, 1994. (Also available through Psychosynthesis Press.)

Hoff, Benjamin.*The Singing Creek Where the Willows Grow: The Mystical Nature Diary of Opal Whitely.* Penguin, 1994.

Macy, Joanna and Anita Barrows, trans. *Rilke's Book of Hours.* NY: Riverhead, 1996.

Roberts, Elizabeth & Amidon, Elias, eds. *Earth Prayers. 365 Prayers, Poems, and Invocations for Honoring the Earth* . HarperCollins, 1991.

Roberts, Elizabeth & Amidon, Elias, eds. *Life Prayers: 365 Prayers, Blessings, and Affirmations to Celebrate the Human Journey.* HarperCollins, 1996.

Systems Thinking

Bateson, Gregory. *Steps to an Ecology of Mind*. Ballantine, 1972.

Berman, Morris. *The Reenchantment of the World*. Bantam, 1984.

Buckley, Walter. *Modern Systems Research for the Behavioral Scientist*. Aldine, 1968.

Capra, Fritjof. *The Web of Life*. Anchor, 1996.

Laszlo, Ervin. *Introduction to Systems Philosophy: Toward a New Paradigm of Contemporary Thought.*, Gordon & Breach, 1972.

Laszlo, Ervin. *The Systems View of the World*. Braziller, 1972.

L'Engle, Madeleine. *A Wind in the Door*. Dell, 1973.

L'Engle, Madeleine. *A Wrinkle in Time*. Dell, 1970.

Lovelock, James. *Healing Gaia: Practical Medicine for the Planet*. Crown, 1991.

Macy, Joanna. *Mutual Causality in Buddhism and General Systems Theory: The Dharma of Living Systems*. SUNY, 1991.

Olds, Linda. *Metaphors of Interrelatedness*. SUNY, 1992.

Sahtouris, Elisabet. *Gaia: The Human Journey from Chaos to Cosmos*. Pocket Books, Simon & Schuster, 1989.

von Bertalanffy, Ludwig. *General System Theory*. George Braziller, 1968.

Wheatley, Margaret J. *Leadership and the New Science: Learning about Organizations from an Orderly Universe*. Berrett-Koehler, 1992.

Spiritual Teachings

Bernstein, Ellen, ed. *Ecology and the Jewish Spirit: Where Nature and the Sacred Meet*. Jewish Lights Publishing, 1998.

Chatwin, Bruce. *The Songlines*. Pan Books, 1988.

Fox, Matthew. *The Coming of the Cosmic Christ: The Healing of Mother Earth and the Birth of a Global Renaissance*. Harper & Row, 1988.

Fox, Matthew. *Original Blessing: A Primer in Creation Spirituality*. Bear & Company, 1983.

Gottlieb, Roger S., ed. *This Sacred Earth: Religion, Nature and Environment*. Routledge, 1996.

Hayden, Tom. *The Lost Gospel of the Earth: A Call for Renewing Nature, Spirit, and Politics*. Sierra Club, 1996.

Jones, Ken. *Beyond Optimism: A Buddhist Political Ecology.* Jon Carpenter, 1996.

Jones, Ken. *The Social Face of Buddhism: An Approach to Political and Social Activism.* Wisdom, 1989.

Kotler, Arnold, ed. *Engaged Buddhist Reader.* Parallax, 1996.

Leighton, Taigen Daniel. *Bodhisattva Archetypes: Classic Buddhist Guides to Awakening and their Modern Expression.* Penguin, 1998.

Neihardt, John G. *Black Elk Speaks: Being the Life Story of a Holy Man of the Oglala Sioux.* University of Nebraska Press, 1961.

Nhat Hanh, Thich. *Interbeing: 14 Guidelines for Engaged Buddhism.* Parallax, 1993.

Nhat Hanh, Thich. *Love in Action.* Parallax, 1993.

Nisker, Wes. *Buddha's Nature.* Bantam, 1998.

Resources for Action

Aberley, Doug, ed. *Boundaries of Home: Mapping for Local Empowerment.* New Society Publishers, 1993.

Aberley, Doug, ed. *Futures by Design: The Practice of Ecological Planning.* New Society Publishers, 1994.

Andrews, Cecile. *The Circle of Simplicity: Return to the Good Life.* HarperCollins, 1997.

Bullard, Robert, ed. *Confronting Environmental Racism: Voices from the Grassroots.* South End, 1993.

Cole, Jim. *Facing Our Future: From Denial to Environmental Action.* Growing Images, 1992.

Daly, Herman and John Cobb. *For the Common Good: Redirecting the Economy Toward Community, the Environment, and a Sustainable Future.* Beacon Press, 1994.

Dominguez, Joe and Vicki Robin. *Your Money or Your Life: Transforming Your Relationship with Money and Achieving Financial Independence.* Penguin, 1992.

Green, Tova and Peter Woodrow. *Insight and Action: How to Discover and Support a Life of Integrity and Commitment to Change.* New Society Publishers, 1994.

Hawken, Paul. *The Ecology of Commerce: A Declaration of Sustainability.* HarperCollins, 1995.

Margolin, Malcolm. *The Earth Manual: How to Work on Wild Land Without Taming It*. Heyday, 1985.

Mills, Stephanie. *In Service of the Wild: Restoring and Reinhabiting Damaged Land*. Beacon, 1995.

Orr, David. *Earth in Mind: On Education, Environment, and the Human Prospect*. Island Press, 1994.

Peavey, Fran. *By Life's Grace: Musings on the Essence of Social Change*. New Society Publishers, 1993.

Shaffer, Carolyn and Kristin Anundsen. *Creating Community Anywhere: Finding Support in a Fragmented World*. Putnam, 1993.

Shields, Katrina. *In the Tiger's Mouth*. New Society Publishers, 1994..

Shutz, Robert. *The $30,000 Solution*. Daniel & Daniel, 1995.

Wackernagel, Mathis and William Rees. *Our Ecological Footprint: Reducing Human Impact on the Earth*. New Society Publishers, 1996.

Journals

Earth First! The Radical Environmental Journal. PO Box 1415, Eugene, OR 97440.

In Context Sustainability Series. Robert Gilman, ed. Context Institute, Langley, WA. Back issues of the beloved quarterly *In Context*, now being published on-line. Web URL: http://www.context.org

YES! A Journal of Positive Futures. PO Box 10818, Bainbridge Island, WA 98110.